W9-CZM-417

THE LIFETIME SPORTS-ORIENTED PHYSICAL EDUCATION PROGRAM

William F. Straub
ITHACA COLLEGE
President, New York State Lifetime Sports Association

53811

PRENTICE-HALL, INC., *Englewood Cliffs, New Jersey*

Library of Congress Cataloging in Publication Data

STRAUB, WILLIAM F   1926–
  The lifetime sports-oriented physical education program.

  Includes bibliographies and index.
    1. Physical education and training.   2. Physical education and training—Curricula.
  3. Physical fitness.
  I. Title.
  GV341.S73   613.7'07   75-33023
  ISBN   0-13-536599-6

To My Mother and Father

© 1976 by
PRENTICE-HALL, INC.
Englewood Cliffs, New Jersey

10 9 8 7 6 5 4 3 2 1

PRENTICE-HALL INTERNATIONAL, INC., *London*
PRENTICE-HALL OF AUSTRALIA, PTY. LIMITED, *Sydney*
PRENTICE-HALL OF CANADA, LTD., *Toronto*
PRENTICE-HALL OF INDIA PRIVATE LIMITED, *New Delhi*
PRENTICE-HALL OF JAPAN, INC., *Tokyo*
PRENTICE-HALL OF SOUTHEAST ASIA PRIVATE LIMITED, *Singapore*

CONTENTS

iii

FOREWORD

During the last seventy-five years, American Society has experienced a convulsive change in living style. At the turn of the century there were few labor-saving devices and no automobiles, airplanes, radios or television sets. The majority of our citizens were engaged in physical labor. Children walked to school. The average American's daily tasks were long, arduous, and physically demanding. Daily activities required sufficient muscular exercise to maintain physical fitness.

In modern America, all this has changed. Most children are bused to school; the work week has shortened; the average job requires little or no muscular effort. Sufficient exercise does not take place, as it did at the turn of the century, by required daily work routines. Today, exercise must be planned as an integral part of one's daily schedule.

Our educational system has failed to communicate this reality. America's school athletic programs do provide unparalleled training and development for gifted athletes, but too often ignore the needs of the average boy or girl. The emphasis has been on team sports which have high spectator interest. With a few exceptions such as swimming and track, school sports participation is of little value as a preparation for exercise habits during adult life, because the opportunity for participation in team games, as football and basketball, is unavailable to most citizens after they are out of school.

It is an almost axiomatic truth that few people will continue an exercise regime throughout life unless the activities are fun. Thus, swimming, jogging, and participation in games that are enjoyable is the best means of insuring the needed amount of exercise for an individual throughout life. Muscular skills are easy to learn when a person is young. Most importantly, the skill, once learned, always remains a part of the person. One who has learned to swim, ride a bicycle, or skate will never forget how to do it. Similarly, a youngster who learns the skills of bowling, tennis, golf or any of the lifetime sports will have the kinesthetic or muscle memory to recall the skill even though many years may elapse between periods of participation. It is, therefore, a responsibility of American education to teach these skills to all young people. This will enable them to enjoy participating in physically active games throughout their lives.

Two American businessmen, Carter Burgess of the American Machine Foundry Company and Jack Hannigan of the Brunswick Corporation, believed so strongly in this concept that in 1965 they established and funded the Lifetime Sports Foundation. The goal of the Foundation was to have the teaching of lifetime sports skills included as an integral part of physical and recreational education. The fact that in only ten years the validity of the goal has been widely accepted by the professional educators is, I know, of great satisfaction to these public spirited gentlemen.

This book by Professor William Straub will become, I believe, the classic text on the subject. It clearly explains the concepts and teaching methodology of the lifetime sports and is scholarly referenced to insure the validity of all materials included. I recommend the text to physical education and recreation professionals and to all parents who have an interest in teaching their children lifetime sports skills.

CHARLES B. WILKINSON

PREFACE

The most significant change that is taking place in physical education today is the trend toward lifetime sports centered instruction. The focus is in keeping with changing societal values which call for a more aware, physically active, better fit nation of citizens. In order to provide experiences so that boys and girls will want to stay physically fit in later life, schools across the nation are redesigning their physical education programs to include a wide variety of lifetime sports. The central purpose of this text is to help school officials make the transition from traditional to lifetime sports-oriented programs.

The lifetime sports concept of physical education has been gaining momentum for the past ten years. Much of the progress toward the objective of inclusion of these sports is due to the work of Charles "Bud" Wilkinson and William E. Noonan, Jr., President and Director, respectively, of the Lifetime Sports Education Project of the American Alliance for Health, Physical Education and Recreation. Many physical educators contend that this program was one of the best grass-roots efforts ever sponsored by AAHPER.

As mentioned above, the purpose of this book is to help physical education teachers and administrators infuse lifetime sports into their physical education programs. Lifetime Sports do not replace physical education—instead, they are an integral part of it. Their values, in contrast to team-sports, lie in that they provide students with skills, knowledge, and attitudes that will enable them to enjoy and profit from physical activity throughout life.

ix

The text takes the reader through a step-by-step approach to the infusion of lifetime sports. First, the lifetime sports concept is explained and justified. Second, a survey of community resources is provided so that off-site facilities and supplementary personnel may be identified and utilized to broaden the scope of the program. Chapters 3 and 4 are concerned with organizational patterns and curriculum construction procedures, respectively. Humanistic, behavioristic, and systems approaches to teaching are covered in Chapter 5, teaching methodology. The best programs, if poorly taught, will not achieve desirable results. Attention is also focused on measurement and evaluation procedures. Two types of assessment are proposed: the progress of the students toward the objectives of the program must be determined; and, the curriculum itself must be assessed to determine if it is meeting the students' interest and needs.

Chapter 7 includes information about how to include lifetime sports for exceptional children, particularly the physically handicapped. Public relations, in an era of economic pressures, are vital to the success of all aspects of education, including physical education. Since P.E. is frequently considered a "frill," it should graduate young men and women who become salesmen for the program.

The planning and design of facilities for the lifetime sports is covered in Chapter 9. New concepts in air and cable support structures, synthetic turf, rooftop fields, and other innovations are presented. Finally, innovations in lifetime sports-oriented programs are covered in Chapter 10. The use of applied research and pilot studies to improve curricular practices is discussed, along with the development of experimental schools.

The author is appreciative of the efforts of many persons who provided valuable input during the development of this book. Special thanks are extended to the members of the New York State Lifetime Sports Association (NYSLSA) for their individual and collective efforts during the seven-year period the author served as President. They helped to make lifetime sports a reality in New York State. Mr. Bernard W. Hungerford, Project Director, State Education Department, made many significant contributions. Charter members of NYSLSA, Dr. G. Hal Chase, Elizabeth Bell, Dr. George H. Grover, the late Dr. Gerald E. Hughes, George Burton, John J. Grant, Robert C. Jackson, and others provided tremendous service to the students, teachers, and administrators of this state. Indirectly, they provided a blueprint for this document with their great coverage and dedication to the physical education of all boys and girls.

Special thanks are extended to Mr. Charles "Bud" Wilkinson, former President, Lifetime Sports Foundation, who wrote the Foreword to the book. I would also like to thank Mr. Norman Fullerton for reviewing the contents of the book and supplying me with helpful suggestions. Appreciation is also given to Teru Uyeyama, Prentice-Hall, Inc., for editing the manuscript and providing me with many helpful suggestions for revision of the document. Finally, acknowledgement is given to Ithaca College, School of HPER, for providing me with a sabbatical leave. It was during this time that the major part of the text was completed.

WILLIAM F. STRAUB

CHAPTER 1

THE LIFETIME SPORTS CONCEPT

The most significant change that is taking place in physical education curricula today is the trend toward teaching the lifetime sports such as tennis, golf, bowling, badminton, and archery. All indications point toward the curtailment of the traditional curriculum of football and soccer in the fall; basketball, wrestling, and gymnastics in the winter; and softball and track and field in the spring. The new physical education is equipping students with the skills, attitudes, and knowledge that will enable them to participate in sports throughout life.

Changes in physical education curricula have come about largely through the efforts of the members of the Lifetime Sports Education Project (LSEP) of the American Alliance for Health, Physical Education and Recreation (AAHPER), and teachers and administrators in elementary and secondary schools. Charles "Bud" Wilkinson and William E. Noonan, Jr., President and Director of the project, respectively, were instrumental in combining the resources of industry and education to make the LSEP one of the best grass-roots projects ever sponsored by AAHPER.

LIFETIME SPORTS DEFINED

The term"lifetime sports"was first utilized by the members of the LSEP. It replaced the term "carryover value activities" that had been popular in the 1950s. Members of the LSEP utilized the term "lifetime sports"to describe the five sports of bowling, archery, badminton, tennis, and golf. At the beginning of the project it was an accurate definition. Today, however, the term"lifetime sports"is a misnomer. The five LSEP sports have been expanded to include a wide variety of activities not usually considered to be sports: camping, aerobic dancing, backpacking, spelunking and orienteering.

There is much confusion among laymen and even among professional physical educators and recreation leaders regarding the terms "play," "sport," and "games." Within recent years scholars such as Roger Caillois, M. J. Ellis, J. Huizinga, Paul Weiss, Elliott Avedon, and Brian Sutton-Smith have attempted to give more specific meanings to these terms.

Despite their attempts to clarify the terms, laymen still utilize them interchangeably. Perhaps we are too involved with activity per se to be concerned with conceptual definitions. Nevertheless, professional physical educators and recreational leaders should differentiate between these terms. Perhaps the statements below will help to clarify their precise meanings.

The conceptual value of a word is always conditioned by the word which expresses its opposite. The opposite of play, for example, is work. Ellis (1973, p. 14) defines play as: "a voluntary, absorbing activity that is not critical or does not contribute to survival." Weiss (1969, p. 14) states: "Play is separate, though, in the sense that it is autotelic, bounded off from the daily pragmatic world." Roger Caillois (1961, pp. 9–10) contends that: "Play is an activity which is free, separate, uncertain, unproductive, governed by rules and make-believe." The Dutch historian, Johan Huizinga (1949, p. 46) says: "Play is a voluntary activity or occupation executed within certain fixed limits of time and place, according to rules freely accepted, absolutely binding, having its aim in itself and accompanied by a feeling of tension, joy and the consciousness that it is different from ordinary life." Avedon and Sutton-Smith (1971, p. 5) are behavioristic in their definition of play. They see play as a type of behavior that is engaged in "for fun's sake." Thus, when children put on mother's high heel shoes, as Caroline Kennedy did to show her father, it is, according to Avedon and Sutton-Smith, for the pleasure of the action without thought to the consequences. The fact that Caroline's behavior disturbed

President Kennedy's news conference had little, if any, consequences at that time.

In contrast to play, sport, according to Paul Weiss (1969, p. 143), is "a traditionalized set of rules to be exemplified by men who try to be excellent in and through their bodies." John W. Loy, Jr. (1969, p. 56), believes that sport is a highly ambiguous term having different meanings for different people. He is of the opinion that sport should be dealt with on separate planes of discourse. For example, he proposes that sport be conceptualized as a game occurrence, as an institutionalized game, as a social institution, and as a social situation or system. As a sociologist, Loy is interested in sport as a microcosm of society—that is, as a mirror of life. For example, different cultures focus on different sports. Sport in the United States, a capitalistic society, is quite different from sport in the USSR, a communistic nation. The Russians, it is reported, identify athletes at a very early age and subsidize them so that they may become very proficient in their particular sport. Amateur athletes in the U.S. do not receive such support. In a word, Loy would suggest that the cultural values of the two countries are different, and sport reflects these orientations.

"A game is any form of playful competition whose outcome is determined by physical skill, strategy, or chance employed singly or in combination" (Loy, 1969, p. 56). Unlike Huizinga (1955), Stone (1955) and Caillois (1961), Loy does not consider game as a subset of play. However, he does recognize the fact that sports are not completely devoid of play. In contrast, Loy sees play, games, and sport as making significant contributions to the socialization process. More recently, Loy and Alan Ingham (1973, p. 269) spoke of the role which play, games, and sport have in the acquisition of social identity, in appropriate role behavior, and in expectations held by members of the social systems to which they belong or aspire to belong.

The controversy goes on regarding the exact meanings of the terms play, games, and sport. And, it is not likely that their definitions will be completely clarified in the near future. This controversy has led some authorities to suggest that the terms defy definition and should be utilized interchangeably. For this text, however, lifetime sports are physical activities in which students may participate throughout most of their life span. More specifically, they are the single and dual sports such as tennis, golf, bowling, badminton, archery, etc.

Some people may disagree with the above definition. There are exceptions, of course. For example, George Blanda, place kicker for the Oakland Raiders is playing football in his late forties. Additionally, some men play half court basketball in their forties and fifties. The position of the author is that these are isolated cases and not true of the population at large. There are attempts, however, to modify team sports so that they may be played longer in life. Slow-pitch softball and no–fast-break basketball are examples of this trend.

WHY LIFETIME SPORTS?

There are many reasons for the trend toward lifetime sports-oriented physical education programs. Basically, lifetime sports came about because the traditional program had failed. The traditional program is largely responsible for the development of a nation of spectators who do not engage in physical activity for the purpose of exercise. A survey by the President's Council on Physical Fitness and Sports (1973) showed that 45 percent of American adults (49 million) never engage in physical activity for exercise. Further, this same survey showed that the most popular adult participatory sports were bowling, swimming, golf, tennis, and skiing. Ironically, these are the sports which are usually given the least attention in our schools. In most states less than half of the schools provide instruction during the regular school day in these activities (AAHPER, 1965). A recent investigation in New York state showed that less than 50 percent of the schools indicated that they provided instruction in tennis and bowling (Straub, Stair, and Hungerford, 1974, p. 8). All too often, the emphasis is placed upon team sports such as football, basketball, wrestling, and baseball. Unfortunately, there is little opportunity to participate in these activities during the adult years. Therefore, it may be concluded that many young men and women are leaving secondary schools poorly prepared for vigorous participation in sports throughout life. Perhaps this is one of the reasons why American men begin to show signs of middle age—obesity, shortness of breath, and clogged arteries—25 or 26 years earlier than they did a generation ago (Lovell, 1975, p. 2).

In addition to the physical fitness values which may be derived from sports participation, there are also social and emotional benefits. Some lifetime sports are better suited to the attainment of these values than others. For example, bowling and archery contribute very little to cardiovascular and cardiorespiratory fitness but they may be very beneficial to those persons who are in need of socialization and emotional health. The opportunity to participate in friendly competition during the adult years becomes increasingly important as one's circle of friends become smaller and smaller. Although the physical fitness and skill acquisition objectives are still considered to be the primary goals of physical education, the social development of the individual should not be overlooked. When one considers the fact that many people lose their jobs because they cannot get along with others, the attainment of social efficiency becomes an important educational goal. Rainer Martens (1975, p. 4), a sport sociologist, lent credence to the above statement when he said: "Our interest in social behaviors is particularly keen today because our physical technology has advanced so rapidly that we have not managed satisfactorily to keep pace with the social impact of these changes; that is, our physical technology has transcended our social technology."

Support for a lifetime sports approach to physical education came from Lawrence E. Morehouse, Professor of Exercise Physiology, University of California at Los Angeles. Dr. Morehouse is of the opinion that just about everything we have been doing to promote physical fitness is wrong. Morehouse's System, in contrast to traditional regimens of exercise, stresses a gentle approach to fitness and weight control. He claims there is no need to punish oneself. In contrast, Morehouse advocates "no sweat" exercises that may be accomplished in 10-minute bouts, three time a week. He bases his radical approach on research spanning more than forty years. As an advisor to the National Aeronautics and Space Administration (NASA), he helped to develop exercise programs for America's astronauts in space.

When one considers the fact that "at least 80 percent of the adult population isn't exercising sufficiently or properly to arrest physiological decay," something must be done (Morehouse, 1975, p. 18). Morehouse goes on to say that this problem has come about because exercise, as it is generally taught and practiced, is simply boring; it is punitive, dangerous, and ineffective (Morehouse and Gross, 1975, p. 18). The thought that exercise, physical activity if you will, should be a pleasurable experience seems to have escaped us. In brief, the science of physical fitness up to this point in time has concerned itself primarily with athletes.

Most everyone will agree that the athlete is a different person, psychologically and physiologically from the nonathlete. Morehouse, et al., is of the opinion that exercise regimens have been developed for persons who are at the extremes of the fitness continuum, the superbly fit athlete at one end and hospital patients on the mend at the other. In the center of the spectrum is the overwhelming majority of nonathletes who are healthy and capable of exertion and yet do not exercise at all (Morehouse and Gross, 1975). What Morehouse and Gross are saying, of course, is that: "Inactivity will kill you!" The lifetime sports approach suggests strongly that exercise of the right type and intensity should result in an alert, vigorous, and lengthy life.

The psychological values which may be derived from physical activity are well-known. Reports from Veterans Administration Hospitals also suggest that physical activity may help to alleviate anxiety, release aggressive feelings, reduce guilt feelings, and resolve feelings of inferiority. In brief, the research and conceptual literature suggest clearly that improvement in physical fitness, self-concept, and social efficiency may be attained through participation in the lifetime sports.

Further documentation for the need for lifetime sports-oriented physical education programs comes from the growing amount of leisure time. The shorter work day and week, more vacation time, and earlier retirement ages suggest a need for instruction in sports which may be played throughout life. Man's quest for leisure is now becoming a reality. The fundamental question remains, however, how will he spend his leisure time? The most logical place to prepare students to make worthy use of leisure time is in the schools. The aim of education should be to educate for life.

PHILOSOPHY OF THE LIFETIME SPORTS CONCEPT

The lifetime sports concept of physical education suggests a philosophy based upon the need for physical activity throughout life. The emphasis, in this approach, is placed upon physical education for *all* students—not just for those persons who already possess high neuro-muscular skill. Interscholastic athletics are an important aspect of the physical education programs but, since only a very small percentage of students may participate, they are of secondary importance to class instruction and intramural sports participation.

Attitude formation is an important dimension of the lifetime sports concept. It is unfortunate that so many persons who participate in sports play so competitively during their adult years. Many persons approach these games with a life or death philosophy. They still believe that they must "win one for the Gipper." And, as a result of this philosophy, sport, all too often, becomes a frustrating series of emotional traumas. Needless to say, the lifetime sports approach discourages highly competitive, dog-eat-dog competition. In contrast, stress is placed on enjoyment, socialization, and self-fulfillment through physical activity of the right type and intensity.

Quality instruction in a broad range of lifetime sports at beginning, intermediate, and advanced levels is absolutely essential. It is suggested that one of the primary reasons for lack of physical activity during the adult years is lack of skill. Usually, people do not participate in sports as adults unless they have mastered some of the basic fundamentals. Unfortunately, teacher preparation institutions, in general, have not equipped their students well to teach the lifetime sports. As a result, instruction in these sports is often poor. The members of the LSEP realize this problem and during the past ten years have conducted hundreds of clinics for elementary and secondary teachers. Consequently, it appears that the quality of instruction in such sports as tennis, golf, bowling, badminton, and archery has improved significantly. Perhaps quality instruction may be one of the reasons why participation in tennis, swimming, and skiing has doubled in recent years (Lovell, 1975, p. 2). Lovell also reports that today the physical fitness scores of boys and girls are higher than those previously scored by their older brothers and sisters.

The need for physical education is supported by the growing body of medical evidence which indicates that lack of exercise makes you a more likely candidate for heart attacks, diabetes, backaches, nervous tension, obesity, psychosomatic disorders, and numerous other ailments (VanHuss, et al., 1960, p. 8). The facts of the matter are that our schools must play a significant role in reversing this unfortunate trend.

PHYSICAL EDUCATION'S CONTRIBUTION
TO GENERAL EDUCATION

Physical education has the potential to become an integral part of general education and contribute to the attainment of its objectives. Worthy use of leisure time (one of the Seven Cardinal Principles of general education), physical fitness, skill, social and emotional health, and enjoyment are important objectives of lifetime sports-centered instruction. They are also important goals of general education.

Lifetime sports comprise an important part of the total physical education program. They possess the potential to help develop a nation of adults who are more physically fit, fun-loving, and productive citizens. In brief, when physical educators change their focus toward the development of the great masses of boys and girls in our schools they will perform a great service for education.

SUMMARY

Lifetime sports are those physical activities in which students may participate throughout most of their life span. Actually, the term is a misnomer since activities, not usually considered to be sports such as camping, aerobic dancing, backpacking, etc., may be included in lifetime sports-oriented physical education programs.

There is much confusion among laymen and even among professionals regarding the precise meanings of the terms "play," "sport," and "games." Play, according to Ellis, is "a voluntary, absorbing activity that is not critical or does not contribute to survival." Paul Weiss says that "sport is a traditionalized set of rules to be exemplified by men who try to be excellent in and through their bodies." John W. Loy, Jr. defines a game as "any form of playful competition whose outcome is determined by physical skill, strategy, or chance, singly or in combination." Despite the attempts to clarify these terms, the controversy continues regarding their exact meanings.

The lifetime sports-oriented approach to physical education is needed because the traditional program of team sports has failed to prepare students for participation in enjoyable physical activity during the adult years. Many students leave our schools with the idea that physical activity is only for the star athlete, those persons who possess high neuromuscular skill. In contrast, the lifetime sports concept suggests that exercise is for everyone, including those persons who have various handicaps. Lawrence E. Morehouse's system is particularly suited to lifetime sports-oriented approaches to physical education. Morehouse's "no sweat" exercises and "fun-loving" approach to fitness is in keeping with the idea that sports participation has the potential to enhance life.

STUDY QUESTIONS

1. Define lifetime sports.
2. Define play, sport, and games.
3. Why should lifetime sports be included in the physical education program?
4. What is the lifetime sports concept of physical education?
5. Why is quality instruction essential to participation in sports that may be played throughout life?
6. What is physical education's unique contribution to the objectives of general education?

REFERENCES

American Alliance for Health, Physical Education and Recreation. *Lifetime Sports Offered in Secondary Schools*. Washington, D.C.: AAHPER, 1965.

AVEDON, E. M., and B. SUTTON-SMITH. *The Study of Games*. New York: John Wiley & Sons, Inc., 1971.

CAILLOIS, R. *Man, Play, and Games*. Glencoe, Ill.: The Free Press, 1961.

ELLIS, M. J. *Why People Play*. Englewood Cliffs, N.J.: Prentice-Hall, Inc., 1973.

HUIZINGA, J. *Homo ludens—A Study of the Play Element in Culture*. Boston: Beacon Press, 1955.

LOVELL, J. A. "Tennis, Yes; Swimming, Yes; but Skip Cigarettes, Please," *The New York Times*, Jan. 12, 1975, p. 2.

LOY, JR., J. W., and G. S. KENYON. *Sport, Culture and Society*. New York: Macmillan, 1969.

LOY, J. W., and A. G. INGHAM. "Play, Games, and Sport in the Psychological Development of Children and Youth," in G. L. Rarick, ed. *Physical Activity: Human Growth and Development*. New York: Academic Press, 1973.

MARTENS, R. *Social Psychology and Physical Activity*. New York: Harper & Row, Publishers, 1975.

MOREHOUSE, L. E., and L. GROSS. *Total Fitness in 30 Minutes a Week*. New York: Simon and Schuster, 1975.

President's Council on Physical Fitness and Sports. "National Adult Physical Fitness Survey," *Newsletter*, May 1973, 1–27.

RARICK, G. L., ed. *Physical Activity—Human Growth and Development*. New York: Academic Press, 1973, pp. 257–302.

STONE, G. P. "American Sport: Play and Display," *Chicago Review*, 9, (1955), 83–100.

STRAUB, W. F., D. L. STAIR, and B. W. HUNGERFORD. "The Status of Lifetime Sports Instruction in New York State Secondary Schools," *New York State Journal for Health, Physical Education, and Recreation*, in press.

VAN HUSS, W., J. FRIEDRICH, R. MAYBERRY, R. NIEMEYER, H. OLSON, and J. WESSEL. *Physical Activity in Modern Living*. Englewood Cliffs, N.J.: Prentice-Hall, Inc., 1960.

WEISS, P. *Sport—A Philosophic Inquiry*. Carbondale, Ill: Southern Illinois University Press, 1969.

CHAPTER 2

SURVEY
OF
COMMUNITY RESOURCES

Once you have decided on a lifetime sports-oriented approach to physical education, the next logical question is: How do you begin to establish the program? The contents of this chapter are devoted to answering this important question.

THE CURRICULUM

Schools exist to help students acquire the interests, skills, attitudes, and knowledge to enable them to live happy and productive lives. The vehicle that is utilized to help students acquire these competences is the curriculum. In American schools, the curriculum refers to the school's total program, i.e., academic courses and extra-class activities such as band, orchestra, glee club, intramural, extramural, and interscholastic sports. Curriculum is described as: ". . . a body of experiences that lies between objectives and teaching methods" (Willgoose, 1974, p. 78). In other words, the curriculum is utilized to help students, faculty, and administrators realize the objectives of the program.

The physical education curriculum is a part of the total school curriculum and contributes to the objectives of the total educational program of the school. More specifically, the physical education curriculum is comprised of all those experiences utilized to help students acquire physical fitness, neuromuscular skills, social efficiency, knowledge of games and sport, the effects of exercise on the organism, and attitudes toward physical activity. The class instructional, intramural, extramural, and interscholastic aspects of the program make up the physical education curriculum. The central purpose of this text is to show that lifetime sports are an important part of the curriculum in elementary and secondary schools, colleges and universities.

SURVEY OF THE ACTIVITY INTERESTS
OF STUDENTS

Curriculum construction should begin with a survey of the interests and needs of students. Curriculum building may be compared to the development of offensive and defensive systems of play for interscholastic or intercollegiate sports teams. The fundamental rule is: one should never specify the type of offense or defense until the capabilities of the players are known. The same rule applies to curriculum construction; the curriculum should not be delineated until the interests and needs of students are known.

It is a relatively easy task to assess the interests of students. You may use a survey instrument such as a checklist and ask each student to check off those sports in which he has the greatest interest. Some physical education teachers and directors secure this information informally by talking with students, other teachers, and parents. Observation of children and young adults during their free play will also provide data about their particular activity interests.

Assessing the activity interests of elementary age boys and girls (grades 4, 5, 6) may be obtained through the use of an inventory developed by the members of the Bureau of Research, New York State Education Department. This Activity Interest Questionnaire (Appendix A) was utilized by Judith S. Rosenstein (1974) to develop guidelines for a physical education curriculum for sixth grade children attending The South Colonie Central School District, Albany, New York. Mrs. Rosenstein found that the lifetime sport rated most highly by these boys and girls was swimming. Outdoor activities such as ice skating, hiking, horseback riding, and bicycling were also important to both boys and girls.

The Lifetime Sports Interest Inventory (LSII) (Figure 2–1) may be used to assess the interests of students attending secondary schools. To avoid the voluminous task of collating large amounts of data, use random sampling procedures instead of having each student in school complete the inventory. Since interests of students vary depending on maturational levels, a stratified sampling procedure should be utilized. That is to say, a random sample of male and female students should be drawn from each grade level. Another approach is to sample classrooms and select "x" number of students from each room.

There are many examples of interest surveys in physical education. Mary Young (1970), for example, found a positive relationship between attitudes toward physical education and physical fitness and personal-social adjustment of high school girls. At the junior high level, Richard Kay, et al. (1972) found a significant positive relationship between interests and abilities in sports and level of self-concept. And at the adult level, Dorothy Harris (1970) concluded following her study that physically active middle-aged men had parents who encouraged their participation in sports. It seems that positive attitudes toward physical activity formulated early in life become part of the life style of persons during their adult lives.

Telephone surveys may also be utilized to determine the interests of students. This is an effective and quick way of evaluation. Select a random sample of students and then telephone them to determine their interests. There is some evidence, according to Carl Willgoose (1974), that some physical education programs are turning students off. However, with greater flexibility in the selection of activities becoming a reality and the trend toward enjoyable approaches to fitness, these attitudes may disappear. Despite the negative attitudes on the part of some students, it is likely that for the great majority of boys and girls, physical education is one of the most popular activities in school. In support of this position, Sara Staub (1975) found that a large percentage of high school boys and girls reported that they spent much of their free time in sports participation.

In large school systems where access to data processing equipment is readily available, interests of students may be secured on data cards and then processed electronically. Computer print-outs may be secured by grade level and sex so that changes in interests may be determined. Since measurement and evaluation procedures seem to be lacking in many schools, the use of computers to process physical fitness, skill, and attitude data has considerable merit. Greyson Daughtrey and John Woods (1971) report that computers are being utilized to generate physical education master schedules in some colleges and secondary schools. Evidently, however, the practice is not extensive in physical education at this time.

Lifetime Sports Interest Inventory

Name: _____ Age: _____ Sex: Male ( )
                                                            Female ( )

Grade: _____ Height: _____inches Weight: _____pounds

Instructions: After the name of each sport or activity listed, place a check ( ) in one of the columns in order to show how much you are interested. If you have considerable interest you will want to check "Strong Interest". If you have very little interest, check "Little Interest" or "No Interest." A check in the middle column indicates that you had difficulty making up your mind.

Sport	Strong Interest	Some Interest	Indifferent (Don't Care)	Little Interest	No Interest
1. Archery					
2. Badminton					
3. Bicycling					
4. Boating					
5. Boccie					
6. Bowling					
7. Camping					
8. Canoeing					
9. Curling					
10. Dance - Folk					
11. Dance - Modern					
12. Dance - Square					
13. Fencing					
14. Figure Control					
15. Fishing					
16. Flycasting					
17. Golf					
18. Gymnastics					
19. Handball					
20. Hiking					
21. Horseback Riding					
22. Horseshoes					
23. Judo					
24. Karate					
25. Kayaking					
26. Orienteering					
27. Sailing					
28. Scuba Diving					
29. Shooting					
30. Shuffleboard					
31. Skating - Ice					
32. Skating - Roller					
33. Skiing - Snow					
34. Skiing - Water					
35. Softball - Slow Pitch					
36. Snow Shoeing					
37. Squash					
38. Swimming					
Diving					
39. Tennis - Deck					
40. Tennis - Regular					
41. Tennis - Table					
42. Weight Training					
43. Other -					

Figure 2-1 Lifetime Sports Interest Inventory

NEEDS OF STUDENTS

The early physical educators were medical doctors who brought students into their office-gymnasiums and assessed their strength, flexibility, agility, cardiovascular and cardiorespiratory endurance and then prescribed exercise regimens based upon the results of these examinations. The individualized nature of these programs was clearly apparent. In essence, the curriculum was designed for each student.

As professional physical educators replaced the M. D.'s and physical education became a required subject in elementary and secondary schools, curricular emphases shifted away from individualized instruction. This change was dictated, in part, by large class size and the importance attached to interscholastic athletics. Physical education's relationship to general education was also being stressed. "Education of and through the physical" was the slogan utilized to delineate these programs (McCloy, 1940, p. 71). Unfortunately, however, less and less attention was being given to the assessment of the needs of each student. And, in many schools today, student needs are given little consideration by curriculum builders. The mass production approach to physical education has become very apparent.

The reason for the lack of attention to the needs of students by physical educators is caused largely by the amount of time needed for testing, record keeping, and curriculum development. As a result, many of today's programs appear to be based on interest alone. This trend is reflected in the "elective" or what others call "selective" aspects of these programs. Students enrolled in programs simply elect those sports which appeal to them. Although selective-elective opportunities should be provided, a far better approach requires students to select within categories of activities based upon their needs. For example, if a student is lacking in shoulder girdle strength, he would be asked to select within a list of activities that would help him develop this fitness component. Gymnastics, weight training, and other activities may be utilized to improve this fitness component.

The President's Council on Physical Fitness and Sports have evaluated activities (Figure 2–2) in terms of their contributions to the components of physical fitness. Note the high ratings given to the lifetime sports, particularly tennis, handball, and aerobic dancing. Although the contributions which sports participation makes to flexibility, balance, coordination, cardiorespiratory and cardiovascular endurance, etc., are well known among physical education teachers, their contributions are not apparently recognized among laymen. Figure 2–2 should be utilized by students and adults who desire to improve various fitness components.

WHAT SOME SPORTS DO FOR YOU . . .

(Star indicates beneficial effect)

ACTIVITY	HEART	MUSCLE ENDURANCE	MUSCLE POWER	COORDI-NATION	BALANCE	FLEX-IBILITY
Aerobic Dancing	*	*	*	*	*	*
Archery			*			
Badminton	*	*		*		
Bicycle Riding	*	*	*		*	
Bowling				*	*	
Canoeing (bow)	*	*			*	
Canoeing (stern)	*	*	*	*	*	
Fly Fishing	*	*	*			
Golf (walking)	*	*		*		
Golf (with cart)				*		
Handball	*	*	*	*	*	*
Hiking	*	*	*		*	
Horseback Riding			*		*	
Jogging	*	*			*	
Long, Brisk Walk	*	*				
Mountain Climbing	*	*	*	*	*	
Rowing	*	*	*	*		
Sailing	*		*	*		
Short Walk	*					
Softball		*		*		
Square Dancing	*	*		*	*	
Surf-Casting		*	*	*	*	
Swimming	*	*	*	*		*
Table Tennis	*			*		
Tennis	*	*	*	*	*	*
Upland Game Hunting	*	*			*	
Walk-Run-Walk	*	*			*	

Figure 2-2 Contributions of Various Sports to the Components of Physical Fitness (From Fales, 1974, p. 23)

Another excellent source is Larson's *Fitness, Health, and Work Capacity: International Standards for Assessment.*

Once the objectives of the program have been determined, a comprehensive assessment schedule must be initiated to determine the student's current status and progress toward these objectives. Physical fitness, skill, knowledge, attitudes toward physical activity, and enjoyment appear to be the major objectives of contemporary programs. The procedures for assessing these objectives will be presented in Chapter 6.

SURVEY OF COMMUNITY RESOURCES

A major tenet of the lifetime sports concept is that the resources of the community should be utilized to build the best possible program. Resources include: (1) facilities, such as horseback riding stables, ski slopes, swimming pools, hiking trails, bowling lanes, horseshoe pits, camping areas, golf courses, etc. and (2) personnel, i.e. persons available on a part-time or full-time basis to teach, serve as teaching aids, or otherwise assist with the administration of the program.

Although interests and needs of students should be the primary concern in establishing lifetime sports-oriented physical education programs, practical considerations such as facilities, staff, time allocation, and finances will always dictate, in part, the activities that may be provided. Within recent years, however, many school districts have significantly improved their programs by making better use of community resources.

The survey of community resources should be conducted prior to the curriculum building process. Once these data are available, along with information regarding the interests and needs of students, curriculum builders may proceed to construct the curriculum.

Some curriculum builders, such as Norman Fullerton (1975), are opposed to this construction process. Fullerton, Director of Physical Education for the Greece Central Schools in Greece, New York, suggests that at first an "ideal" curriculum should be constructed. Modifications are then made depending on facilities, staff, budget, equipment and supplies, etc. By first building the ideal curriculum, parents, members of boards of education, administrators, and other interested persons may be shown the inadequacies of the present program. When it comes time to allocate funds, Fullerton contends that his approach will lead to greater allocations for physical education. There is considerable merit in this approach, but the time involved may be prohibitive for some directors and their staffs.

The Lifetime Sports Community Resources Inventory (LSCRI) (Figure 2–3) may be utilized to secure this information. The director of physical education and his staff should collect these data with great care, because accurate information needs to be secured so that the results of the survey are realistic. Part II of the LSCRI may be used for a detailed assessment of those facilities that may be of particular value to your

Lifetime Sports Community Resources Inventory

Part I: Facilities

Evaluator: _____ Date: _____

Community: _____

Instructions: In the spaces provided place a ( ) in the brackets if the facility may be available in your community or surrounding near-by communities.

	Indoor	Outdoor
Archery range	_____	_____
Badminton courts	_____	_____
Bicycle paths	_____	_____
Boating marina	_____	_____
Boccie courts	_____	_____
Bowling lanes	_____	_____
Camping area	_____	_____
Curling	_____	_____
Dance studio	_____	_____
Deck tennis courts	_____	_____
Fencing area	_____	_____
Golf course	_____	_____
Golf driving range	_____	_____
Putting green	_____	_____
Handball courts	_____	_____
Hiking trails	_____	_____
Horseback riding stable ..	_____	_____
Orienteering course	_____	_____
Rifle range	_____	_____
Sailing marina	_____	_____
Shuffleboard courts	_____	_____
Skating-ice rink	_____	_____
Skating-roller rink	_____	_____
Squash courts	_____	_____
Ski-cross country	_____	_____
Ski-downhill	_____	_____
Swimming pool	_____	_____
Tennis courts	_____	_____
Others:	_____	_____

Part II: Detailed Facilities Analysis

Evaluator: _____ Date: _____

Instructions: Carefully complete each of the statements below. Be very accurate in answering each statement.

Name of facility: _____

Address: _____

1. What type(s) of Lifetime Sports can be taught within this facility?

_____

Figure 2-3 The Lifetime Sports Community Resources Inventory

17

2. What is the distance of facility from school? _____ miles

3. Name and address of owner of facility. _____
   _____

   a. Telephone Number: ____-_____
      code

4. Name of the manager of facility. _____

   a. Telephone Number: ____-_____
      code

5. Cost for use of the facility. $_____

6. Number of persons facility may accomodate: _____

7. Equipment or supplies available: _____
   _____

8. Time(s) in which facility may be utilized: _____
   _____

9. Safety factors.

   a. Are there any hazards that may result in injuries to students?

      Yes No Comment: _____
      _____

   b. Are exits properly marked and readily accessible to building
      occupants?

      Yes No Comment: _____
      _____

10. Are alcoholic beverages sold on premises?

    Yes No Comment: _____
    _____

11. Does the owner(s) have insurance coverage?

    Yes No Comment: _____
    _____

Summary: What is your opinion about the desirability of utilizing this
facility for class instructional and/or intramural purposes?

    Comment: _____
    _____
    _____

Evaluator: _____
                signature

Figure 2-3 (*Continued*)

18

Part III: Human Resources

Date: _____

I. Demographic data.

Name: _____
              last   first   initial

Address: _____
                     street

_____
         city   state   zip

Telephone: _____ Age: _____ years
                  code

Height: _____ Weight: _____lbs.

Health status: _____

II. Educational qualifications.

a. High School: _____

b. College:

name	date attended	degree
_____	_____	_____
_____	_____	_____
_____	_____	_____

c. Certification (list the subject(s) that you are certified to teach).

_____   _____

_____   _____

_____   _____

III. Former employer(s)

name of firm	dates	address
_____	_____	_____
_____	_____	_____
_____	_____	_____

IV. Sports participation and officiating background.

a. Interscholastic sports played in high school.

_____ _____ _____

_____ _____ _____

b. Intercollegiate sports participation.

_____ _____ _____

_____ _____ _____

Figure 2–3 *(Continued)*

c. Officiating experience.

_____   _____   _____

V. <u>Other data</u>.

Include any other information that you feel may be of value to us in
deciding on your qualifications for this position.

_____

_____

_____

_____

_____
signature

Figure 2–3 *(Continued)*

program. You will need more specific information about these facilities
and their operation before deciding on the feasibility of utilizing them
for class instruction, intramural, or interscholastic purposes. Part III of
the LSCRI may be utilized to assess the human resources of your community. Since the quality of the program is directly related to the
competences of teachers, great care must be taken in the selection of
personnel. Frequently, even when facilities and equipment are lacking,
good teachers can conduct programs of excellent quality. Therefore, one
of the most critical decisions in the educational process is made when
teachers are assigned as instructors.

It is with this thought in mind that prospective employees are asked
to complete detailed information about their qualifications to serve as
teachers, teacher aids, or supervisors. Figure 2–3 (Part III) shows the form
necessary to secure this information. Before completing this part of the
LSCRI, you will need to identify the names of persons who may be able to
assist you with some aspect of your program. Depending on the size of
your community and how well you know its citizens and their special
talents, the results of this part of the analysis should be very beneficial to
your program. If you are not well established in the school district you
may wish to confer with other people who may help you uncover the
names and addresses of these persons. A personal interview with the
applicant for a position is always desirable before deciding to include him
in your program. It is also a good practice to talk with former employers,
school and college officials, and other knowledgeable persons about the
applicant's qualifications for a particular job. The authenticity of the
applicant's credentials, e.g. degrees, teaching certification, etc., should
always be established prior to employing the individual. It is a good
practice to have the school physician give the applicant a complete physi-

cal examination to determine if he is medically fit to perform the vigorous participation that is sometimes needed to teach the lifetime sports.

LEGAL CONSIDERATIONS

When off-school site facilities are utilized it is desirable to have the school attorney prepare an agreement between the parties involved. Figure 2–4 shows an agreement which was developed by Irwin Rosenstein (1975) for this purpose. As shown, the agreement specifies the time the facility will be utilized, the cost to be paid the owner, equipment and supplies necessary, responsibilities of the parties involved, etc. Putting these statements in writing is good business practice and will protect both parties from misunderstandings that may result from the use of the facility.

SUMMARY

The purpose of this chapter is to show persons who are interested in implementing a lifetime sports-oriented physical education program how to determine the interests and needs of students and survey community resources. The Lifetime Sports Interest Inventory (LSII) and the Lifetime Sports Community Resources Inventory (LSCRI) were developed for these purposes. The LSCRI consists of three parts which may be used to make a detailed assessment of the facilities and personnel in your community. The importance of securing the most qualified persons to teach the lifetime sports was stressed throughout the chapter. Legal considerations must be considered before utilizing community facilities. Rosenstein (1975) has developed an agreement form that may be utilized by school district officials when they negotiate with owners of various community facilities.

The arduous practice of determining the current status of the program has been completed and attention will now be focused on organizational patterns before the actual task of curriculum construction is begun.

AGREEMENT

Between _____ School District

and _____ Community Facility

Relating to the Use of the Facility for Physical Education

This AGREEMENT is made and entered into this _____

day of _____, 19___, by and between the

_____ School District of _____

County, hereinafter referred to as the "District," and

the _____ Community Facility, here-

inafter referred to as the "Community Facility."

It is mutually agreed as follows:

1. The Community Facility shall make available to the District for use for physical education purposes for a specified period of time facilities that may be required to conduct the activity being taught.

2. A schedule shall be established, setting forth the exact time that the Community Facility can be used by the District. Any use not set up in the schedule must be requested by the District in writing in order to maintain clear lines of responsibility and liability.

3. The normal operating and maintenance costs involved in the use of the facility will be the responsibility of the Community Facility.

4. The Community Facility when used by the District for physical education shall be under the supervision of Community Facility personnel. However, all District personnel assigned to the Community Facility shall be and shall remain acceptable at all times, and shall remain responsible at all times to the board of education of the school district and the chief administrative officer of the Community Facility.

5. The District and the Community Facility will mutually agree to provide such equipment and supplies needed for teaching the physical education activity. Such equipment and supplies shall remain the property of the party furnishing the same.

6. The cost of operating and maintaining the facility shall be the responsibility of the Community Facility.

7. The Community Facility will pay for all supervisory and custodial services. The cost of paying for instructional personnel shall be mutually

Figure 2–4 Sample Agreement between School District and Owner of Off-school Site Facility (From Rosenstein, 1975)

agreed upon by both the District and the Community Facility.

8. Each party hereto shall maintain its own insurance with respect to its liability under the program.

9. In order to implement the cooperation of the parties hereto, the Director of Physical Education of the District shall meet from time to time with representatives of the Community Facility to establish policies and to decide any questions which may arise.

The term of this agreement shall be for a period of _____ (days) (weeks) (months) beginning ___month ___day, 19___ and shall terminate on ___month ___day, 19___ .

This agreement shall bind the successors of the parties hereto, unless notice of termination is given by one party to the other.

The parties hereto have caused this agreement to be executed as of ___month ___day, 19___ .

_____Community
                        Facility
BY _____
Chief Administrative Officer

_____ School District of

_____ County

BY _____
        Superintendent

Figure 2–4   (*Continued*)

STUDY QUESTIONS

1. Define curriculum.
2. Why should the physical education curriculum be an integral part of the total school program?
3. What experiences make up the physical education curriculum?
4. Why is it important to survey community resources?
5. Why should the interests and needs of students be considered prior to building the curriculum?
6. What factors need to be considered prior to the use of community resources?
7. Why is it important to carefully determine the capabilities of resource persons before they are utilized in your program?

8. Why is it important to draw up a legal agreement between the parties involved prior to the use of off-school-site facilities? What factors should be considered in such an agreement?

REFERENCES

DAUGHTREY, G., and J. B. WOODS. *Physical Education Programs: Organization and Administration.* Philadelphia: W. B. Saunders Company, 1971.

FALES, JR., E.D. "The Name of the Game is Health," *Parade,* September 1974, pp. 22–23.

HARRIS, D. V. "Physical Activity History and Attitudes of Middle-Aged Men," *Medicine and Science in Sports,* 2 (Winter 1970), 203–8.

KAY, R. S., D. W. FELKER, and R. O. VAROZ. "Sports Interests and Abilities as Contributors to Self-concept in Junior High School Boys," *Research Quarterly,* 43 (May 1942), 208–15.

LARSON, L. A., ed. *Fitness, Health, and Work Capacity: International Standards for Assessment.* New York: Macmillan Publishing Co., Inc., 1974.

McCLOY, C. H. *Philosophical Bases for Physical Education,* New York: F. S. Crofts & Co., 1940.

ROSENSTEIN, I. "Use of Community Facilities," in *Teaching Lifetime Sports.* Albany, N.Y.: The University of the State of New York, State Education Department, Bureau of Secondary Curriculum Development, 1975.

ROSENSTEIN, J. S. "Physical Education Activity Interests of Sixth Grade Boys and Girls." Unpublished Master's thesis, Ithaca College, 1974, p. 55.

STAUB, SARA. "Attitudes toward Physical Activity of High School Boys and Girls Enrolled in Traditional and Lifetime Sports-Oriented Physical Education Programs." Unpublished Master's thesis, Ithaca College, 1975.

WILLGOOSE, C. E. *The Curriculum in Physical Education.* Englewood Cliffs, N.J.: Prentice-Hall, Inc., 1974.

YOUNG, M. L. "Personal-Social Adjustment, Physical Fitness, Attitude Toward Physical Education of High School Girls by Socioeconomic Level," *Research Quarterly,* 41 (December 1970), 593–99.

CHAPTER 3

ORGANIZATIONAL PATTERNS

The lifetime sports-oriented approach to physical education requires some type of flexible scheduling. That is to say, large blocks of time are needed to dress, shower, learn sport skills and game strategies, and to make use of off-school site facilities. It is an understatement to say that one of the major problems with instruction in physical education in the past, and even in many schools today, is the brief length of the period. For example, in the traditional fifty-minute period, less than thirty minutes of on-court time is available after time for dressing and showering is deducted. When some form of flexible scheduling is utilized, this problem is usually avoided.

Before proceeding with the actual task of constructing the curriculum, you should organize the school day into blocks of time. The scheduling plan will dictate, in part, the type of physical education curriculum that may be provided. As mentioned above, if students are to be bused to nearby facilities off the school site, a block of time longer than the traditional fifty-minute period is usually required. Some type of flexible scheduling should be developed by school administrators to enable students to utilize these facilities. Since the goal of instruction is to provide experiences through which students learn, a scheduling plan should be developed to accomplish this objective. Technological advances such as the computer may be used to help bring greater flexibility to school programs.

Education, in general, is calling for more flexibility, relevance, and individuality in the teaching-learning process. Within recent years, greater attention has been given to the individual differences of learners, and this practice has resulted in a more flexible pattern of organization for instruction. And, even within traditional scheduling plans, there appears to be increased flexibility. Ewald B. Nyquist (1973, p. 3), Commissioner of Education and President of the University of the State of New York, spoke to this point when he said: "I am especially impressed with the extent of creative pioneering and imaginative reforms in curriculum offerings and educational programs in the schools of the state." In his inaugural address Commissioner Nyquist said the one single thing he wished to accomplish during his tenure was to see the educational system become more humanistic.

Changes in instruction have also taken place in physical education. Independent study, team teaching, coeducation, graded and nongraded classes, the use of trained paraprofessionals, and other innovations are now common practice in many schools. The objective is the effective utilization of time structures to create optimum learning environments to provide greater quality, more efficiency, increased economy, and fewer failures.

OPTIONAL LEARNING ENVIRONMENTS

There is growing support in physical education for carefully planned, conducted, and evaluated programs that represent responsible experimentation. This trend is in keeping with the concept that educational systems which seek to permit every individual to achieve at his maximum potential must provide multiple options. And, although there is currently a trend toward re-establishment of the traditional school, there is also some evidence that traditional education has not served some individuals well. The number of drop-outs, or give-ups, attest to the failures of our schools to meet the interests and needs of some boys and girls.

Since 1968, we have witnessed the development of a wide variety of alternative schools within public school systems. It is true that some of these programs have not lasted very long for one reason or another. All too often they become known as "alternative to schools" rather than as viable forms of education. However, when well-designed and well-operated, they serve to complement traditional forms of education. To avoid the "alternatives to school" problem, and qualify as an alternative school, the following criteria were established: (1) there must be a number of options available to students; (2) it must be an integrated program, not just a single class or part of a school day, and (3) parents and students must be involved in the planning, development, implementation, and evaluation of the program. Additionally, alternative schools usually make extensive use of community resources, focus on learning-oriented programs, emphasize open education practices, and feature individualized, problem-centered instruction. These characteristics incidentally are also suggested in lifetime sports-oriented approaches to physical education.

OPTIONAL LEARNING ENVIRONMENTS IN PHYSICAL EDUCATION

Although optional learning environments have not been utilized extensively in physical education, there is growing interest in their use. The Trump report (1961), sponsored by the National Association of Secondary School Principals, stresses the requirement of a basic curriculum for all students, with in-depth instruction for some pupils and far more flexibility in scheduling arrangements. Three types of instruction, according to Trump and Boynham (1961), should be provided. They are: (1) large group, (2) small group, and (3) independent study. The report also stresses the need for the recognition of the students' individual differences and for complete evaluation, not only of the pupil but also of the curriculum.

Trump (1971) delineated a scheduling plan for physical education. He claims that some of the best teaching in physical education occurs in interscholastic athletics, but he also claims that many coaches lose their expertise when they move into the classroom. Under the Trump plan there would be large-group weekly motivational lectures followed by small-group discussions during which students get a chance to interact with teachers regarding their individual programs. The remainder of the time is spent in independent study where teachers and support personnel serve as resource persons. The use of community facilities and resource persons are integral parts of Trump's system.

TYPES OF SCHEDULING PLANS

Basically, there are two types of scheduling plans, traditional and flexible. Each type has advantages and disadvantages. The plan that is selected for a particular school will depend on such factors as the educational philosophies of the community, teachers, and administrators; finances; use of off-site facilities, etc. Carl Willgoose (1974), in citing Alfred North Whitehead, the noted philosopher, warns against the assumption that a particular plan, pattern, time allocation, or sequence of topics will guarantee the fulfillment of desired objectives. What Willgoose is alluding to is of course the fact that the teaching-learning process is far more complicated than that and a multiplicity of variables must be considered when planning the curriculum.

Traditional Plan

Under this plan all classes meet the same number of minutes each day for the entire semester. Each teacher is assigned a given number of students for a fixed period of time during the school day. A typical schedule is shown in Figure 3–1. Regardless of what is being taught, the same amount of time is allocated for instruction and the teacher-pupil ratio remains constant for all classes within a given subject matter area.

The primary advantage of this schedule is its regularity. A routine is established that is comfortable for students, administrators, and faculty. The constant change in time allocations, a feature of flexible scheduling,

Time	Monday	Tuesday	Wednesday	Thursday	Friday
8:00 - 8:55	Science	--	--	--	--
9:00 - 9:55	English	--	--	--	--
10:00 - 10:55	Social Studies	--	--	--	--
11:00 - 11:55	Study	--	--	--	--
12:00 - 12:55	Lunch - Homeroom	--	--	--	--
1:00 - 1:55	Physical Education	--	--	--	--
2:00 - 2:55	Industrial Arts	--	--	--	--
3:00 - 3:55	Spanish	--	--	--	--

Figure 3–1 The Traditional Time Schedule

is avoided. Students, faculty, and administrators adapt quickly to the routine of the school day. Everyone knows where he or she should be at a particular time, and hopefully they are in attendance. Disciplinary problems and the wasting of time are said to be avoided or at least lessened under this schedule.

The major disadvantage of the traditional schedule is its failure to allow for flexibility. Off-site instruction is often limited and variations in time allocations within the school day are usually not permitted. The rigidity of the traditional plan and the demand for educational reform have caused many administrators to adopt some form of flexible scheduling.

Flexible Plan

Time periods and the composition of classes are based on the learning requirements of the students, the subject matter to be taught, and the method of teaching most appropriate to the learning task. And, although flexible schedules vary greatly from school to school, they are based usually on short time segments, commonly called modules. Modules may vary from ten to twenty minutes in duration. Flexibility is achieved by placing "mods" together to provide appropriate lengths of time for instructional purposes. Time allocations for instruction may vary from day to day and from subject to subject.

Figure 3–2 is an example of a flexible modular schedule for a secondary school student. As shown, varying blocks of time are allocated for different experiences. At the end of one week, a new schedule will be generated based upon the needs of the student. A unique feature of this plan is the varying blocks of time for subjects and the independent study opportunities.

A physical education modular class schedule for a junior high school is shown in Figure 3–3. A feature of this plan is that all students may be scheduled for large-group instruction at one time. Extra periods are utilized for small-group laboratory sessions where extra help may be given.

As with most types of schedules, there are a number of inherent problems associated with flexible scheduling. Helen Heitmann (1971) identified problems that she encountered when using flexible scheduling:

1. Not all students feel secure in or can profit from unscheduled class time. Special counseling and supervision of these students are needed.
2. Some state laws and local regulations require a daily period of physical education.

TIME	M	T	W	Th	F
8:00	English	Indep. Study	English	Social Studies	English
8:30				Indep. Study	
9:00	Indep. Study	Math	Guidance	Math	Social Studies
9:30			Social Studies		
10:00	Math	English	Math	English	
10:30	Indust. Arts	Typing	Indust. Arts	Typing	Math
11:00	Boys' Chorus		Boys' Chorus	Physical Education	
11:30	Indep. Study		English		
12:00	L	U	N	C	H
12:30	Social Studies	Social Studies	Indep. Study	Indep. Study	Guidance
1:00			Study	Study	
1:30	Physical Education				Physical Education
2:00		Indust. Arts	Physical Education	Indust. Arts	Education
2:30			Education		English
3:00					Boys' Chorus

Figure 3–2 A Sample Student Modular Schedule for One Week with Thirty-minute Modules (From Heitmann, 1971, p. 13)

3. Staffing requirements may be greater than under the traditional system. (A teacher's schedule under a modular system is shown in Figure 3–4.)
4. A period of acclimation, organization, and public relations must be undertaken before the program can be successfully implemented.

SCHEDULING THE LIFETIME SPORTS

Under traditional schedules, one of the most serious problems that physical education teachers have faced is the brief length of time available for instructional purposes. When time is utilized for dressing and showering, only about thirty minutes in a fifty-minute period is available for instruction; for this reason alone, some type of flexible scheduling is desirable. In addition, as mentioned previously in Chapter 2, a flexible scheduling plan will make it possible for students to leave the school site

TIME	MOD	M	T	W	Th	F
8:30- 8:50	1	7th L.G. Sec. A-B	7th Sec. A-B	7th Sec. A-B	7th Sec. A-B	7th Sec. A-B
8:50- 9:10	2	7th L.G. Sec. C-D	Small Groups	Small Groups	Small Groups	Small Groups
9:10- 9:30	3	Open	7th Sec. C-D	7th Sec. C-D	7th Sec. C	7th Sec. D
9:30- 9:50	4	Lab.	Small Groups		Indep. Study	Indep. Study
9:50-10:10	5				Open Lab	Open Lab
10:10-10:30	6	6th L.G. Sec. A-B	6th Sec. A-B	6th Sec. A-B	6th Sec. A-B	6th Sec. A-B
10:30-10:50	7	6th L.G. Sec. C-D	Small Groups	Small Groups	Small Groups	Sm. Grs.
10:50-11:10	8	Open Sec. C-D	6th Sec. C-D	6th Sec. C-D	6th Sec. C-D	6th
11:10-11:30	9	Lab.	Small Groups	Small Groups	Small Groups	Small Groups
11:30-11:50	10	Adapted P.E.L.G.	Adapted P.E.	Adapted Ind. St.	Adapted P.E.	Adapted P.E.
11:50-12:10	11		Small Groups		Small Groups	Small Groups
12:10-12:30	12	OPEN LABORATORY				
12:30-12:50	13	8th Sec. A-B	8th Sec. A-B	8th Sec. A-B	8th Sec. A-B	8th Sec. A-B
12:50- 1:10	14	Large Group	Indep. Study	Small Groups	Small	Small
1:10- 1:30	15	8th Sec. C-D	8th Sec. C-D	Groups	Groups	Groups
1:30- 1:50	16	Large Group	Indep. Study	8th Sec. C-D	8th Sec. C-D	8th Sec. C-D
1:50- 2:10	17			Small Group	Small Group	Indep.
2:10- 2:30	18			Group	Group	Study
2:30- 2:50	19	OPEN LABORATORY				
2:50- 3:10	20	(Conferences, remedial help, practice)				

6th grade Sections A,B,C,D   Grouped according to needs

7th grade Sections A,B   Average ability
  Sections C,D   High interest and ability; self-motivated; beginning independent study.

8th grade Sections A,B   Average ability; beginning independent study
  Sections C,D   More highly skilled and motivated

Figure 3–3 Sample Junior High School Physical Education Modular Schedule (From Heitmann, 1971, p. 14)

for instruction at community recreational facilities, e.g. bowling lanes, golf courses, ski slopes, riding stables, etc.

If it is impossible to change the traditional scheduling procedure,

TIME	M	T	W	Th	F
8:00	P.E. 10 Sec. 4,5,6	P.E. 10	P.E. 10	P.E. 10	P.E. 10
8:30	With other Staff	Sec. 4	Sec. 4	Sec. 2	Sec. 3
9:00		P.E. 10	P.E. 10	P.E. 10	Plan
9:30	Open Mod. P.E.	Sec. 5	Sec. 5	Sec. 4,5,6 With other	P.E. 10
10:00	Counselling	P.E. 10	P.E. 11	Staff	Sec. 6
10:30	P.E. 11	Sec. 6	Sec. 1	P.E. 10	Plan
11:00	Sec. 1	Plan	Plan	Sec. 1	
11:30	L	U	N	C	H
12:00					
12:30	P.E. 10	P.E. 10		Open mod.	P.E. 10
	Sec. 1,2,3		Plan	P.E.	Sec. 2
1:00	With other	Sec. 2		Counselling	
1:30	Staff	P.E. 10			P.E. 10
2:00		Sec. 3	P.E. 10	Plan	Sec. 1
			Sec. 1,2,3		
2:30	Plan	Plan	With other		P.E. 10
3:00			Staff		Sec. 3

Figure 3–4 Sample Teacher Schedule under a Modular Schedule for One Week with Thirty-minute Modules (From Heitmann, 1971, p. 33).

there are a number of alternative plans that may be adopted to improve instruction and/or intramural participation in the lifetime sports. Basically, these plans may be considered extensions of flexible schedules. Many school officials have utilized them to help accomplish desirable educational objectives.

The use of an activity period at the end of the school day is one way of bringing a little flexibility to traditional schedules. This type of flexibility is particularly desirable in rural school districts where the busing of most students is required. The activity period may be utilized by physical educators for intramurals in the lifetime sports. The use of community facilities may also take place during this period. Some administrators, however, have complained that the activity period creates disciplinary problems where pupils are running all over the building unsupervised.

Extending the school week to six days and the school year have also been proposed by some educators. Neither proposal has met with the approval of students, teachers, or parents. Despite some objections, vacation time and Saturdays have been utilized extensively by coaches of interscholastic sports teams for practices and games. In those communities where Departments of Recreation exist, greater use of school facilities has been made during the early evening hours, Saturdays, and summer vacation periods. Some school districts are conducting excellent summer programs in the lifetime sports of golf, tennis, camping, boating, swimming, and other activities.

Another way to bring flexibility to the physical education curriculum is to schedule large numbers of students at one time. This system works well in schools where a large number of teaching stations and staff members are available. For example, a large school district may schedule two hundred and fifty students for physical education each period of fifty minutes during a seven-period day. Students may be assigned or be given the opportunity to select from the nine different activities that are being taught each period.

The double period also has been used advantageously in some schools in courses like physical education and industrial arts. This method is particularly useful in those schools which have short periods of less than fifty minutes. The double period, however, should not reduce the twice a week physical education period. It may be desirable in a five periods per week system to schedule regular length periods on Monday, Tuesday, and Wednesday, and a double period on Friday.

Some schools have scheduled evening classes for upper level high school students and utilized study hall time for additional instruction and practice in physical education activities. When not abused, these practices have considerable merit. Since many of the most qualified teachers in the community will have day-time jobs, utilization of evening classes will enable them to participate as instructors in lifetime sports classes.

SUMMARY

The lifetime sports-oriented approach to physical education requires some form of flexible scheduling so that use may be made of community resources. As mentioned throughout this chapter, one of the major problems in scheduling physical education classes has been the brief length of the instructional period. In a traditional period of fifty minutes, less than thirty minutes of time is usually available.

Optional learning environments are now being developed to permit every individual to achieve at his maximum potential. Selective-elective opportunities in physical education are an outgrowth of this trend. However, alternate forms of education must be based upon sound educational procedures. If not carefully planned, developed, implemented, and supervised, alternative schools may become alternatives to school. Trump and his associates have developed a system that may be used in physical education.

Basically, there are two types of scheduling procedures, traditional and flexible. Traditional schedules divide the school day into equal blocks of time for instructional purposes. A seven-period day of fifty-minute periods is a typical example of a traditional scheduling plan. Flexible scheduling procedures are based upon the learning requirements of students, the subject matter to be taught, and the method of teaching most appropriate to the learning situation. Large- and small-group instruction, independent study, and other instructional innovations may be utilized in conjunction with flexible scheduling plans.

Even within traditional plans, some flexibility may be achieved by lengthening the school day, providing evening and Saturday classes, and having summer sessions for instructional purposes.

STUDY QUESTIONS

1. Describe a traditional scheduling plan.
2. Describe a flexible scheduling plan.
3. What are the advantages and disadvantages of flexible and traditional scheduling procedures?
4. Which plan is most appropriate for instruction and laboratory experiences in the lifetime sports?
5. How may some flexibility be achieved within a traditional scheduling plan?
6. Describe the Trump plan.
7. What are the characteristics of alternative schools?

REFERENCES

American Alliance for Health, Physical Education and Recreation. *Organizational Patterns for Instruction in Physical Education.* Washington, D.C.: AAHPER, 1971.

HEITMANN, H. M. "Rationale for Change," in *Organizational Patterns for Instruction in Physical Education.* Washington, D.C.: AAHPER, 1971.

NYQUIST, E. B. Preface In *Providing Optional Learning Environments in New York State Schools.* Albany, N.Y.: The University of the State of New York, State Education Department, 1973.

TRUMP, J. L. NASSP Model School Program for Health, Physical Education, Recreation. In *Organizational Patterns for Instruction in Physical Education.* Washington, D.C.: AAHPER, 1971.

TRUMP, J. L., and D. Baynham. *Guide to Better Schools: Focus on Change.* Chicago, Ill.: Rand McNally & Company, 1961.

CHAPTER 4

CURRICULUM CONSTRUCTION

The actual task of constructing the curriculum is a time-consuming job. Many variables must be considered. And, since the curriculum provides the experiences that enable students to achieve the objectives of the program, the curriculum must be developed with great care. All too often, the curriculum is thrown together haphazardly without serious attention being given to the interests and needs of boys and girls. Administrative feasibility and the interests of teachers appear to be the salient features of these unfortunate programs.

HOW TO BEGIN

Whether building an elementary or secondary school curriculum; one of the first steps is to establish the objectives of the program. And, since objectives will vary in each school district depending on the interests and needs of students, there is no one single curriculum for all schools. Each school district must build its own curriculum after it has surveyed carefully the interests and needs of pupils, community resources, finances, and other practical matters.

The objectives of the program are derived after the interests and needs of students have been determined. Physical fitness, knowledge, attitudes, and skill test results will also provide curriculum builders with essential information that should be used in this process. If, for example, these data show that students are lacking in flexibility, strength, endurance, agility, or some other physical fitness component, then activities should be included to develop these capacities. In a word, the curriculum evolves from the careful evaluation of test results and the subjective evaluations of staff members.

The practice of giving tests and then "storing" the data without ever having analyzed it is deplorable and represents a disjointed approach to curriculum construction. Some teachers and administrators say that they do not have the time to test. Others indicate that they give tests but do not utilize these data. As a result of these approaches, their curriculums are usually nothing more than a conglomeration of activities established for the purpose of meeting the physical education requirements.

There are other teachers and administrators who approach the task of curriculum construction more scientifically. Since measurement usually precedes evaluation, these persons first administer interest, skill, knowledge, and fitness tests. They then analyze these data to determine their applicability. The curriculum is then constructed based upon the information obtained from test results. Since we are entering an age of accountability in education, this practice is strongly recommended.

Despite the importance of practical considerations such as facilities, staff, finances, etc., the variable that greatly influences the contents of the curriculum is the philosophical beliefs of the director of physical education and his staff. Their opinions about the place of physical education in our schools will have a great effect upon the contents of the curriculum. If, for example, the director and his staff are team sports oriented, then team sports will probably comprise a large part of the total curriculum. If, on the other hand, the staff is lifetime sports oriented, then the lifetime sports likely will be stressed.

One of the most important rules for curriculum builders is that the program should have *balance*. That is to say, all aspects of physical education should be given appropriate time within the curriculum. Figure 4-1 shows some aspects of physical education that need to be considered during the curriculum building process. The amount of time that is given to each area will depend, in part, on such factors as students' interests and needs, facilities, teaching competencies of staff members, community resources, to name a few.

Figure 4–1   Areas of the Secondary School Physical Education Curriculum

A serious problem today in many school districts is the lack of continuity throughout the curriculum from grades K–12. All too often, in districts that do not have directors of physical education, there is little communication between staff members at elementary, junior, and senior high school levels. Each faculty member does his own thing and as a result there is much repetition in curricular content. The fundamentals of movement, which should form the basis for the secondary program, often are not acquired during the elementary years. When the pupils reach high school their experiences have been so varied that there is little basis on which to build a sound secondary curriculum. In a word, the curriculum should be developed for grades K–12, to avoid repetition and lay the foundations for a sound secondary curriculum.

The solution to this problem is to appoint a full-time director or coordinator of physical education who has district-wide responsibilities. However, even in districts that have directors, curricular continuity is sometimes lacking. Merely having a director is not enough. The solution to the problem depends on that person's orientation. It is commonly known, for example, that most directors spend approximately 80 percent of their time coordinating interscholastic athletics. With interscholastic sports for girls becoming more and more popular, it is anticipated that this time allocation will increase. In a word, the facts of the matter are that very little attention is given to up-grading class instruction, intramural, and extramural opportunities in physical education. And, this unfortunate practice will likely continue unless we change our focus from the education of a few highly skilled athletes to improved instruction for the great masses of boys and girls in grades K–12. In brief, we have the wrong emphasis.

If you want quality physical education as well as quality athletics, find yourself a director who has the interest and expertise to do the job. Then provide him with the facilities, staff, equipment, and supplies so that he may complete his assignments. Too often, school districts have a director in name only. Actually, they have directors of athletics—not of physical education.

The fault also lies with the directors themselves. They frequently refer to themselves as directors of athletics rather than directors of physical education. There is some indication that they could delegate some of the routine tasks involved in athletic administration to competent secretaries or paraprofessionals. Assignment of a regular staff member on a part-time basis is also suggested. There is little doubt that directors are overworked. Just keeping up with developments in junior and senior high school boys' and girls' athletics is a full-time job. The time required for the purchase and repair of equipment and supplies, budget preparation, scheduling, transportation, assignment of officials, supervision of contests, etc., is tremendous. Nevertheless, the fact remains that these duties are sometimes in conflict with the responsibilities which directors of physical education must perform.

TEACHING THE "WHY" AS WELL AS THE "HOW"

During the past several years there has been an attempt to teach the "why" of physical activity as well as the "how" to participate. It was theorized that teaching the effects of physical activity on the organism would lead to greater participation in sports during the adult years. Although there may be some support for this belief, definitive evidence is lacking. Knowing the "why" of physical activity does not insure that students will lead physically active lives as adults. Apparently, there are other factors that also influence the participation of persons during the adult years. Time, health, money, and attitudes of friends toward sports participation, and other factors appear to influence physical activity in later life.

Teaching has always been a race against time. Many teachers and directors will say that time does not permit them to teach the knowledge content of their profession. When only two fifty-minute periods are allocated per week for instruction, they believe that it should be spent in vigorous physical activity. Perhaps this is the right approach but there are other options open for those teachers who believe in the knowledge acquisition concept. First, program instruction modules may be developed for students who desire to learn more about the effects of physical activity. Second, utilization may be made of what the late J. B. Nash (1948, p. 36) called the "teachable moment" in physical education. This practice calls for the teacher to teach an important aspect of physical education when the right situation develops. If, for example, during a particular class a student asks a question about endurance, strength, speed, etc., the teacher supplies the information at that particular time. The danger in this approach is that the teachable moment may never develop.

Some teachers promote independent or self-directed study to help students acquire knowledge about the effects of physical activity. AAHPER's award-winning publication, *Knowledge and Understanding in Physical Education* (1969), is an excellent source for those teachers who desire to teach the "why" as well as the "how" of physical education.

THE CURRICULUM BUILDING EXPERIENCE

The best way to acquire curriculum building skills is to actually attempt to build a course of study. The learning is in the doing! Just talking about or reading about curriculum is helpful but not enough to master the techniques involved. Therefore, a hypothetical situation will be developed to help students acquire these competencies.

Suppose that you were hired as a director of physical education for a medium-size rural school district. One of the first requests of the superintendent of schools is to build a new physical education curriculum for grades K–12.

After a period of acclimation, you begin this assignment. Figure 4–2 shows a curriculum construction checklist that may be of value to you as you undertake this task. As shown, the first step in the construction process is to form a committee composed of students, teachers, administrators, and community citizens. The purpose of this committee is to assist you and your staff with the curriculum building task. Too often curriculums are constructed in isolation without receiving appropriate input from students, parents, teachers, and other members of the community. The advantage of this procedure is not only that the course of study will be more realistic but that it will likely be implemented. A fundamental of democratic administration is that those persons who are affected by decisions should have a say in formulating them.

The Curriculum Construction Checklist

( )   1.   Form a curriculum construction committee composed of students, teachers, administrators and community citizens.

( )   2.   Review curriculum literature, e. g., books, periodicals, research reports, etc.

( )   3.   Visit school districts which have outstanding programs.

( )   4.   Become thoroughly familiar with the present curriculum, e. g., facilities, staff, equipment and supplies, etc.

( )   5.   Survey community resources.

( )   6.   Establish the philosophy of the program.

( )   7.   Determine the interests and needs of students.

( )   8.   Establish the objectives of the program. What skills, attitudes, and knowledge should the student possess at graduation from the program.

( )   9.   Determine the present status of the objectives of the program, e. g., physical fitness, skill, knowledge, attitudes, etc.

( ) 10.   Institute pilot programs.

( ) 11.   Evaluate pilot programs.

( ) 12.   Plan curriculum to accomplish the objectives of the program.

( ) 13.   Implement curriculum.

( ) 14.   Evaluate curriculum in terms of the objectives which were established for the program.

( ) 15.   Redesign curriculum to better meet the interests and needs of pupils.

Figure 4–2

It will be helpful if committee members research and read extensively materials regarding the latest innovations in elementary and secondary curriculums. These materials will provide valuable background information for all committee members when they are asked to make important decisions about the most appropriate course of study to be constructed. Books, periodicals, research reports, and other materials may be utilized to accomplish this task. The film, "All the Self There Is,"[1] is an excellent introduction to the lifetime sports approach.

Visitations to school districts having outstanding programs will also prove to be invaluable to those persons involved in the curriculum building process. These visitations, if chosen carefully, will enable committee

---

[1] Available from AAHPER, 1201 Sixteenth Street N.W., Washington, D.C., 20036.

members to obtain ideas about facilities, teaching methods, curriculum content, budget, etc. In New York state, plans are being developed by the members of the New York State Lifetime Sports Association (NYSLSA) to designate Lifetime Sports Model Schools where teachers, students, and administrators may go to observe outstanding programs in operation.

Obviously, one of the most important steps in the curriculum building process is to become thoroughly familiar with the present curriculum. Therefore, you should decide to spend considerable time visiting the schools in your district—for example, three elementary schools and one one-thousand-pupil junior-senior high school.* During these visitations you talk with students, custodians, teachers, and administrators, survey indoor and outdoor facilities, and get to know some of the residents of the communities in which the schools are located. Studying the competencies of your staff members is one of the most important facets of the data gathering process. Once you are acquainted with your new situation, you will be better able to make intelligent decisions about the program and its operation.

Following these discussions and observations, you decide to draw some tentative generalizations about your new situation. You note that the socioeconomic level of the community appears to be middle class. Many of its residents make their living dairy farming and working in small industries within the three small towns that comprise the school district. The people are friendly and appear to be interested in quality educational opportunities for their children, but also they are concerned about rising school taxes that have come about due to the bond issue for the new junior-senior high school building. The tax rate in the district has risen each year due to inflation and the demands of the teachers for higher pay.

From studying written materials provided to you by the superintendent of schools and the principals of the four schools within the district, you note that the physical education curriculum consists mainly of team sports. These sports activities are introduced, in some instances, at grade three and continue to be taught each year until the end of the twelfth grade. Your observations in all schools and conversations with staff members confirm the belief that the program is largely composed of team sports.

The indoor and outdoor facilities appear to be adequate. The high school building was built three years ago when three neighboring communities centralized to provide a more comprehensive program for their children. An elementary school, grades K–6, is located in each of the

---

* The school district is nonexistent. It is proposed here to make the curriculum building experience realistic.

three towns which comprise the new central school district. Each elementary school has a gymnasium, outdoor activities areas, and all-weather play surfaces. One full-time physical education teacher is assigned to each elementary school. Elementary pupils receive instruction in physical education three times a week. The length of each period is thirty minutes. Boys and girls are separated at grade four for instructional purposes. Although some attempt in recent years has been made to provide a coeducational dance unit, the program was not very successful; getting the boys to cooperate was one of the major problems.

Further study and observation show that the elementary program is traditional in nature. It was composed largely of team sports, such as flag football, soccer, basketball, softball, and track and field. Some attention was given to movement exploration but the teachers are not very skilled in this approach to physical education since they are former secondary people who are now teaching at the elementary level. Two men coach at the senior high level after school, and the one woman teacher has to go home immediately after school to take care of her two small children. As a result, there are no intramural activities provided in any of the three elementary schools.

The junior-senior high school facilities include a two-station gymnasium, an auxiliary gymnasium, locker and shower rooms, offices, etc. Provisions for instruction in aquatics were not provided. A pool was originally proposed but had to be eliminated from the building plans when costs rose, due to inflation. An additional bond issue for the pool was defeated by the taxpayers.

The high school curriculum is also traditional in nature. Team sports comprise most of the course of study. Coeducational, selective, and elective opportunities are not provided because the two men teachers do not believe in them. They are largely coaching-oriented and believe that the participation of girls will lower the skill level of the male students.

The one female instructress is young, having graduated from college only three years ago. She is trying to develop an interscholastic program for girls but is having difficulty with facilities, equipment, budget, and equal practice time during the after-school hours. After a long fight in which the superintendent of schools was consulted, the board of education mandated that one half of the gymnasium must be set aside for practice for girls' teams immediately after school.

The boys' interscholastic sports teams have had reasonable success. Except for the varsity basketball team, they have finished in the top half of the eight-team league during the past three years. A feeder system is now being developed in all sports at the junior high school level to provide opportunities for these students. Also there has been some talk of competition among the three elementary schools for fifth and sixth grade boys.

Except for physical fitness test results, testing and evaluation have not been an integral part of this program. Pupils who were found lacking in physical fitness were not provided with remedial classes. In a word, physical fitness tests were given but these data were not utilized.

As an outsider coming into this situation you are able to draw several conclusions about this program. Your own philosophy of physical education and its place in general education will naturally shape your reactions. If, for example, you are team sports oriented you may conclude that the program is adequate. If you are, on the other hand, lifetime sports oriented you probably will find the program deplorable. Hopefully, you have a philosophy that calls for a balanced curriculum and will shape the new course of study to meet this objective.

Generalizations

Following your period of observation and study, you sit down and write your reactions to the program. Some of your reactions are as follows:

ELEMENTARY

- A new elementary curriculum needs to be designed and implemented to better meet the interests and needs of boys and girls. In order to do this, inservice educational opportunities for teachers will need to be provided.
- Since the three schools are located within a radius of ten miles, it may be desirable to rotate the three teachers from school to school to better utilize their individual and collective talents. For example, the one female teacher may be asked to teach a unit of dance at each school. One of the men teachers is particularly skilled in gymnastics. He could teach this unit at each of the three schools. Of course, there are some disadvantages to this approach but it is one way of improving instruction in various areas of the curriculum. Physical education is such a broad field that it is inconceivable that one person can be an expert in every aspect of it. Using the most qualified teacher, regardless of sex, does improve instruction.
- You are also dissatisfied with the fact that intramural sports are not provided for intermediate grade boys and girls. The practice of using elementary teachers for after-school coaching is robbing the elementary boys and girls of much needed activity. After school, intramural sports programs need to be established in each of the three schools for the fourth, fifth, and sixth grades.

- Facilities, equipment, and supplies appear to be adequate. The rotation of equipment, e.g. gymnastics apparatus, from school to school may also be desirable. At the present time all schools have some apparatus but not enough to keep students active throughout the thirty-minute period.
- There is a need for outdoor playgrounds to be developed at each school. Climbing, swinging, and other apparatus are not provided. Figure 4–3 shows a playground that was developed at Ithaca Commons, Ithaca, New York for this purpose.
- From the limited test data available it appears that the level of physical fitness is, generally speaking, adequate. However, provisions have not been made for handicapped boys and girls who are currently being excused from physical education classes.
- The attitudes of pupils toward physical education appear to be positive. Most of the boys and girls look forward to coming to class. The teachers have good rapport with the pupils. The level of enthusiasm is clearly positive as one views classes in operation.

Other generalizations of course could be drawn. But, for now, you decide that these are your first impressions. Putting your ideas down on paper or tape recording your reactions as you observe classes will be of great value when you finally have to make definitive judgments about this program. Gathering all the facts is one of the first steps in the curriculum building process.

Figure 4–3 Playground structures such as the above are being constructed in cities so that the urge to play may be satisfied. Ithaca Commons, Ithaca, New York.

Some of your reactions to the secondary curriculum are as follows:

- The need for additional teaching stations and staff is clearly apparent. There are no tennis, handball, or squash courts. The elimination of the natatorium was a serious mistake since aquatic activities are an important part of a balanced physical education curriculum. Perhaps a survey of community resources will help to solve some of these problems. You note with interest that the YMCA has a pool that may be available for school use. There are also bowling lanes, riding stables, ski slopes, tennis courts, and a golf course within five miles of the senior high school building.
- You are aware of the absence of lifetime sports such as golf, tennis, and bowling with high carry-over value from the curriculum. Obviously, the curriculum will need to be restructured to better meet the interests and needs of *all* the pupils.
- From previous experience at another school you have learned that one of the most important factors influencing the quality of the program is the competencies of the teachers themselves. You have noted that even when facilities and equipment are sometimes limited a good teacher may provide quality instruction. You are concerned about the fact that your three high school instructors all graduated from the same university and that their philosophical beliefs are quite similar. More diversity of opinions and viewpoints regarding the role of physical education in our schools would be desirable. Perhaps inservice education may help to improve this problem.
- At the present time there seems to be an overemphasis on interscholastic athletics. You note with alarm the absence of an after-school intramural program for junior and senior boys and girls. There used to be intramural activities for girls but they were eliminated when girls' interscholastic sports were introduced three years ago. The boys never did have intramurals. All facilities are utilized for interscholastic team practices and games immediately after school. You ponder the solution to this problem and wonder what would be the reactions of the coaches if you set aside the first hour after school for intramural sports. Additionally, you wonder if there may be facilities in any of the three towns that may be used for interscholastic practices or intramural activities.

The above concepts are your main concerns at the present time. Obviously, more experience in the district will enable you to draw other generalizations.

Next Steps

Following these observations, you and the members of your Curriculum Committee decide to make a complete survey of community resources (Step 5 in the Curriculum Construction Checklist). Go about this task systematically so that the information that you collect will be accurate.

To formulate the philosophy of the program you decide to involve your entire staff in a workshop session. They should relate the program and its role to the entire educational process. You provide them with reading materials and decide to invite a well-known authority in the philosophy of physical education to speak at one of the workshop sessions. Then, after much deliberation you get the philosophy of the program formalized (Step 6).

You proceed to Step 7—to determine the students' interests and needs. To do this you may administer the Lifetime Sports Interest Inventory (LSII) and Kenyon's Attitudes Toward Physical Activity Inventory (KATPAI) tests to the students. These tests are given to a stratified random sample of boys and girls, grades seven through twelve. The stratification is based upon grade level, and random samples of boys and girls are selected from each grade. As soon as you know what the interests and needs of the students are, you may proceed to establish the objectives of the program. Consult AAHPER's position paper, *Guidelines for Secondary School Physical Education* (1970), and supply each member of the Curriculum Construction Committee with a copy of this document. The establishment of the objectives of the program will be the topic of consideration at the next meeting. At this meeting members of the committee may adopt some of the objectives listed in this document and formulate others to meet the needs of their own boys and girls. After a series of meetings, the committee establishes general and specific objectives to be approved by the staff members, administrator, and members of the board of education.

Following the Curriculum Construction Checklist (Figure 4–2), you and your committee members determine the present status of the physical fitness, skill, and knowledge objectives. You should make sure that you have baseline data available to compare test data with, when it is time to evaluate the program again.

Since the trend toward competency-based education calls for the development of skills, knowledges, and attitudes, you are well aware of the importance of determining the current status and growth of students toward these worthy goals. After a careful study of these data you and your committee members decide to initiate a pilot program in cross country skiing.

Ample space for the pilot program is available near the school, skis and boots are leased from a local firm, and an expert instructor is secured on a part-time basis from a local ski resort area. Having adopted a six-weeks unit of skiing, you and your committee members will want to evaluate the results of this program at its conclusion. Much enthusiasm has been generated by students who elected this activity. The contributions to cardiorespiratory and cardiovascular fitness are clearly evident. The out-of-door concept has given you another teaching station so that other activities may be taught inside. The inservice educational value to your staff members who assisted with this program is clearly apparent. You also notice the improved attitudes of students in this program. Discipline and motivation were not a problem. The pupils were there because they wanted to be. You ponder the question whether your entire program should be elective.

The pilot cross country ski program was so successful that you and your committee members decide to conduct another pilot project, a six-week bowling unit at a nearby bowling establishment. You work out the details and implement the program. Class size is limited to thirty pupils, and the school district elects to pay the cost of the lane rental fee. Local residents are beginning to talk about the "new" physical education program at the high school. The program is being spoken of as innovative in nature.

Again, post pilot study evaluation shows that the program was very successful. The lifetime sport concept of physical education appears to be the right direction for your school. You are now ready to initiate a lifetime sports-oriented approach to physical education. The best features of the old traditional program will be retained, but basically the program will be composed largely of the lifetime sports. Selective-elective opportunities for students will be an integral part of the new curriculum.

It is now time to get the new curriculum down on paper. Following six months of meetings and pilot testing it becomes increasingly apparent that a compromise between a completely traditional and lifetime sports approach will be necessary. The committee and staff members vote to implement a selective-elective lifetime sports program for grades 11 and 12. Due to the insistence of coaches of team sports, the rest of the program will remain, at least for the present, traditional in nature.

Figure 4–4 shows the curriculum that was developed at this particular school. It combines the best features of both the lifetime sports and traditional programs. Juniors and seniors will select-elect one of the four sports during each of the seven six-week blocks. In compliance with Title IX, freshmen and sophomore boys and girls (except in contact sports) will be assigned to coeducational classes, and will be required to participate in the activities shown. As shown, grade level scheduling is established for grades nine and ten. These boys and girls are scheduled for physical education in the mornings and juniors and seniors take it in the afternoons.

For juniors and seniors, the first period of each block is utilized for

Grade	Fall Block I	Fall Block II	Winter Block III	Winter Block IV	Winter Block V	Spring Block VI	Spring Block VII
Boys 9	Flag Football	Soccer	Basketball	Wrestling	Folk & Sq. Dancing	Track & Field	Softball
Boys 10	Soccer	Flag Football	Wrestling	Basketball	Weight Training	Softball	Track & Field
Girls 9	Field Hockey	Soccer	Basketball	Volleyball	Folk & Sq. Dancing	Track & Field	Softball
Girls 10	Soccer	Field Hockey	Volleyball	Basketball	Slimnastics	Softball	Track & Field
Coeducation 11 & 12	Beginning Tennis Beginning Golf Beginning Archery Orienteering	Bicycling Horseback Riding Sailing Karate	Handball-Paddleball Beginning Badminton Beginning Fencing Beginning Swimming	Cross Country Ski Volleyball Scuba Bowling	Downhill Ski Modern Dance Gymnastics Self Defense	Life Saving Inter. Badminton Table Tennis Deck Tennis Horseshoes	Inter. Tennis Inter. Golf Inter. Archery Camping-Boating

Figure 4–4 Combination Traditional and Lifetime Sports-Oriented Program

scheduling purposes. Students meet with their advisors and select an activity based upon their interests and needs. Students who fail to maintain acceptable levels of physical fitness may be assigned to activities designed to improve the fitness component(s) they are lacking. Since there are only three full-time instructors, a resource person is utilized to teach one of the four activities during each of the seven blocks. At least one of the four sports is scheduled off the school site. A golf course, bowling lane, swimming pool, and other facilities are being utilized for this purpose. All classes are coeducational and are taught by the most qualified instructor, regardless of sex. Beginning and intermediate levels of instruction are provided in golf, tennis, badminton, and archery. All the activities were selected by the members of the curriculum committee after the interests and needs of pupils were determined.

Figure 4–5 shows a selective-elective lifetime sports curriculum for students in grades nine through twelve. Beginning, intermediate, and advanced levels of instruction are provided. All sports are coeducational, and the most qualified teacher, regardless of sex, is assigned to each activity. Maximum use is made of community resources, both facilities and support personnel. Intramurals are provided after school in a variety of individual, dual, and team sports.

After this program has been in operation for a year it should be evaluated and changes should be made where they are needed. Evaluation procedures are discussed in Chapter 6.

SUMMARY

The curriculum provides the experiences so that students may accomplish the objectives of the program. Basically, the curriculum evolves after a survey has been made of finances, facilities, equipment and supplies, competencies of teachers, and most of all the interests and needs of students. In this chapter, a hypothetical situation was developed so that students could obtain valuable experience in the curriculum building process. Each student is encouraged to construct a sample curriculum for a school system which he knows well. A curriculum construction checklist was developed to assist students with this task.

	Fall	Fall	Winter	Winter	Winter	Spring	Spring
Grade	Block I	Block II	Block III	Block IV	Block V	Block IV	Block VII
9 & 10	Golf (B) Tennis (B) Archery (B) Orienteering	Sailing (B) Horseback Riding (I) Softball Swimming (B)	Volleyball (B) Badminton (B) Handball-Paddleball (B) Fencing (B) Swimming (B)	Bowling (B) Folk & Sq. Dance Karate (B) Cross Country Ski (B) Diving (B)	Downhill Ski (B) Bowling (I) Gymnastics (B) Winter Camping Diving (B)	Weight Training Squash Recreational Games (Shuffleboard, Table Tennis, Horseshoes)	Golf (I) Tennis (I) Archery (I) Camping (B)
11 & 12	Golf (A) Tennis (A) Archery Orienteering	Sailing (I) Horseback Riding (I) Bicycling Water & Small Craft Survival	Volleyball (I) Badminton (I) Handball-Paddleball (I) Fencing (I) Life Saving	Scuba Bowling (A) Modern Dance Judo (B) Cross Country Ski (I)	Downhill Ski (I) Water games -Water polo Gymnastics (I) Volleyball (I) Snow Shoeing	Slimnastics Squash (I) Deck Tennis Bait & Fly Casting	Canoeing Tennis (A) Water Ski Softball Backpacking

Figure 4-5 Selective-Elective Coeducational Lifetime Sports-Oriented Physical Education Program, Grades 9 and 10, 11 and 12

Lifetime sports-oriented curriculums are appearing with increasing regularity. Selective and/or elective opportunities for students are an integral part of these programs. The task of constructing the curriculum is never finished. As the interests and needs of the students change, so should the curriculum; continual evaluation is needed. Evaluation should be an integral part of the curriculum building process.

STUDY QUESTIONS

1. Identify and describe the essential steps in the curriculum building process.
2. What baseline data should be collected before curriculum construction takes place?
3. Identify the major divisions of the secondary school physical education program, i.e., what are the major activities to be taught?
4. Why is it important to teach the "why" as well as the "how" of physical activity?

REFERENCES

American Alliance for Health, Physical Education and Recreation. *Knowledge and Understanding in Physical Education.* Washington, D.C.: AAHPER, 1969.

————. *Guidelines for Secondary School Physical Education—a position paper.* Washington, D.C.: AAHPER, 1970.

KENYON, G. S. *Values Held for Physical Activity by Selected Urban Secondary School Students in Canada, Australia, England and the United States.* Washington, D.C.: U.S. Department of Health, Education, and Welfare, Office of Education, 1968.

NASH, J. B. *Physical Education: Interpretations and Objectives.* New York: A. S. Barnes & Co., 1948.

CHAPTER 5

TEACHING
METHODOLOGY

Lifetime sports-oriented approaches to physical education require teachers who are not only knowledgeable of the subject matter to be taught but are sensitive to the feelings of boys and girls. The best curriculum, if poorly taught, will not accomplish the objectives of the program. Unless students enjoy physical education, there is little chance that they will continue to be active physically during the adult years. Morehouse's system (1975), which requires a gentle approach to fitness, is in keeping with the lifetime sports concept of physical education. Tolerable increments in physical activity and small reductions in calories, Morehouse has shown, will produce significant gains in fitness. In a word, we must use teaching methods that are palatable to students.

The purpose of this chapter is to present a variety of teaching styles so that teachers may learn to behave in different ways. Optional learning environments require teachers who are able to present the subject matter in a variety of styles. Since students come from diverse backgrounds, it is likely that they will learn more easily if the teacher can adapt a style that is palatable to them. Teachers who are able to utilize different styles of teaching are better able to meet the interests and needs of a greater number of students.

TEACHERS—BORN OR MADE?

It has often been said that great teachers are born, not made. Although there is little doubt that intelligence and personality are important determinants of teaching success, it is well recognized today that much of the teacher's behaviors are learned. In fact, empirical evidence suggests that we tend to teach the way we were taught. If we had good models to emulate the chances are that we will incorporate much of their behaviors into our own teaching styles. Proponents of this theory suggest that professional preparation institutions should seek out the best master teachers and then assign their student teachers to those schools in which these teachers are located. From an intuitive point of view, there is considerable merit in this practice. Research evidence, however, is lacking.

Student evaluations of teachers suggest that personality plays a major role in teaching success. It is commonly known that some students rate teachers very high because they are kind, considerate, easy graders, and place the feelings of students above the acquisition of subject matter. If student opinion alone is to be considered the criterion for success, there is little doubt that teachers who possess pleasing personalities will be considered master teachers. However, parents, administrators, and members of boards of education do not always agree with the opinions of students. They feel that students go to school not to be entertained but to be educated. Therefore, these persons require that the performances of students must be considered in the evaluation of teachers. Accountability, holding teachers responsible for educational outcomes, is a movement in this direction.

Probably, teaching success is not an either/or matter. That is, teachers are not born or made. It is likely that success in teaching requires a delicate mix of inherited and acquired abilities. This position suggests that personality and intelligence are required but imitation learning also plays a major role in the acquisition of the skills required for master teaching status.

TEACHING—ART OR SCIENCE?

Sciences, such as anatomy and physiology, differ from the arts, such as dance, music, painting, etc., because they are concerned with the observation and classification of facts. Scientists, in contrast to artists, try to establish verifiable laws that will bring order to the universe. Artists see little reason to test hypotheses through carefully conducted research investigations. They are more concerned with the application of skill to produce beauty in paintings, sculpture or prose. In a word, artists acquire skill largely through experience; scientists acquire skill through research.

Is teaching an art or is it a science? Most authorities would agree that although the art of teaching is well developed, the science of teaching is still in its infancy. Only within recent years have researchers begun to study systematically the many variables that interact to bring about increments in motor skill, knowledge, understanding, and attitudes toward physical activity. Behavioral assessment of teachers is a new and growing area of interest and concern among students of pedagogy.

The recent upswing of interest in the analysis of teaching behavior may be attibuted to (1) the growing dissatisfaction among teachers with their own teaching behaviors; (2) the concern of taxpayers about the worth of their investments in education; (3) the failure of a large number of pupils to acquire the basic skills required to perform complex neuromuscular coordinations in sports and games.

TEACHING AND LEARNING

Teaching and learning, although highly related, are not synonymous terms. Teaching refers to the procedures used by teachers to help pupils learn. Learning is defined as a relatively permanent change in performance usually brought about through practice. Practice may be either physical or mental—that is, increments in physical performance may result from mentally rehearsing the skill to be learned.

As mentioned previously, the analysis of teaching behavior is becoming an important part of the teaching-learning process. Psychologists contend that the behavior of the teacher is one of the most important factors that influences learning. It is the opinion of the author that teachers must become proficient in the application of different styles of teaching if optimum learning is to take place. And, as teachers learn to behave in different ways, they will become better able to meet the interests and needs of their students. The types of methodologies teachers use will depend on such factors as class size, skill level of pupils, material to be learned, available equipment and facilities, etc. One of the central purposes of this text is to identify and describe various types of teaching methods which are appropriate for instruction in the lifetime sports.

TEACHING STYLES

How many styles of teaching are there? Probably, as many as there are teachers. Each teacher, after a period of experimentation, evolves his own style—one that works best for him. It's like throwing the curve ball; no two pitchers seem to grip the projectile the same way. Although all pitchers are likely to have a fast ball, slider, curve ball, and change of pace, the twenty-game winners have perfected the control of these pitches. Master teachers, like twenty-game winners, possess a repertoire of styles that they use when the situation presents itself. In brief, the best teachers, like the best pitchers, have unusual sensitivity. They gather feedback from their environment and utilize it to shape their teaching or pitching behaviors.

For practical purposes, teaching styles, or ways of presenting subject matter to students, may be classified into three categories. They are (1) humanistic, (2) behavioristic, and (3) systems approaches to instruction. In the pages to follow we will examine each of these styles and point out their strengths and weaknesses. But, before we do so, let us review some of the historical milestones in the development of teaching behaviors in physical education.

As mentioned previously, the early physical educators were medical doctors who emphasized the preventative aspects of physical education. They were concerned largely with the development of strength, flexibility, endurance, agility, and other components of fitness. Fresh air and breathing exercises were integral parts of these programs. Even as early as 1904, Dudley Allen Sargent, M.D. (1904, p. i), Director of the Hemenway Gymnasium, Harvard University, was concerned about the physical decay resulting from what he called "the strains of modern life."

As time passed and draft rejection statistics led to required physical education programs in our schools, physical education teachers found that they could no longer cope with the large number of boys and girls who needed to be serviced. As a result, new teaching methods had to be developed to enable teachers to teach large classes. And, although a number of different styles of teaching were used, the most common approach was referred to as the "command" style. That is, the teacher issued a command and the pupils executed it. Calisthenics, performed to the numbers, is a perfect example of command style or what some persons have called stimulus-response (S–R) teaching. Figure 5–1 shows an example of this type of teaching.

Even today, according to Mosston (1966, p. 19), command style teaching is still the most frequently utilized method of teaching physical education. There is, however, growing evidence that during the 1960's physical education teachers began to alter rigid and authoritarian approaches to instruction. More and more teachers began to change their

Figure 5–1 Professional preparation in physical education in the 1920s was characterized by formal Indian club drills and calisthenics. Teaching methods in public schools reflected this emphasis (Courtesy of Ithaca College, School of Health, Physical Education and Recreation, Ithaca, New York).

teaching behaviors to make them more acceptable to today's liberated youth. Humanistic approaches to instruction have appeared with increasing regularity within recent years and it appears that this trend will continue. In the humanistic approaches to teaching physical education, the pupil, not the teacher, is the center of the teaching-learning process.

Humanistic Styles

Humanistic approaches to education have occurred with increased regularity during the 1960s and 70s. Physical educators have also begun to adjust their teaching methods to include less formalized instruction. A recent survey (Straub, Stair, and Hungerford, 1974) shows that one of the most significant changes in physical education instruction in New York State during the past eight years was the switch toward less formal teaching. This change is in keeping with Muska Mosston's (1966) thesis that students should become self-directed learners.

Humanistic educators such as Carl Rogers believe that traditional systems of education have failed to develop a fully functioning person. Instead, Rogers contends, our educational system as a whole is the most traditional, conservative, rigid, and bureaucratic institution of our time

(Rogers, 1969, p. vii). As a result of lock-step teaching methods, he believes that education is faced with incredible challenges, different from and more serious than it has ever met before. And, if educators fail to change their system, education may be taken over by profit-making corporations who can be more innovative and more responsive to social needs and demands.

Rogers identifies two types of learning. The first he refers to as learning from "the neck up," which involves the mind only. That is, there is no feeling or personal meanings, and it has no relevance for the whole person. Unfortunately, according to Rogers, this type of learning is the most prevalent in our schools today.

The second type of learning is characterized by personal involvement for the learner. Humanists refer to this type of instruction as significant, meaningful, experiential learning. The learner, not the teacher, is at the center of the teaching-learning process. Since learning has significance for the person, it proceeds rapidly and is not easily forgotten. Experiential learning, in contrast to traditional instructional methods, has a quality of personal involvement. It is self-initiated, provides a sense of discovery, of reaching out, of grasping. Thus, comprehension comes from within. And, as with Mosston's later styles, e.g., the individual program, it is evaluated by the learner. It is up to the individual, not the teacher, to judge whether education is meeting his needs, whether it leads toward what he wants to know. The locus of evaluation lies within the person; its essence is meaning!

Rogers goes on to say that education in the United States, by and large, is locked into a traditional and conventional approach that makes significant learning improbable if not impossible. Conventional education is characterized by prescribed curriculum, similar assignments for all students, lecturing, standard tests, and instructor-chosen grades as a measure of learning.

Humanistic education, in contrast to conventional education, has the following characteristics:

1. The curriculum is self-chosen.
2. Each student has an opportunity to establish his or her own assignments.
3. Lectures constitute the most infrequent mode of instruction.
4. Standardized tests lose their sanctified place.
5. Grades are either self-determined or become a relatively unimportant index of learning.

These characteristics are in sharp conflict with those of the traditional system of education as it exists today in most schools. The focus in humanistic styles of teaching is the active learner as opposed to the passive learner. The basic premise that Rogers and his associates are fostering is that education belongs fundamentally to the students. In their system it is up to the learner to choose his goals, to act on his choices, and then live with the consequences.

Basically, humanistic education is nonthreatening in character. The emphasis is on learning rather than teaching. Students are encouraged rather than continually threatened with examinations. Encouragement is provided by the teacher through personal involvement with students. Frequently conferences are held during which time students receive specific feedback about the work they have asked the teacher to review for them. The role of the teacher is to release human potential and encourage professional growth. This is done through trusting the pupil rather than through evaluative or punitive action. Tailoring the curriculum to meet the needs of the individual enables teachers to individualize instruction.

Once students perceive that they are free to follow their own goals, most of them invest more of themselves in their effort. They are motivated to work harder; they retain and use more of what they have learned than in conventional classes. When they are trusted to learn they become free to think, to feel, to express, to behave, and to be. Rogers is of the opinion that traditional forms of education do little in the way of fostering these worthy goals.

Application to Teaching Physical Education.   Humanism means a concern for the person above all else. The emphasis in humanistic approaches to education is on the individual's social and emotional well-being. The connection between physical education and social and emotional well-being came about following the early emphasis on physical health. In the 1930s "education through the physical" was fostered. Today, although physical health and fitness are important objectives of physical education, it is widely recognized that physical education possesses the potential to contribute to social, emotional, and intellectual development. Improvement in self-esteem and self-actualization should be important goals of modern physical education programs.

How does one teach humanistically? Mosston's spectrum of styles (1966) provides an important framework for humanistic approaches to instruction. The freeing process, which is characteristic of Mosston's styles, brings out each person's unique human potential. It is an unfolding process that focuses on creativity. This focus is in keeping with humanistic psychology's emphasis on the cultivation of creativity.

According to Donald R. Hellison (1973), there are four goals which may be utilized to help educators shape instruction in physical education toward humanism. They are (1) self-esteem, (2) self-actualization, (3) self-understanding, and (4) social considerations. Self-esteem refers to the feelings of competence or incompetence that derive from a person's subjective perceptions of his own experience. Psychologists recognize the relationship between how a person feels about his body and his self-esteem. Self-actualization (Maslow, 1962) is growth toward fulfillment of one's special potentialities and talents. Physical education has the potential to help people to identify and develop specific physical abilities. Today, we speak of the peak experiences provided by the vertigo sports, e.g., sky diving, ski jumping, etc. It has been suggested that these sports may be an important antidote for the drug problem since they provide moments of total involvement in an experience. Self-understanding leads to answers to the questions: Who am I? Am I competent? Self-understanding forms the basis for the identification of needs, abilities, and interests.

The social significance of sports participation is well known. It provides opportunities for interaction—for socialization of the individual. If played humanistically, sports participation may lead to greater sensitivity toward others and to cooperation. Humanistic approaches to physical education place winning in a secondary role to such important outcomes as self-esteem, self-actualization, self-understanding, and social considerations.

Although, by and large, we are still a work ethic–oriented culture, there are signs that humanistic thought is beginning to make an impact on our lives. Man's capacity for self-reflection has led to greater flexibility within society in recent years. The system is becoming amenable to change, and physical education, as part of this system, is going to have to change if it is to contribute significantly to social and emotional well-being.

Humanistic methodology is based on the assumption that each person is unique with special talents and capacities. Therefore, each person is potentially better able than anyone else to discern what is most meaningful for him and how he learns best. Therefore, in order to implement this philosophy, physical educators need to provide a wide range of opportunities within a nonthreatening environment. To do this it will be necessary to move away from structured styles of teaching to individualized approaches. The responsibility for learning is shifted gradually from the teacher to the student. Mosston's spectrum of styles (1966) provides the framework for this transition. Under humanistic education, students assume full responsibility for planning, executing, and evaluating their own physical education programs.

Behavioristic Styles

Behavioristic approaches to teaching have arisen from the application of Skinner's (1974) operant psychology. Some people believe that they are in complete opposition to humanistic approaches to instruction; that is, operant psychologists such as Skinner believe in shaping the environment to bring about the required response. In contrast to humanistic styles, acquisition of subject matter becomes the measuring rod for teaching success.

Operant behavior, in contrast to respondent behavior, e.g., Pavlovian or classical conditioning, is based on the principle that behavior is strengthened or weakened on the basis of its consequences: the events that follow a given response. These consequences are called reinforcers. They either increase (positive reinforcer) or decrease (negative reinforcer) the probability of a response occurring again. For example, coaches' praise may serve as a positive reinforcement for some athletes, whereas being taken out of a game after not playing well may be a negative reinforcer.

Operant Psychology

The application of psychology to physical education is not new since coaches, from as early as Rockne's era, recognized the need to prepare their teams psychologically as well as physiologically for competition. However, it is only within recent years that Brent Rushall and Daryl Siedentop (1972) have provided physical education teachers and coaches with the specific procedures for doing so. Until the contribution of these authors, psychological preparation of athletes and the application of psychology to teaching physical education had been based largely on hunches and half truths. By arranging the environment, it is now possible to shape behaviors that may be utilized in sports and games. For example, providing students with tokens after they have reached certain goals is one of the ways in which behaviorists shape behaviors to bring about increments in performance. Of course, working for rewards is not new in a capitalistic society such as ours. Picking up one's pay check is a further example of a token economy system. Most of us would not work unless we got paid for it. Teachers who utilize behavioristic styles believe that students should also be rewarded for their efforts. The primary concern of behaviorists is to bring about changes in behavior through reinforcement procedures.

Physical education teachers and coaches are just beginning to recognize the important contributions which operant psychology can make to their discipline. Behavior modification procedures have proven to be effective in improving swimming performance (Rushall, 1967). Operants are behaviors that have been developed primarily by events which follow them. In other words, the occurrence of a behavior is caused by the history of reinforcement associated with that behavior. For example, in the development of strategies for the sport of badminton, pupils will tend to develop and apply those strategies which produce desired results. They will tend to avoid those strategies which do not enable them to play well.

Skinner (1969) has suggested that the interaction between behavior and the environment should specify (1) the occasion upon which a response occurs, (2) the response itself, and (3) the reinforcing consequences. These three factors are referred to as the contingencies of reinforcement. For example, in establishing the behavior for forehand drive in tennis, the teacher should (1) specify when the stroke is to be used, (2) describe and demonstrate the mechanics of the stroke, and (3) decide on the reinforcers, e.g., teacher's praise, material reinforcers, etc., that are to be used in shaping the desired behavior. The formulation of behavioral objectives and the use of measurement and evaluation techniques (Chapter 6) to determine operant levels are central to this type of instruction.

Application of Operant Psychology to Teaching Physical Education. With growing emphasis on accountability in teaching physical education as well as in other subjects in education, the application of operant psychology to teaching methods fits in well. The concept of accountability means that teachers are held responsible for educational outcomes. In other words, taxpayers are demanding that educators be productive. In this sense, teachers are required to measure the student's level of performance prior to instruction, formulate desirable performance objectives, and measure the student again at the end of the unit of instruction. Teaching success, in this system, is based upon bringing about desirable changes in behavior. Competency-based teacher education (CBTE) is also based upon the concept of accountability. Additionally, the contract system of education which is being used by commercial companies is based upon holding educators responsible for educational outcomes.

Naturally, the trend toward accountability in education raises some serious questions. For example, who is to determine what outcomes will be developed? Should it be the teacher, the members of the board of education, the principal, the superintendent of schools, the parents, or the students themselves? With increased leisure time becoming a reality, many parents are demanding that their children gain competencies in sports that may be played throughout life.

The application of the criterion of productivity in physical education will force teachers to define clearly their aims and objectives in terms of measurable behavioral outcomes. Throwing out a ball and letting them play will not be good enough for economy-minded taxpayers who are demanding their money's worth for their tax dollar. The goal of teaching will become the development of terminal behaviors which are observable and measurable. The application of the principles of operant psychology to teaching physical education provides physical education teachers with a powerful tool for meeting the criterion of accountability.

It is beyond the scope of this overview of teaching methodologies to provide a detailed explanation for the application of operant psychology to teaching physical education. For a much more detailed explanation, the reader should consult Rushall and Siedentop's text, *The Development and Control of Behavior in Sport and Physical Education*. However, I would be remiss if I did not mention some of the basic principles of operant conditioning approaches to teaching physical education.

CONTINGENCY MANAGEMENT

The teacher's success in applying operant psychology to the teaching of physical education will depend, to a great extent, on the application of contingency management procedures. As mentioned previously, contingency refers to the relationship between a behavior and a consequence (Rushall and Siedentop, 1972). Contingency management refers to changing behavior by controlling and altering the relationship between the response, the setting in which the response occurs, and the reinforcing consequences. More specifically, in a lifetime sports teaching situation, contingency management refers to the use of token and point systems and the use of grades as reinforcers. Physical education activities frequently serve as reinforcers for desirable behaviors emitted by pupils in other academic areas.

In order to control and alter behavior the following contingency management guidelines (Rushall and Siedentop, 1972, p. 175) should be followed:

1. *Behaviors must be defined in observable and measurable terms.* For example, in the sport of bowling, the pupil should deliver the ball with a velocity of 40 feet/second.

2. *Terminal behaviors must be specified clearly.* In order to receive the reinforcer—for example, teacher's praise—the student should know exactly what is required.

3. *Continuous measurement is necessary.* Once objectives have been established, progress toward these objectives must be measured and evaluated. Entry behaviors, progress toward objectives, and terminal behaviors are carefully measured.

4. *The target behavior must be the one that is reinforced.* Reinforcement should be provided to pupils as they approach the terminal behaviors that have been specified prior to the beginning of instruction. For example, in those skills where both speed and accuracy are important such as the tennis serve, both of these components should be reinforced throughout the learning period.

5. *The contingency must be clearly stated.* The contingency, relationship

between a given behavior and its consequences, must be clear. For example, after having served the badminton bird into the proper service area in eight out of ten attempts, the pupil will be given fifteen minutes of game competition against an opponent of his choice.

6. *The contingency must be fair.* The reward that is given must be commensurate with the behavior that is emitted, that is, if the learning of a particular task required great effort over a long period of time the reward must be something the individual strongly desires.

7. *At the outset, tasks should be small and reinforcement frequent.* The quickest way to establish a given behavior is to reward the pupil every time he approximates the desired response. Once behaviors are well established, other types of reinforcement schedules may be used. At the beginning, teachers should specify tasks in which pupils may succeed with reasonable effort and skill.

Application of Contingency Management. There are three categories of contingency management programs: (1) simple task-reward systems, (2) token systems, and (3) contract systems.

The simplest contingency management system requires that a reinforcer be presented immediately after the successful completion of a task. If the task is to shoot an arrow from a distance of 100 yards into the bullseye, then the student should be rewarded as soon as this goal is accomplished. Under this system, the learning process calls for the acquisition of a series of tasks. Usually, tasks become increasingly difficult as the learning process continues.

Token systems require that teachers provide students with "chips" when they behave in appropriate ways. For example, a chip may be awarded to the student when he serves an ace in tennis, drives the green in golf, strikes out in bowling, or executes a lob that lands on the end line in badminton. At the end of a given period of time, chips may be turned in for back-up reinforcers, e.g., field trips, candy, toys, etc. This type of award system is not unusual since our entire economic system uses tokens which we call money. Money, in and of itself, has little value. However, its reinforcing value comes when it is turned in for things desired by the person who possesses it. See Figure 5–2 for an example of this system. Point systems may be used instead of token systems. When an entire school system uses a token system, a general store is usually set up where students may exchange their tokens for available reinforcers. Additionally, play time serves as a powerful reinforcer for some boys and girls. In essence, students buy time to engage in their favorite activities.

The contract system is the most sophisticated form of contingency management. Basically, this system requires that a contract be made between the teacher and the student. The contract specifies that a specific reinforcer will be given to students following the completion of given tasks. In this sense, contract systems are extensions of token systems.

BEGINNING HANDBALL TASKS

Task	Procedure	Criterion for passing task
1. Drive off back wall (Preferred hand)	Stand 6' from back wall/ toss ball against back wall/fit to front wall	3 out of 4 hits below red line
2. Same as #1 (non-preferred hand)	Same as #1	3 out of 5 hits below red line
3. Side wall drive (Preferred hand)	Stand in center of court 6' from back wall/toss ball against side wall/ hit to front wall	3 out of 4 below red line
4. Same as #3 (non-preferred hand)	Same as #3	Same as #3
5. Lob serve	Stand anywhere in service area/make a legal serve	3 out of 4 serves land within 3' of side wall and don't bounce out from back wall more than 6'
6. "Z" serve	Same as #5/serve front, side, floor, back, and side sequence	3 out of 4 that hit in sequence
7. Scotch toss serve	Same as #5/serve front, side, floor, back, and side sequence	3 out of 5 that hit in sequence
8. Drive serve	Same as #5	3 out of 4 that hit within 3' of side wall or within 3' from floor on the side wall
9. Corner carom shot (Preferred hand)	Stand in center court 6' from back wall/instructor will toss a "z" ball/ return to front wall	3 out of 4 below red line
10. Same as #9 (non-preferred hand)	Same as #9	3 out of 5 below red line
11. Three wall drive	Stand in center court 6' from back wall/toss to side or back wall/hit a front, side, side, floor sequence	3 out of 4 that hit in sequence
12. Passing shot	Same as #11/hit passing shot	3 out of 4 that hit within 3' of side wall
13. Corner kill shot	Same as #11/hit a side-front kill shot	3 out of 5 that hit within 2' of floor
14. Rules and strategy test	Take before or after class in Room 120	90%

Contingency: All tasks must be passed satisfactorily in order to receive a passing grade and to enter the ladder tournament.

Figure 5–2 Contingency Task Plan for a Beginning Handball Class at the College Level (From B. S. Rushall and D. Siedentop, *The Development and Control of Behavior in Sport and Physical Education,* Philadelphia: Lea & Febiger, 1972, p. 183)

Figure 5–3 shows a contingency bowling contract. This contract may be a part of a larger contract related to the physical education requirement in school. It is of interest to note that this contract requires knowledge and understanding behaviors as well as skill.

Learning experiences themselves frequently serve as reinforcing agents for some pupils. One of the important tasks which contingency managers perform is to determine the most effective reinforcers for each pupil.

CRITICISM OF OPERANT PSYCHOLOGY

There have been many criticisms of the use of operant psychology for educational purposes. Humanists, such as Carl Rogers (1969) and George Angell (1969), are perplexed by modern mechanistic-deterministic views of man. Rogers and his followers contend that conditioning procedures utilized in behavioristic approaches to education are incompatible with personal freedom and preparation for life in a democratic society.

One of the major criticisms of operant psychology is that students fail to internalize what they have learned—in other words, students should learn for the sake of learning. However, Skinner believes that learning for learning's sake is unrealistic. After all, teachers and other workers do not work only for the enjoyment derived from their jobs. Another criticism of operant psychology, as mentioned previously, is: Who is to determine what behaviors are to be developed? Modern approaches to education would seem to suggest that the students themselves should have a say in what is to be learned. A third criticism is that animal research cannot be generalized to human behavior. Most of Skinner's early work was done with pigeons. On the other hand, the application of operant psychology principles have helped bedridden children to a state of normalcy. For example, the hospital syndrome, the tendancy to become helpless, may be lessened by reinforcing hospital patients when they perform in various ways, e.g., make bed, clean room. These incidents demonstrate the power of operant conditioning and refute some of the criticism directed toward its use.

In a recent book, *About Behaviorism,* Skinner (1974) answers his critics. Skinner contends that all the criticisms of behaviorism is wrong. Much of the problem, he believes, is due to the misunderstanding of behaviorism. According to Skinner, the major problems of the world can be solved only if we improve our knowledge of human behavior. Traditional views of behavior have not produced societies which can live in harmony with one another. Behaviorism, Skinner contends, offers a promising alternative.

Contract 1 (Level 4-20 point value)

Bowl six games at any lane. Keep your score. Copy your game scores on the enclosed sheet in this packet. On a separate paper, state the two basic rules for scoring. List the symbols used in scoring and tell their meaning. Your score will be graded for accuracy.

Contract 2 (Level 3-15 point value)

Research and write a paper on the history of bowling using at least three resources. The paper should be double spaced, preferably typed, and should include a bibliography.

Contract 3 (Level 2-10 point value)

Learn the correct way to pick up a ball, how to hold the ball, and be able to demonstrate the hand positions, footwork, and release. Further, be able to demonstrate the position of the hand that creates a hook ball, a straight ball and a back up ball. Evaluation will be based on an oral explanation to the instructor.

Contract 4 (Level 5-25 point value)

Observe the Ft. Pierce Women's City Bowling Tournament for an hour or an hour of league bowling. Report in writing how this type of bowling differs from open bowling.

Contract 5 (Level 3-15 point value)

From the enclosed rule book put out by WIBC, find out what special prizes are given in sanctioned leagues. Illustrate the patches and/or pins and explain what they are given for.

Contract 6 (Level 4-20 point value)

Visit any lane and have the proprietor show you the automatic pin setter in operation, how to operate the ball cleaner, how to turn on the teleprompter, how to reset the pins, where the trouble bell is located, where the foul light indicator is located, and how the foul line operates. When you feel that you are ready, take short quiz over this information from the instructor.

Contract 7 (Level 2-10 point value)

Make a poster showing a lane diagram. Enlarge and make off-set drawings of the approach area and the pinfall area. Write a short paper telling of the use one could put this information to when bowling.

Figure 5-3 Bowling Contracts (From Rushall and Siedentop)

67

Contract 8 (Level 1-5 point value)

Locate my posted average at the lane. Explain in a brief paragraph how this figure was computed. (Information of which league to look for is given the student).

Contract 9 (Level 5-25 point value)

Practice spare bowling of a single pin until you can make 4 out of 10 shots. (Have the proprietor take all but one pin out of the rack, and shoot at any set that the automatic pin spotter sets.)

When you are ready to test yourself, try ten consecutive shots and record your score as either a miss or a spare. Use the form enclosed in this packet.

Contract 10 (Level 1-5 point value)

Compile a list of at least 15 bowling terms and give a definition of each/

Contract 11 (Level 1-5 point value)

Work the bowling crossword puzzle found in this packet and turn it in to the instructor.

Contract 12 (Level 5-25 point value)

Take a written multiple choice examination over bowling which will cover the following: etiquette, scoring, handicaps and averages, technique, termino-logy, history. You must score 85% or above to receive the contract point value.

Contract 13 (Level 3-15 point value)

Secure a bowling film and show to your class. Prepare a 10 question quiz over film and administer to class.

Contract 14 (Level 2-10 point value)

Do the large bulletin board in the Physical Education locker room with a bowling motif. The assignment will be judged on the basis of originality of presen-tation, eye appeal, balance, color, significance or value.

Contract 15 (Level 1-5 point value)

Find out what is considered to be proper as bowling attire. Model for the class and explain why this type of gear or clothing is used.

Contract 16 (Level 1-5 point value)

Be able to demonstrate the proper stance, the four step delivery, and what position the hands are in with each step.

Figure 5-3 (Continued)

Contract 17 (Level 1-5 point value)

Using a real bowling ball, (1) show how to select a ball which fits your hand, (2) be able to show how one can tell the weight of the ball selected, (3) show how you can identify the ball you are using. Evaluation will be a verbal demonstration to the instructor.

Contract 18 (Level 3-15 point value)

Write a paper describing the following: Moonlight Bowl - Headpin tournament - 3-6-9- tournament.

Contract 19 (Level 2-10 point value)

Watch a professional bowling match on TV, on Saturday afternoon at 3:30 on Channel 4 - write a one page report of your reaction or observations.

Contract 20 (Level 2-10 point value)

Bowl a 3 game set with a partner - watch for her errors. List on a paper movements which were done well, and those movements which were improper.

Contract 21 (Level 5-25 point value)

Read a book on bowling and give a brief resume of the contents. Write a critique of the book.

Figure 5-3 *(Continued)*

Systems Approach

A systems approach to teaching physical education is a way of conceptualizing the various components of the teaching-learning process, that is, models are used to show the sequential steps taken by teachers to bring about changes in the behaviors of students.

Systems approaches were first accepted by industrial psychologists to show the interrelationships of man-machine systems. In an industrial sense, systems may be viewed as men and machines working together to accomplish a common goal—to produce a given product. Professional, intercollegiate, and interscholastic athletics may be thought of as systems. They may be conceptualized as being composed of men, players, managers, coaches, and others, on the one hand, and machines (rebound devices, tennis racquets, blocking sleds, ski simulators, and so on), on the other. A characteristic of all systems is that they be productive, and in this sense, systems approaches show the interrelationship of the components that comprise the total system. Being systematic, rather than random, is one of the important contributions systems approaches bring to the study of behaviors within man-machine systems.

Educators, for the most part, have not used systems approaches to conceptualize the teaching-learning process. Recently, however, Singer and Dick published a text,[2] which describes the application of systems approaches to teaching physical education.

Figure 5–4 shows a systems approach model for teaching physical education that was proposed by Dick in 1968. Dick visualizes the teaching-learning process as being comprised of the following sequential factors: (1) goal identification, (2) instructional analysis, (3) identification of the students' entry skills, (4) development of performance objectives, (5) development of evaluation instruments, (6) instructional strategy, (7) selection of media, (8) development or selection of instructional materials, (9) formative evaluation, and (10) revision of instruction. Let us consider each of these components separately.

GOAL IDENTIFICATION

Dick's model (Figure 5–4) shows that the first step teachers should take as they prepare for instruction is to identify instructional goals; that

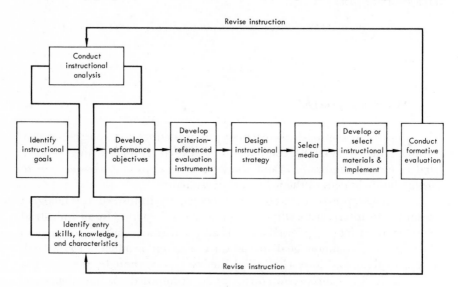

Figure 5–4 Systems Approach Model for Teaching the Lifetime Sports (Modified from Singer and Dick, 1974, p. 59)

---

2 Robert N. Singer and Walter Dick. *Teaching Physical Education: A Systems Approach* (Boston: Houghton Mifflin Company, 1974).

is, to clarify what one wishes to teach. Probably it would be more appropriate today to talk about what they would like students to learn. Some authorities (e.g., Mager, 1962) have argued that too much emphasis has been placed on teaching; far too little attention has been devoted to learning. In a behavioristic sense, teachers should be able to describe specifically the behaviors that they want students to obtain as a result of having taken a particular course.

In a lifetime sport such as tennis, the goal of a particular unit of instruction may be: to engage successfully in a game of tennis in which the player observes appropriately the rules of the game. The more specific the goal, the greater the chance that it will be realized. All behaviors should be observable and measurable. The procedures followed to write behavioral, instructional, or performance objectives will be covered in Chapter 6.

INSTRUCTIONAL ANALYSIS

Once goals are specified, instructional analysis begins. That is, each objective is considered separately by asking the question: What is it that the learner has to do in order to perform the task? For example, consider the goal stated above for the unit of instruction in tennis: The learner will be able to participate effectively as a player in a game of tennis. Figure 5–5 shows an instructional analysis of this important objective. As shown, if a person is to play the game of tennis, he or she must be able to serve,

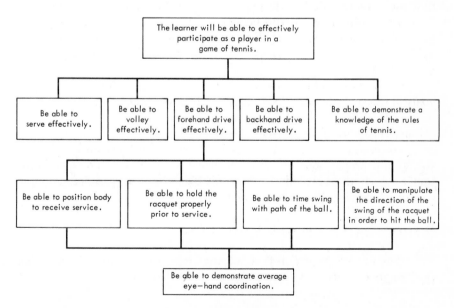

Figure 5–5 A Partial Instructional Analysis of a Goal for Tennis (Adapted from Singer and Dick, 1974, p. 62)

volley, execute a variety of strokes (forehand, backhand, smash, lob, etc.), and demonstrate a knowledge of the rules. Level two of Figure 5–4 shows a further breakdown of each of the five skills. There are subordinate learning experiences that must be accomplished if the first level skills are to be mastered. This process, although time-consuming, has much value. It clearly identifies those skills that are most critical for the achievement of the terminal objectives.

IDENTIFICATION OF ENTRY SKILLS

Assessment of the student's skills, knowledge, and attitudes should be made before performance objectives are established. After all, the instructional program should be based upon the interests and needs of students. In addition, if we know the abilities of the students, we will know where instruction should begin. Assuming that all students are alike fails to enable us to move along the spectrum of styles (Mosston, 1966),[3] toward the individual program and problem solving. If the concept of accountability is to be implemented, this type of assessment is also needed.

IDENTIFICATION OF PERFORMANCE OBJECTIVES

Various types of objectives have been named to indicate what it is that the student will be asked to learn. In a Skinnerian sense the term "behavioral objective" should be utilized. Since some educators object to the mechanistic connotation, the term performance objective is used here so that it is in keeping with the trend toward humanistic instruction in physical education.

Performance objectives should be stated only after instructional goals and student's skills have been established. Since attention will be focused in the next chapter on how to construct performance objectives, this material will not be presented here.

For each of the subordinate skills (Level two) shown in Figure 5–5, you should prepare one or more performance objectives. The conditions under which the behavior is to occur, e.g., game or practice, and the terminal behavior should always be stated.

DEVELOPMENT OF EVALUATION INSTRUMENTS

The model (Figure 5–4) shows that immediately after formulating performance objectives, instruments for evaluation of each objective

---

[3] Mosston refers to his seven teaching methods as a "spectrum of styles."

should be devised. This procedure is quite different from the one usually used by teachers. Most of the time teachers pull together some kind of a test after they have taught the course or unit of instruction.

Criterion-referenced testing is an evaluation procedure that takes into account the direct relationship between the performance objective and the measuring instrument. Singer and Dick (1974) contend that evaluation must be tied directly to the goals and objectives of instruction. In a lifetime sports sense this would mean that the goal—to play tennis effectively in a game—would relate directly to some measure of assessing game playing performance, e.g., ladder tournament. The advantage of designing measuring instruments prior to instruction is to help teachers plan effective instructional strategies.

DESIGNING INSTRUCTIONAL STRATEGY

Designing instructional strategy calls for the teacher to decide how the subject matter is to be taught. In other words, should humanistic, behavioristic, or systems styles be used? Naturally, the philosophy of the teacher, subject matter to be taught, student characteristics, class size, and available equipment and facilities all need to be taken into consideration before determining what style is to be used. Skinner would say that a teacher's history of success and failure with various teaching styles will also influence his choice.

Regardless of the teaching style, the teacher will need to determine the sequence of instructional events. For instance, is the service in badminton to be taught before the lob, or smash, or some other aspect of the game? Motor learning research results suggest that skills with similar motor patterns be taught sequentially (Robb, 1972). Since interference is one of the factors that inhibits the learning of new skills, this strategy seems to make sense. The hierarchy of goals and subgoals (Figure 5–4) will help teachers in establishing effective instructional strategies. For example, one of the objectives for archery instruction may be to have students acquire a knowledge of the rules. Since this is a cognitive skill, an effective teaching strategy may be for the teacher to mimeograph the rules, give them to students, and ask them to study them. To internalize the rules, practice in officiating may be required. The use of media, e.g., video tape, to help students learn various skills also plays an important part in facilitating skill acquisition.

SELECTION OF MEDIA

The use of devices such as video tape, closed-circuit television, loop films, computers (computer assisted instruction), and teaching machines to improve instruction is well-known. The old saying that "a good picture is worth a thousand words" is still true. Whenever possible the teacher should use effective visuals to enhance the learning process. Friedrichsen (1956) found that having students study loop films of incorrect performances significantly improved skill acquisition in gymnastics over a control group of subjects who viewed only loops that showed the correct form.

Usually only one media is used—the teacher. Today, however, teachers have at their disposal a wide range of devices to help improve instruction. The activation of all the senses—visual, auditory, kinesthetic —is now possible through multi-media devices. The use of video tape makes it possible for students to acquire feedback immediately after the execution of a skill. Since knowledge of results is one of the most important factors that influences learning, these devices should be used whenever possible. However, media should not be utilized indiscriminately.

DEVELOPMENT OR SELECTION OF INSTRUCTIONAL MATERIALS

The next step in the instructional planning process is to either develop or select instructional materials such as books, tennis balls, golf clubs, etc. Great care should be taken in the selection of these devices. Too often, when teaching young children, adult size equipment is used during instruction. Since pupils often do not possess the necessary strength to handle this large size, decrement in performance results.

The development and use of smaller balls, lower baskets, and shorter racquets have enabled young children to improve their skills and gain greater enjoyment in a wide variety of sports. In the development of hand-eye coordinations required in catching various types of balls, teachers have found that these behaviors are learned faster if fleece balls are used early in the skill acquisition process. In brief, selection of the appropriate materials will enhance learning.

CONDUCTING FORMATIVE EVALUATION

Formative evaluation refers to the procedures used to determine the quality of instruction. These procedures will be presented in Chapter 6, Measurement and Evaluation. Usually, the opinions of students, fellow teachers, and administrators are weighed to assess the effectiveness of instruction. Based upon the results of these evaluations, the instructional process should be revised to better meet the interests and needs of students. Figure 5–3, the systems model, shows the feedback loops that carry the evaluative information back to the beginning of the system for re-analysis.

Systems approaches to teaching physical education provide teachers with models for use in planning the instructional process. Being systematic, rather than random, means that all components of the instructional process and their interrelationship of goal identification, instructional analysis, entry skills of pupils, performance objectives, criterion-referenced evaluation, design of instructional strategy, media selection, instructional materials, and formative evaluation must be specified. There are other models that could have been presented; for example, Ann Gentile's model (1970), as shown in Figure 5–6, provides another way of conceptualizing the learning of a motor skill. Readers will also find John Nixon's and Lawrence Locke's "Research on Teaching Physical Education" (1973) interesting and informative.

SUMMARY

Good teaching is absolutely essential if the objectives of lifetime sports-oriented approaches to physical education are to be realized. No matter how good the curriculum, if it is taught without great sensitivity, the program will not be a success. In a word, great teachers make physical education a "special" subject in our schools.

Basically, there are three broad approaches to teaching physical education. They are (1) humanistic, (2) behavioristic, and (3) systems styles. Humanistic styles place emphasis on the individual and how he or she feels about the learning experiences.

In contrast, behavioristic methods focus on the acquisition of subject matter. Contingency management procedures are used to shape the environment to bring about desired responses. This approach is in keeping with the growing concern for accountability and competency-based teacher education. Token and point systems are integral parts of what B. F. Skinner calls operant conditioning. Brent Rushall and Daryl Siedentop have shown how to apply operant psychology to the development and control of behaviors in sports and physical education. However, behaviorism is not without its critics.

Systems styles of teaching view the teaching-learning process as being composed of step-by-step procedures. In this chapter Singer-Dick's model was demonstrated. Their system conceptualizes the components

PHASE I
CRITICAL EVENTS IN MOTOR LEARNING
STUDENT SEQUENCE

STUDENT	Goal Behavior Activated	Identifies Relevant Stimuli	Formulates Motor Plan	Emits Response 1	Processes Feedback	Decides Nature of Next Response	Emits Response 2	TO PHASE II
TEACHER	STAGE 1	STAGE 2	STAGE 3	STAGE 4	STAGE 5	STAGE 6	STAGE 7	POSTACTIVE EVENTS / TEACHER

PREACTIVE DECISIONS

Create Environment.
Plan Instruction.

Research on:
Schedules
Special Training
Equipment and Environment
Class Size
Ability Grouping
Coeducation
Teacher Planning

STAGE 1 — Clarify Goal. Establish Motive and Learning Set.
Research on: Motivation, Goal Clarity

STAGE 2 — Select, Present and Analyze Practice Task.
Research on: Wholes and Parts, Level of Difficulty, Progression, Simulation, Demonstration, Practice without Instruction, Programmed Learning, Verbal Behavior, Principles, Attention and Distraction

STAGE 3 — Provide Directions for Performance.
Research on: Motor Plans, Speed and Accuracy Sets

STAGE 4 — Support and Observe Practice.
Research on: Systematic Observation, Manual Assistance

STAGE 5 — Direct and Augment Feedback.
Research on: Open and Closed Skills, Knowledge of Performance, Knowledge of Results, Feedback Media

STAGE 6 — Guide Adjustment of Performance.
Research on: Learning Strategies, Incentive Motivation, Mental Practice

STAGE 7 — Pace and Sequence Practice.
Research on: Distribution of Practice, Mastery and Advanced Phases of Practice

POSTACTIVE EVENTS — Analyze, Evaluate and Adjust Instruction.
Research on: Critical Incidents, Descriptive Analyses

TEACHER SEQUENCE
CRITICAL DECISIONS AND INTERVENTIONS TO FACILITATE MOTOR LEARNING
PHASE I

Figure 5–6 A. M. Gentile's Model for Conceptualizing the Learning of a Motor Skill (From A. M. Gentile, "The Nature of Motor Skill and Skill Acquisition: A Working Model." Paper delivered at the Post Doctoral Invitational Seminar in Motor Learning, Columbia University, Teachers College, New York, June 1970)

that comprise the instructional process into goal identification, instructional analysis, entry skills, performance objectives, etc. Evaluative procedures make up an integral part of the instructional process. Formative evaluation, the evaluation of the teaching process, is an important part of Singer and Dick's system.

Finally, it is a basic premise of the author that teachers can learn to behave in different ways so that they may provide students with a variety of environments in which to learn. Alternative forms of education, not *to* education, are a growing interest and concern among students of the educational process. The development of optional learning environments will play a central role in physical education in the years ahead.

A second premise of the author is that all styles of teaching have the potential to contribute significantly toward desirable educational outcomes. The style that the teacher chooses will depend on the teacher's philosophy, his beliefs about the educational process, and goals that are to be achieved. Laurence Morehouse and Leonard Gross, for example, advocate a gentle approach to exercise. Other factors, such as the capabilities of students, attitudes and beliefs of members of the community, board of education, and administration also shape teaching behaviors. But, despite all of the above factors, the teacher must determine how students best learn and adopt instructional strategies to bring about desirable changes in behavior.

STUDY QUESTIONS

1. What is the difference between teaching and learning?
2. Are great teachers born or made?
3. Is teaching an art or is it a science, or both?
4. How many different styles of teaching are there?
5. What are the characteristics of humanistic, behavioristic, and systems approaches to teaching? What are their similarities and differences?
6. Show the application of each of the above styles to teaching physical education.
7. What is operant psychology? Show its application to teaching physical education.

8. Describe contingency management and show its application to teaching physical education.

9. What are some of the criticisms of operant psychology?

10. What is a performance objective?

11. Describe the concept of accountability.

12. Why is it important for teachers to develop alternative approaches to teaching?

13. What factors should be considered when selecting media, e.g., video tape?

REFERENCES

ALLEN, D. W., and K. RYAN. *Microteaching*. Reading, Mass.: Addison-Wesley Publishing Co., Inc., 1969.

ANGELL, GEORGE. "Physical Education and the New Breed," *Journal of Health, Physical Education and Recreation*, 40 (1969), 25–28.

BLOOM, BENJAMIN, ed. *Taxonomy of Educational Objectives*. New York: David McKay Co., Inc., 1956.

BRUNNER, JEROME S. *The Relevance of Education*. New York: W. W. Norton & Company, Inc., 1971.

DOUGHERTY, NEIL J. "A Comparison of the Effects of Command, Task and Individual Program Styles of Teaching in the Development of Physical Fitness and Motor Skills." Unpublished Doctoral dissertation, Temple University, 1970.

————. "A Plan for Analysis of Teacher-Pupil Interaction in Physical Education Classes," *Quest* (Winter, 1971), pp. 39–48.

FLANDERS, NED A. *Analyzing Teaching Behavior*. Reading, Mass.: Addison-Wesley Publishing Co., Inc., 1970.

Friedrichsen, F. W. "A Study of the Effectiveness of Loop Films as Instructional Aids in Teaching Gymnastic Stunts." Unpublished Master's thesis, State University of Iowa, 1956.

GARDNER, JOHN W. *Excellence*. New York: Harper and Row, Publishers, 1961.

GENTILE, A. M. "The Nature of Motor Skill and Skill Acquisition: A Working

Model." Paper delivered at the Post Doctoral Invitational Seminar in Motor Learning, Columbia University, Teachers College, June 1970.

GOBLE, F. G. *The Third Force—The Psychology of Abraham Maslow.* New York: Grossman Publishers, 1970.

GOLDBERGER, MICHAEL. "Studying Your Teaching Behavior," *Journal of Health, Physical Education and Recreation,* 45: 3 (1974), 33–36.

GREENBERG, HERBERT O. *Teaching with Feeling.* Toronto, Ontario: Collier-Macmillan Canada Ltd., 1969.

HELLISTON, DONALD R. *Humanistic Physical Education.* Englewood Cliffs, N.J.: Prentice-Hall, Inc., 1973.

HOLT, JOHN. *How Children Learn.* New York: Pitman Publishing Corporation, 1967.

———. *How Children Fail.* New York: Pitman Publishing Corporation, 1964.

KNEER, MARION E. "How Human are You?" *Journal of Health, Physical Education and Recreation,* 45: 6 (June 1974), 32–34.

LEONARD, GEORGE B. *Education and Ecstacy.* New York: The Delacorte Press, 1968.

MAGER, R. F. *Preparing Instruction Objectives.* Palo Alto, Calif.: Fearon Publishers, 1962.

MASLOW, W. H. *Toward a Psychology of Being.* New York: Van Nostrand Reinhold Company, 1962.

MOREHOUSE, LEONARD E., and LEONARD GROSS. *Total Fitness in 30 Minutes a Week.* New York: Simon and Schuster, 1975.

MOSSTON, MUSKA. *Teaching Physical Education.* Columbus, Ohio: Charles E. Merrill Publishing Company, 1966.

NIXON, JOHN E., and LAWRENCE F. LOCKE. "Research on Teaching Physical Education," in R. W. W. Travers, ed. *Second Handbook of Research on Teaching.* Chicago: Rand McNally & Company, 1973, pp. 1210–42.

ROBB, M. D. *The Dynamics of Motor-Skill Acquisition.* Englewood Cliffs, N.J.: Prentice-Hall, Inc., 1972.

ROGERS, CARL R. *Freedom to Learn.* Columbus, Ohio: Charles E. Merrill Publishing Company, 1969.

RUSHALL, BRENT S. "Personality Profiles and a Theory of Behavior Modification for Swimmers," *Swimming Techniques,* October 1967.

RUSHALL, BRENT S., and DARYL SIEDENTOP. *The Development and Control of Behavior in Sport and Physical Education.* Philadelphia: Lea & Febiger, 1972.

SAFRIT, MARGARET J. *Evaluation in Physical Education.* Englewood Cliffs, N.J.: Prentice-Hall, Inc., 1973.

SARGENT, D. A. *Health, Strength and Power.* Boston: H. M. Caldwell, 1904.

SINGER, ROBERT N., and WALTER DICK. *Teaching Physical Education: A Systems Approach.* Boston: Houghton Mifflin Company, 1974.

SKINNER, B. F. *About Behaviorism.* New York: Alfred A. Knopf, Inc., 1974.

————. *Beyond Freedom and Dignity*. New York: Alfred A. Knopf, Inc., 1971.

————. *The Technology of Teaching*. New York: Appleton-Century-Crofts, 1968.

STRAUB, WILLIAM, DAVID STAIR, and BERNARD HUNGERFORD. "The Status of Lifetime Sports Instruction in New York State Secondary Schools," in press.

Webster's Collegiate Dictionary. Springfield, Mass.: G. & C. Merriam Company, 1947.

WEINBERG, CARL, ed. *Humanistic Foundations of Education*. Englewood Cliffs, N.J.: Prentice-Hall, Inc., 1972.

CHAPTER 6

MEASUREMENT
AND EVALUATION

Sound, practical measurement and evaluation procedures must be utilized if teachers and administrators are to accomplish the goals of the lifetime sports-oriented physical education program. The concern is with changing the behaviors of learners so that they may be equipped to participate in enjoyable physical activities throughout life. Unless students acquire desirable skills, knowledges, and attitudes, it is unlikely that they will want to participate in sports during the adult years. Empirical observations of adult participants suggest that they acquired these competencies at an early age.

Although courses in tests and measurement, and measurement and evaluation have been an integral part of undergraduate and graduate professional preparation curriculums respectfully for many years, it is surprising that there is a lack of sound measurement and evaluation procedures in our schools. The major problem seems to be that teachers do not believe that there is adequate time allocated for the use of comprehensive measurement and evaluation techniques. As a result, students are not provided with definitive information about their current status and growth toward worthy educational objectives, such as physical fitness, skill, knowledge, and attitudes toward physical activity. And, when knowledge of results is lacking, learning does not take place as readily as it does when definitive feedback is present. The assumption is that effective teaching requires a clear conception of the desired learning outcomes (Gronlund, 1970).

In this chapter the principles and procedures of the evaluation process are presented in three parts: identifying and defining behavioral objectives; selecting evaluation instruments that most effectively appraise learning outcomes; and utilization of measurement and evaluation to improve instruction.

MEASUREMENT AND EVALUATION DEFINED

Before proceeding with the above format, several terms will be defined in order to avoid some of the misconceptions that frequently hamper developers of measurement and evaluation techniques. Operational definitions bring greater clarity and therefore reduce the ambiguity often associated with the use of measurement and evaluation procedures.

"Measurement is defined as the process of assigning a number to some property of an entity" (Safrit, 1973, p. 1). Julian Stanley (1964, p. 24) refers to measurement "as the administration and scoring of tests." And, a test, according to Lee Cronback (1960, p. 21), "is a systematic procedure for comparing the behavior of two or more persons." Thus, measurement in physical education involves giving tests of physical fitness, skill, knowledge, and attitudes so that students may be provided with definitive information about their current status and growth toward the objectives of the program.

"Education is a process which changes the learner" (Bloom, Hastings, and Madaus, 1971, p. 8). To determine if changes occur, measurement followed by evaluation must take place. In this context, evaluation is the process of making judgments about the results of measurement. When teachers answer questions or assign grades to students based upon the results of measurement, they are performing evaluation. Bloom, et al. (1971, p. 8) summarized these thoughts well when he said: "Evaluation, . . . , is the systematic collection of evidence to determine whether in fact certain changes are taking place in the learners . . . ."

Unfortunately, evaluation has been most frequently utilized only to assign grades or classify students for instructional purposes. Little attention has been given to the important role evaluation should play in the improvement of teaching and learning. Basically, two types of evaluation are needed. First, evaluation should be an integral part of the teaching-learning process. Therefore, evaluation should take place while the instructional unit is in process. For example, when learning the tennis serve students want to know if they are gripping the racquet correctly, tossing the ball properly, positioning the racquet at certain check points throughout the swing, etc. This type of evaluation is called formative evaluation. Second, it is also desirable to evaluate progress at the end of each instructional unit. For example: Have the objectives which were established prior to instruction been realized? This type of evaluation is referred to as summative evaluation.

One of the distinguishing characteristics of formative and summative evaluation is their purpose. Since summative evaluation takes place at the end of the instructional unit, it is used to assign grades, predict success in future courses or on the job, provide knowledge of results for students, etc. Formative evaluation, on the other hand, is used to provide students with feedback while the unit is in process. It also helps teachers to shape learning experiences so that optimum learning will take place.

BEHAVIORAL OBJECTIVES

With the trend toward accountability in education, increasing use and attention have been given to behavioral objectives. Accountability refers to the practice of holding teachers responsible for educational outcomes. In a physical education context, accountability means that teachers would be held responsible for growth in skill, knowledge, attitudes, and physical fitness.

In order to hold teachers responsible for results, clear-cut objectives must be established prior to the start of the teaching-learning process. The emphasis is placed on observable behaviors that can be determined objectively. In other words, overt, rather than covert, behaviors are emphasized. Therefore, behavioral objectives should be established for each unit of instruction so that definitive measurement and evaluation procedures may determine if changes in behavior are taking place. Determination of the student's status prior to the start and again at the end of each unit is required if intelligent decisions are to be made about progress toward the goals of instruction.

Peter Werner (1973) raised several important questions about the formulation and use of behavioral objectives. You may find these questions and their answers useful as you attempt to prepare behavioral objectives for the lifetime sports. First, Werner asks: What is a behavioral objective? Second, how are behavioral objectives classified in each of the educational domains? Third, what do behavioral objectives do that a common, old-fashioned objective cannot accomplish? And, fourth, to whom are these behavioral objectives useful? Let me try to answer these questions.

Definition

An educational objective is a statement of proposed change in the learner (Mager, 1962). One of the principal tasks of school administrators and teachers is to decide how they want the student to change and what part they may play in enabling him to do so (Bloom, Hastings and Madaus, 1971). When learning outcomes are stated in terms of observable behaviors that students will emit, they are referred to as behavioral objectives. Thus, as a teacher of tennis, you may state that one of your behavioral objectives is: Given balls and a racquet, the student will serve five out of eight services from the service position behind the endline into the opponent's right service court. This statement is a behavioral objective since it is stated in terms of the student's observable behavior. And, the objective fulfills two fundamental criteria that should be met in the writing of behavioral objectives: (1) it states what is to be learned; and (2) it tells the student how to recognize when learning has taken place. In the tennis serving example, the tennis service is learned when a student can serve five out of eight services into the opponent's service court. This objective may be realistic for beginners but would be inappropriate for high level performance since velocity, spin, and placement of the service within the service court were not specified. In summary, behavioral objectives are statements that communicate clearly a desired action on the part of the learner (Werner, 1973).

Classification

Behavioral objectives are classified into three domains—cognitive, affective and psychomotor. In planning instructional materials, the teacher should prepare behavioral objectives for each of these domains. Cognitive behaviors consist of knowledge, comprehension, application, analysis, synthesis, and evaluation (Bloom, et al., 1956). In a lifetime sports context, cognitive objectives would be written for knowledge of the rules, strategies, and ethics.

The affective domain is concerned with the development of interests, desirable attitudes, values, commitment, and willpower (Krathwohl, 1964). This area of student development has not been given the attention which it rightfully deserves. Many students are apparently leaving our secondary schools without an indepth knowledge and appreciation of the effects of exercise on their bodies. As a result, a large number of students fail to maintain optimum levels of physical fitness throughout life.

Perhaps one of the reasons why little attention has been given to the attainment of affective outcomes is that they are less tangible and not easily measured. Since physical education provides unique opportunities for students to develop desirable attitudes, interests, appreciations, and values, it is unfortunate that we do not place greater emphasis on the attainment of these goals. Perhaps, as Julian Stanley (1964) points out, teachers are not well prepared to provide learning experiences for the attainment of affective behaviors.

The psychomotor domain deals with physical, motor, or manipulative skills. The demonstration of a motor skill is the dominant characteristic of the student's response (Gronlund, 1970). Although a handbook has not been developed by Bloom or Krathwohl for this domain, Ann Jewett (1971) has proposed a taxonomy of educational objectives. The major categories within Jewett's system are generic, ordinative, and creative movements.

A psychomotor behavioral objective for an archery unit would be as follows: The student will be able to brace the bow, nock the arrow, come to the full-draw position, anchor, and release the arrow so that it hits the bull's-eye from a distance of thirty yards. In contrast to the gross motor coordinations required above, putting in golf requires fine motor control. A behavioral objective for this skill is as follows: The student will putt the ball into the hole from a distance of ten feet. It is obvious that physical education contributes to the development of simple and complex psychomotor behaviors. Fox and Sysler (1972) have prepared behavioral objectives for eleven lifetime sports.

Traditional versus Behavioral Objectives

When consulting the measurement and evaluation literature you frequently find the terms: behavioral, instructional, and performance objectives. All of these terms have one thing in common. They attempt to communicate clearly a desired action on the part of the learner; that is, they try to help the learner assess his own progress toward desirable outcomes. The factor that makes behavioral objectives so valuable to educators is that they are stated in behavioral terms. The action on the part of the learner is clearly visible. You can actually see him serve, putt, throw, field, etc. And, as a result, they may be measured objectively.

One of the most important long-range objectives of lifetime sports-oriented physical education programs is to develop and maintain physical fitness throughout life. Although this is a worthy objective, it is not stated in behavioral terms, i.e., it is not stated so that the behavior may be measured objectively. For example, how will the person demonstrate that he is physically fit? What type of fitness are we talking about? In other words, this objective is too vague—it is not possible to measure the desirable behavior. If the objective were restated so it read: Men of thirty years of age must run the six-hundred-yard course in two and one-half minutes, then it would be classified as a behavioral objective.

Selection of Behavioral Objectives

When formulating behavioral objectives the teacher must make choices, because in a given unit of instruction it is impossible to cover all the aspects of each sport. One of the major advantages of providing beginning, intermediate, and advanced levels of instruction is that course content is separated for each level of instruction. Therefore, it is easier to write objectives for each unit.

When forced to make choices, Tyler (1951) recommended that: (1) data be collected about students, such as their present abilities, knowledge, skill, etc., (2) societal demands be determined so that the educational process may prepare students to live effectively in contemporary life, (3) specialists in various subject fields be consulted to determine what competencies are needed. Naturally, the teacher's philosophy, the philosophy of the administration, and situational variables such as facilities, equipment, and supplies also will influence the objectives which you will select.

Gronlund (1970, p. 29) lists criteria for the selection of objectives. The following criteria for appraising the adequacy of the objectives to be included are:

1. *Do the objectives indicate learning outcomes that are appropriate to the instructional area?* For example, in a given lifetime sport, what should be taught and at what level of instruction? Knowing the sport well and the capabilities of students will help you to answer this question.

2. *Do the objectives represent all logical learning outcomes of the instructional area?* In other words, have objectives been formulated for each of the three domains—cognitive, affective, and psychomotor? Is there a proper balance among the three areas? In the past many teachers have been guilty of not giving appropriate attention to the attainment of cognitive and affective behaviors.

3. *Are the objectives attainable by these particular students?* As mentioned previously, the objectives should be written for a particular group of students. Knowing the abilities, interests, and desires of students is absolutely essential if objectives are to be realistic.

4. *Are the objectives in harmony with the philosophy within the school*

in which the instruction is to be given? Knowing the philosophy of your school and operating within its structure is important to your success in that system. Whether you like it or not, you will be forced to work within established guidelines. Unfortunately, as Gronlund points out, many school districts have not formulated clear statements of philosophy. Therefore, it is a good policy to ask school administrators to comment on the objectives which you have formulated prior to utilizing them.

5. *Are the objectives in harmony with basic principles of learning?* Will the attainment of objectives result in retention, transfer, and motivation of the learner? Are the students mature enough and do they possess the background to accomplish the desired goals of instruction?

In summary, the selection of objectives for a particular unit of instruction should be made with great care. The objectives should be realistic and in keeping with the philosophy of the school system in which you are working. Objectives should be developed for cognitive, affective, and psychomotor behaviors so that the learner will develop abilities that he may use throughout life.

Writing Behavioral Objectives

The construction of behavioral objectives is not an easy task. Most teachers find that considerable practice is necessary before they become skilled in writing objectives in behavioral terms. The most common error in stating objectives is to state learning outcomes in terms of teacher behavior rather than in terms of student behavior (Gronlund, 1970). Mager provides a three-step approach to the formulation of objectives. They are as follows:

1. Identify the terminal behavior.
2. Further define the behavior by describing the important conditions under which the behavior will be expected to occur.
3. Specify the criteria of acceptable performance by describing how well the learner must perform to be considered acceptable (Mager, 1962, p. 12).

Using the above suggestions let us try to establish a behavioral objective for each of the three domains—cognitive, affective, psychomotor —for the sport of tennis. Our first attempt in writing objectives for each of the three results in the statements shown in Table 6–1.

Obviously, according to Mager's criteria, these statements are not behavioral objectives. They are too vague and it is impossible to measure the terminal behaviors as they are now stated. Additionally, the condi-

---

Table 6–1

Content of a Tennis Unit

---

1. Knowledge of rules   (Cognitive domain)
2. Appreciation of the effect of physical activity on the organism   (Affective domain)
3. Development of skills: serving, ground strokes, volleying, etc. (Psychomotor domain)

---

tions under which the behaviors are to be emitted are not specified. Much refinement is needed. Table 6–2 shows our second attempt to write these statements in behavioral terms.

Table 6–2

Incomplete Behavioral Objectives for Tennis

---

1. Student is able to explain the concept "let." (Cognitive domain)
2. Student feels better after vigorous physical workout. (Affective domain)
3. Given a ball and racquet the student will serve the ball five out of eight times into the opponent's service court. (Psychomotor domain)

Some improvement is shown in meeting Mager's criteria but further rewriting is needed. The psychomotor objective (#3) does not specify under what conditions the service must be made. For example, mention is not made about the position of the server at the time of service.

The cognitive objective (#1), knowledge of the "let," comes closer to meeting Mager's criteria. The terminal behavior is specified—knowledge of the "let"—but further refinement is required to meet criteria two and three. For example, under what conditions should the student be able to recognize the "let"? Should it be on a written examination (multiple choice) or under game conditions?

Writing behavioral objectives for the affective domain is more difficult than writing psychomotor or cognitive objectives. Affective behaviors are more internalized and less tangible than cognitive or psychomotor responses. How a person feels, what he values and perceives as important, are personal matters and not easily measured. Covert rather than overt behaviors are much more difficult to assess. Popham and Baker (1970) have suggested that the following guidelines be used when writing objectives for the affective domain. First, think of an individual who possesses the behavior and an individual who does not. Second, describe a situation in which the two individuals will react differently to the behavior to be developed.

Applying Popham and Baker's suggestions to the problem of writing a behavioral objective for the appreciation of the effect of physical activity on the organism, we should proceed as follows: First, select an individual who possesses this behavior and a person who does not. Obviously, the person who is in good physical condition by working out systematically and controlling food intake would probably have internalized the behavior we are trying to instill in our students. This statement is particularly true if the individual had emitted this behavior over a long period of time. Hopefully, the model will be the teacher—but this is not always so. Sedentary, overweight, obese individuals probably do not possess the behavior we are looking for. The next step is to observe the overt behaviors of the two individuals to determine how they differ. For example, the person who has gained an appreciation of the effect of exercise on the organism may participate actively in physical activity; he may watch his diet to control food intake. These and other behaviors may differentiate between the two individuals. Thus, after making these observations, you formulate behavioral objective #2 found in Table 6–3 for the affective domain. Again, you will note that these behaviors are observable and that they require overt, rather than covert, responses on the part of students. Further refinement of this objective would specify the intensity of the physical activity.

The relationship between affective and cognitive behaviors has been stressed by Krathwohl, Bloom, and Masia (1964). Bloom, Hastings, and Madaus (1971) pointed out that each affective behavior has a cognitive technique. Utilization of interview techniques can result in an appraisal of how much internalization has taken place. However, observations of overt behaviors are usually more appropriate for assessing affective responses.

Affective behaviors may be arranged on a continuum from merely being aware of a phenomenon at the end of the scale to the highest point in the hierarchy when the phenomenon becomes a part of an individual's life. For example, the person may be aware that exercise causes certain physiological changes such as increased heart rate, blood pressure, etc. This behavior represents the lowest position on the continuum. When the individual internalizes the value of physical activity so that he actually works out and controls food intake to keep in good physical condition, he is functioning at the highest point on the continuum. In other words, the value of physical activity has become a part of him and it now guides his conduct.

Table 6–3 shows a further reshaping of objectives for cognitive, affective, and psychomotor behaviors. It is apparent now that they are more easily measured than they were in the beginning of our coverage of this topic. Gronlund's Checklist (Appendix B) may be utilized to determine the adequacy of objectives after they have been formulated.

Table 6–3

Behavioral Objectives for Tennis

---

1. Under game conditions, the student calls "let" correctly ten out of ten times. (Cognitive)
2. Student maintains optimum body weight through the regulation of food intake and participation at least three times per week in vigorous physical activity. (Affective)
3. Given balls and a racquet, the student serves with high velocity ten out of fifteen services from the server's position behind the endline into the opponent's right service court. (Psychomotor)

In summary, throughout this section it was emphasized that learning outcomes should be stated in terms of observable student behaviors. The procedures for preparing, selecting, and using behaviorally defined objectives were described and illustrated. Ideally, these procedures should be used by all teachers for each course or instructional unit. The assumption was made that effective teaching and testing requires a clear conception of the desired learning outcomes.

SELECTION OF EVALUATION INSTRUMENTS

The advancement of a profession depends, in part, upon the development of valid and reliable measuring instruments. Usually, professional advancement occurs when instruments have been developed to systematically assess phenomena related to a given discipline. Physical education, an emerging discipline, will probably reach full professional status when better instrumentation is developed. At the present time, physical education suffers from a dearth of valid and reliable measuring instruments.

The selection of appropriate tests to measure the various objectives of physical education is an important part of a comprehensive measurement and evaluation program. Usually, the teacher on the job does not have the time to construct tests and must rely on instruments already developed. In doing so, however, the teacher should be sure that those selected meet several criteria. Ruth Glassow and Marion Broer (1938) spoke about the importance of meeting the criteria of validity and reliability. They contend that after the validity and reliability of the instruments have been established, the "goodness" of the test depends upon the technique and skill of the test administrator. Unless the test is given according to the procedures listed in the test manual its validity and reliability will have little significance. Glassow, et al. (1938, p. 43), concluded: ". . . instruments of measurement must be chosen with judgment and used with the skill and precision demanded by each instrument."

Barrow and McGee (1971) raised several important questions that should be answered before selection is made of evaluation instruments: it should be determined (1) why you are giving the test, (2) what information is needed, and (3) what use will be made of the test results. Once you have answered the above questions, criteria for the selection of tests should be established. Most all of the measurement authorities indicate that the following criteria should be used:

1. *Validity*—A test is considered valid if it measures what it purports to measure. When we are measuring shoulder girdle strength, we are not measuring muscular endurance. Validity is the single most important criterion to be met in test selection. Mathews (1963, p. 19) states: ". . . we should make certain that it (the test) does an accurate job of measuring what it was designed to measure."

2. *Reliability*—If a test is reliable it will produce nearly the same results each time it is given under like conditions (Barrow and McGee, 1971). Reliability does not insure validity, that is, a test may produce nearly the same results but it may not be measuring what it is supposed to measure. Lee Cronback (1960) refers to reliability as the consistency of scores throughout a series of measurements. For example, if a person runs five one-hundred-yard dashes with nearly the same scores, the test is considered to be reliable since it produces nearly the same result each time it is given under like conditions.

3. *Objectivity*—If a test is objective it may be administered by several different testers under the same conditions and produce nearly the same results. Reliability and objectivity refer to the consistency of the measurement for any given test (Mathews, 1963). Obviously, testers must pay close attention to administration procedures if results are to be meaningful. Each test must be given in the same way to produce high objectivity coefficients. Objectivity is enhanced by clear test directions and precise scoring methods.

4. *Administrative feasibility*—Practical matters, such as class size, time

allocation for testing, equipment and supplies, cost of the instrument, etc., most always enter into the selection of evaluation instruments.

5. *Norms*—Tests should include up-to-date norms so that comparisons may be made. Most students want to know how their performances compare with other students at local, state, and national levels. When selecting tests, teachers should make sure that the test provides norms for the age level with which they are working. Gronlund (1965) suggests that five basic questions should be answered to determine the adequacy of normative data. They are:

   a. Are the norms relevant for the students?

   b. Are the norms based on a representative sample?

   c. Are the norms up-to-date?

   d. Are the norms comparable from test to test?

   e. Are the norms adequately described?

We have already talked about question one: the relevancy of the normative data to the students to be tested. Question two is concerned with the representativeness of the normative group to the students to be tested. If, for example, we are concerned with the assessment of attitudes toward physical activity, we should not use normative data from students in another country. Cultural differences would probably rule out the use of data collected outside the United States.

One of the difficulties with the selection of appropriate tests is that their norms are outdated. Currently, AAHPER is developing new norms for its Youth Fitness Test. Since physical fitness scores have improved for school age boys and girls since the 1960s, states that have developed their own tests should also follow this practice.

Question four refers to the use of the same sample for each item in a given test battery. For example, if we desire to assess tennis performance and the test battery selected consists of items such as the service, forehand drive, backhand drive, etc., data for each item should have been collected using the same sample. Gronlund (1965, p. 298) suggests that normative data should include: (1) method of sampling; (2) number and distribution of cases included in the norm sample; (3) characteristics of norm group such as age, sex, race, educational level, socioeconomic status, etc.; (4) extent to which standard conditions of administration and motivation were maintained during testing; and (5) date of testing.

Sources for selected sports skill tests for the lifetime sports have been prepared by Margaret Safrit (1973, p. 273) and are listed in Appendix C. When you need to select tests to measure various aspects of lifetime sports-oriented programs, consult this source. But, before using them be sure to subject them to the criteria of validity, reliability, norms, objectivity, and administrative feasibility mentioned previously in this chapter. After all, if you are going to make important decisions about the motor behaviors of students, you will need instruments which will enable you to do so.

SUBJECTIVE EVALUATION

Much of the physical educator's time is spent in making subjective rather than objective evaluations of the students' performances. The quality of these judgments usually depends on the training and experience of teachers. Since there are many characteristics that cannot be measured with objective techniques, teachers should become skilled in the use of this form of evaluation. In addition, subjective evaluations should be applied to complement and supplement objective measures.

In order to increase the quality of subjective evaluations, B. Don Franks and Helga Deutsch (1973, p. 28) suggest that the following questions be answered before subjective evaluations are made.

1. What are the components to be evaluated?
2. Which one should be evaluated subjectively?
3. What rating scale will be used?
4. How will each point on the scale be defined?
5. How many students will be rated at one time?
6. In what situation will the rating be done?
7. What type of rating form will be used?
8. How many raters will be used?

Ebel's (1965, p. 450) definition of measurement lends credence to the use of subjective judgments. He said: "An evaluation is a judgment of merit, sometimes based solely on measurements such as those provided by test scores but more frequently involving the synthesis of various measurements, critical incidents, subjective impressions, and other kinds of evidence." Since time for testing is usually very limited, experienced teachers place considerable emphasis on subjective evaluations of students' performances. A good teacher can usually observe errors in the execution of skills without having to give tests to detect them. When video tape and films are available, teachers should use them to point out to students their mistakes. Knowledge of results is one of the most important factors to influence learning.

The use of rating scales to improve subjective evaluations is particularly important because they enable teachers to make more systematic evaluations. Ellen Vanderhoof (1956) developed a rating scale for golf, and Georgia May Hulac (1958) has developed a rating scale for the tennis serve. These scales are shown in Tables 6–4 and 6–5 respectively.

Table 6–4

Vanderhoof Rating Scale for Golf

---

5. Good	Consistent, relaxed, well-coordinated swing and follow-through. Good stance and grip. Good timing with entire swing in approximately the same place.
4. Above Average	Consistent, coordinated swing and follow-through. Good stance, grip, and timing. Minor errors in plane of swing and use of wrists.
3. Average	Fair form for stance, grip, swing, and follow-through. Fair coordination and timing. Fairly consistent.
2. Below Average	Fair form for stance, grip, and swing. Poor timing and coordination. Inconsistent.
1. Poor	Generally poor form for stance, grip, and swing. Tense and inconsistent.

SOURCE: E. R. Vanderhoof, "Beginning Golf Achievement Tests" (unpublished Master's thesis, State University of Iowa, 1956).

In making these types of evaluations it is important to avoid the "halo" effect (Scott and French, 1959). This problem refers to the amount of bias that may affect the rater's judgments when he lets personality or physical appearance of the student influence his evaluation. Objectivity is one of the earmarks of quality measurement and evaluation programs.

UTILIZATION OF MEASUREMENT AND EVALUATION TO IMPROVE INSTRUCTION

The entire educational process may be conceptualized as a series of steps to bring about changes in the behavior of the learner. Earlier in this chapter, it was pointed out that measurement and evaluation are not a process apart from instruction but rather an integral part of it. This thought is expressed in Ralph Tyler's conceptualization (1951, pp. 47–67) of the instructional process. Tyler indicates that instruction involves:

Table 6–5

Hulac Rating Scale for the Tennis Service

Elements of the serve:

1. Accuracy.
2. Sufficient speed to be effective.
3. Rhythmic swing.
4. Toss and swing coordinated.
5. Ball tossed to proper height.
6. Racquet meets ball at proper height and place.
7. Proper weight transference.
8. Body rotation and follow through.

Score values:

5. Excellent	Serve meets all elements with no apparent errors. Consistent in accuracy and effectiveness.
4. Good	Serve gives general impression of good form but minor variations exist. Consistent in accuracy and effectiveness.
3. Average	Serve meets elements of good form but lacks smoothness and ease or lacks control in some one or two respects which affect serve as a whole. Accuracy and effectiveness fairly consistent.
2. Fair	Acceptable but executes serve with many errors which result in inconsistency in accuracy and effectiveness.
1. Poor	Serve is inadequate.

SOURCE: Georgia May Hulac, "The Construction of an Objective Indoor Test for Measuring Effective Tennis Serves" (unpublished Master's thesis, The Woman's College of the University of North Carolina, Greensboro, 1958), p. 42. Used by permission of the author.

1. *Determination of objectives.* What changes in student's behavior should be brought about?
2. *Determination of content and learning experiences.* What content and learning experiences may be used to change behavior?
3. *Determination of effective organization of learning experiences.* How should content and learning experiences be organized to bring about changes in behavior?
4. *Appraisal of the effects of instruction.* Have learning experiences been effective? If not, how should they be changed?

Obviously, Tyler's fourth step involves the use of measurement and evaluation. Without it, the teacher has no way of determining the validity of his judgments about the effectiveness of learning experiences. Tyler goes on to say that measurement helps the teacher to (1) select objectives, (2) select content, learning experiences, and procedures of instruction, (3) organize learning experiences, and (4) provide supervision and administration of instruction.

The use of educational measurement to help select and refine objectives of lifetime sports-oriented physical education curriculums should be encouraged. Collecting baseline data to determine the interests and needs of students will enable instructors to formulate more realistic and meaningful objectives. Although the careful selection of objectives seems obvious, the fact is that a great many schools and teachers carry on instruction without having a clear conception of the ends to be realized. This practice will hopefully change as a result of the movement toward competency-based education.

Measurement and evaluation contribute significantly to the first step in the educational process—to motivate teachers to select and define objectives clearly so that they may guide the learning process. The second contribution is to provide data for the effective selection of course content and learning experiences. Test results from previous classes may help teachers determine the various performance levels of students. The central question teachers must answer is: What kind of content will be effective for attaining the instructional goals? Once the content has been determined, it needs to be organized into meaningful units. For example, is the service in tennis to be taught prior to the ground strokes? To avoid interference it has been commonly thought that skills with the same basic movement patterns should be taught sequentially. Richard Schmidt (1975, p. 62), however, concluded: ". . . there is no research evidence of the transfer of basic movement patterns from task to task." This does not mean that transfer does not take place. We simply do not at this time have definite evidence to support it.

Educational measurement may also contribute to the process of organizing learning experiences by providing a means for testing organizational hypotheses. In other words, measurement may be used to determine if the way in which course content was organized was effective in meeting the behavioral objectives established prior to the start of the instructional process. The support for good organization of teaching materials was pointed out by the late Charles Harold McCloy in what he called the "fundamentals of physical education" (1940, p. 95).

The contribution of measurement to the supervision and administration of instruction has not been clearly defined. According to Tyler (1951), the supervision of instruction has two major functions. (1) It should provide for the coordination of instructional efforts. As mentioned previously, there is little communication between elementary, junior high, and secondary school teachers. As a result, students reach high school without a base of common movement experiences to build a comprehensive secondary curriculum. (2) Inservice educational opportunities are often left to chance. New teachers are not provided with the supervision they need and desire; therefore, the quality of instruction is not as good as it could be. The use of a measurement program as a supervisory tool to assist teachers and administrators to improve instruction has considerable merit. In the final analysis, the value of measurement and evaluation depends on the use made of the results.

APPRAISAL OF THE TOTAL CURRICULUM

Thus far in this chapter attention has been focused on formative evaluation, i.e., the evaluation that takes place during the teaching-learning process. Also mentioned was a second type of appraisal—to determine if the objectives of the program have been realized. This type of evaluation is called summative evaluation.

Summative evaluation is frequently overlooked by teachers and administrators. Once a class, semester, or school year has ended, teachers and administrators become involved with other things and they fail to determine the effectiveness of instructional techniques. Bookwalter and VanderZwaag (1969) referred to this type of assessment as process evaluation to differentiate it from product evaluation. Bloom, et al. (1971), stressed the importance of summative evaluation by saying that we need to develop a broader view of evaluation—one that contributes to the improvement of teaching and learning.

Basically, summative evaluation helps us answer the important question: How adequate is the program? Is it contributing to the growth of students in physical fitness, skill, knowledge, and attitudes toward physical activity? If it is not, then we will need to change certain teaching techniques, course content, evaluative procedures, etc. Thus, summative evaluation answers the question: How well are we meeting the curriculum objectives established prior to the start of the school year? These data need to be examined as we plan new learning experiences for the next course, semester, or school year.

Throughout this text the author has stressed the need for curricular balance so that pupils are exposed to a wide variety of class instructional, intramural, extramural, and interscholastic experiences. Our evaluative procedures must examine each of these areas to determine if the objectives have been realized. Self-evaluation promotes soul-searching and a restructuring of curricular content, teaching methods, and administrative procedures, so that we may be better able to realize the objectives of our programs.

Many self-appraisal instruments have been developed to help teachers and administrators assess the total program. Perhaps the best known and most widely accepted scale is the La Porte Health and Physical Education Score Card (1951). Karl Bookwalter (1969) reported that he used the instrument in a ten-year national study involving nearly three thousand high schools. This scale is divided into ten curricular areas that are rated from one to thirty points. A total score of two hundred points out of a possible three hundred points is considered to be indicative of a "good" program.

State education departments in Texas, California, Indiana, Florida, New York, and Ohio have also developed evaluative instruments. These instruments are available from the respective state education departments. New York state, through its Cooperative Review Service, provides visitations to school districts on request for this purpose. School district personnel first evaluate their own programs, and then a supervisor is requested to make an on-site evaluation. A written report is prepared by the supervisor that highlights the strengths of the program, areas in need of improvement, and specific recommendations. This report is sent to the chief school officer of the school district for his study and evaluation. The district submits reports to the department periodically on the progress it is making toward the realization of the recommendations that were made by the supervisor during his visitation.

Charles Bucher (1967) has also developed a Checklist and Rating Scale for the Evaluation of the Physical Education Program. Bucher's scale combines the criteria required by several state education departments.

The application of these scales will help directors of physical education and their staff members to determine the quality of their programs. Since the curriculum is the vehicle which has been developed to bring about changes in the behaviors of students, we need to make sure that it is accomplishing this objective. Too often students and teachers are evaluated but for some unknown reason the curriculum itself never receives careful assessment.

GRADING

The lifetime sports-oriented approach to physical education places less emphasis on grades than traditional forms of education. The reason for this philosophy is that physical education must avoid becoming a frustrating, anxiety-producing situation to students when they are in school. If it does, there is little chance that students will want to exercise in later life. Thus, harsh, punitive grading practices are not in keeping with the spirit of the lifetime sports approach. However, evaluation is useful when it is utilized to help bring about increments in knowledge, skill, and attitude formation. But, grades must be given with great sensitivity or they may turn students off for life.

There is little reason to believe that physical education is not an enjoyable, pleasurable experience for many boys and girls while they are in school. It has the potential, however, to reach a far greater number of students and equip them with skills, knowledge, and attitudes so that they may enjoy and profit from exercise and sports during the adult years. But, if we are to accomplish this goal, we must change our emphasis from the few to the many. Let's face it, as we are presently structured, the great majority of boys and girls leave our schools physically uneducated.

Despite the distastefulness of giving grades for some teachers, it is evident that most of us will have to continue to do so. Most school systems require some form of evaluation. In fact, the trend in competency-based education (CBE) is toward more frequent evaluation. To be classified as being competent, you must be able to meet basic criteria. So, faced with the task of giving grades, how are you going to arrive at your marks? And, if they are challenged by parents, administrators, or the students themselves, will you be able to support your evaluative procedures?

Factors Influencing Grading

Like teaching methodology, there are almost as many approaches to grading as there are teachers. Some teachers go to great lengths to arrive at marks; others, it seems, use the "throw-down-the-stairs" approach. Under this system, the names of students who fall on the top step get A's, those that land near the top B's, those in the middle C's, and near the bottom D's and F's. Of course, this is not true, but there is a wide variety of ways in which teachers handle the grading problem.

In Chapter 5, Teaching Methodology, we talked about different styles of teaching. More specifically you may recall that we covered humanistic, behavioristic, and systems approaches to instruction. Grading practices should be in keeping with the philosophical bases of these styles; that is, if we are using humanistic methods, our grading procedures should reflect this philosophy. Likewise, behavioristic and systems styles require different evaluative practices. In a word, teaching methods dictate, in part, the type of grading that is to be utilized.

Humanistic.   As you may recall, the essence of education for the humanist is "meaning." In this system, you are a successful teacher if your students leave your classes feeling good about their experiences. Hopefully, they have become self-directed learners who have the capacity to shape their own destiny. In brief, the students are fulfilled—turned on by life itself.

Many humanists, such as Carl Rogers, see little reason for giving grades at all. In fact, grades may destroy delicate student-teacher relationships that have been established during the course of study. Therefore, Rogers has students evaluate themselves and turn in to him the grade that they feel is appropriate. This statement must include (a) the criteria by which you are judging your work; (b) a description of the ways in which you have met or failed to meet those criteria; and (c) the grade which you think appropriate to the way you have met or failed to meet your own criteria (Rogers, 1969, pp. 61–62). If his estimate is quite at variance with the student's grade, he will talk it over with the student and arrive at a mutually satisfactory grade. Admittedly, Roger's approach is quite different from the one used at the present time in most schools. Besides, you may ask: Where do I get the time for all the conferences when I have 500 pupils? Answer: I don't know!

Behavioristic.   Evaluation plays a central role in behavioristic approaches to instruction. You are a good teacher, in this system, if you bring about desirable changes in the behaviors of students. In a physical education context good teachers enable students to increase their skill, knowledge, physical fitness, and other objectives. Harold H. Morris (1975, p. 74) wrote on this point: "Since lifetime sports programs tend to emphasize the development of specific skills that have been identified as essential to successful playing of an activity, it is only reasonable that students are assessed on how well they have accomplished these skills."

Grades are used frequently as reinforcers in a behavioristic system; that is, they may serve to increase the probability of a response. For example, if a student obtains a grade of "A" in paddle ball, he is more likely to play the sport outside of class or after he leaves school. B. F. Skinner (1968, p. 147) talked about this reinforcement value: "Another ultimate gain is in prestige. The student joins the company of educated men and women with its honors and cabalistic practices; he understands its illusions, enjoys its privileges, shares its esprit de corps."

There are many approaches to evaluation when behavioristic styles of teaching are used. Since the behaviors that are to be developed are specified in observable terms, they are more easily measured than in conventional systems. Token, contract, and point systems are developed to motivate students to high levels of performance. These practices are referred to as contingencies of reinforcement. They possess the potential to bring about the desired response. Courses are frequently set up on a total point basis and students are encouraged to earn points by completing various tasks. Final grades are based upon the total number of points earned throughout the course. Rushall and Siedentop (1972, p. 225) show the application of this type of grading procedure.

Systems. Systems approaches, as outlined by Robert Singer and Walter Dick (1974), represent ways of conceptualizing the teaching-learning process. A model is proposed showing step-by-step procedures for the development of effective teaching strategies. The interrelationship of the component parts of the teaching act are carefully delineated. To be an effective teacher, Singer and Dick (1974, p. 75) contend, you must consider all the activities proposed by the model.

Since clear-cut objectives are established prior to instruction, systems approaches make use of criterion-referenced evaluation. That is, points are awarded for work completed and the student's final grade in the course is based upon the total number of points earned throughout the course and on the final examination. Of course, as Singer and Dick suggest, students should be informed of these totals before the class begins. As you can see, systems approaches require nearly the same grading practices as behavioristic styles of teaching.

Practical Considerations

By now you should have some idea about how grading ties in with the way in which you teach physical education. And, you have also probably learned that the lifetime sports-oriented approach requires sensitive grading practices, for we do not want to turn anyone off if we can help it. We want students to learn to love to participate, regardless of their skill. Humanistic, rather than behavioristic, styles are in keeping with our objectives.

You will probably have to grade your students according to the procedures used in your school system. Below are listed some of the more common grading plans.

Pass-Fail. Under this approach, students receive either a "pass" or "fail" instead of the usual letter grades of A,B,C,D, and F. Criteria for passing are usually established by the teacher and if students meet these requirements, they pass the course. If they do not, they fail. The establishment of realistic criteria is one of the most difficult tasks confronting the teacher in this system. Mastery learning approaches to instruction sometimes utilize this approach. Under this system, the course content is partitioned into units. Students use self-paced learning procedures to pass each unit and the final examination. There is no penalty for failing unit tests. You simply study some more and take it again. As you can see, the emphasis is placed on mastery of the subject matter. Once the course content is learned, pass grades are awarded.

The major disadvantage of pass-fail grading is that students are usually not supplied with definite feedback about their current status and growth toward the objectives of the program. It has been shown that when knowledge of results is lacking learning does not occur as readily as it does when precise feedback is given. Furthermore, students do not usually work as hard when they know they are going to get a "pass" rather than a letter grade.

Letter Grades.   Many school systems use letter grades to communicate to parents, students, members of the board of education, and other interested citizens, the growth of students toward the objectives of the program. Ted Baumgartner and Andrew Jackson (1975, p. 333) spell out procedures for awarding letter grades. Briefly, scores on tests are translated into letter grades and these grades are awarded points; the total points earned determine a student's final mark. Some teachers translate test scores to T-scores so that they may be added to arrive at the final grade.

Numerical Grades.   This system requires that teachers derive a numerical grade for each student. The practice is quite common in many schools, even in physical education. Since this procedure is not appropriate, in my opinion, for lifetime sports-oriented programs, it will not be reviewed here. Rather, what is needed are grading practices which will enable teachers to evaluate large numbers of students in a short period of time. One school system that was faced with this program eliminated letter grades in physical education and awarded credit (1/8) for the successful accomplishment of the objectives of each course (10 weeks). Two credits in physical education are required for graduation.

In summary, teachers communicate their values in their grading procedures. If you are humanistic in orientation, your grading practices usually reflect this approach. Behavioristic and systems styles require more precise grading procedures. Grading, regardless of style, should be based upon cognitive, affective, and psychomotor objectives which were established prior to the start of instruction. If students realize these goals, they should receive high grades. Basing grades on objective, rather than subjective, evidence will enable teachers to support their evaluations when they are challenged by students, administrators, and parents. But in the final analysis, grades are means to an end; not an end in themselves.

SUMMARY

Measurement and evaluation should be an integral part of the teaching-learning process. Once behavioral objectives have been established for the cognitive, affective, and psychomotor domains, curricular content and teaching methods may be developed to bring about a realization of these goals. Measurement, followed by evaluation, helps to assess the effectiveness of these procedures. Safrit has defined measurement as a process of assigning a number "to some property of an entity," while Bloom, et al., described evaluation as a process of systematically collecting evidence to determine whether any behavioral changes are taking place in the learner. Two types of evaluation are needed. The evaluation that takes place while the unit is in process is called formative evaluation. The evaluation that occurs at the end of each instructional unit is called summative evaluation.

The concept of accountability refers to the procedure of holding teachers responsible for educational outcomes. Thus, teachers of physical education are required to bring about increments in knowledge, skill, attitudes, and physical fitness. In keeping with the concept of accountability, behavioral objectives should be established so that changes in behavior may be assessed. The emphasis is placed upon the development of observable behaviors. They are referred to as behavioral objectives. Guidelines were cited to help teachers formulate appropriate behavioral objectives for the lifetime sports. The assumption was made that effective teaching and testing require a clear conception of the desired learning outcomes.

The selection of appropriate tests to assess behavioral outcomes comprises an important part of a comprehensive measurement and evaluation program. Physical education has suffered from a lack of valid and reliable measuring instruments. It was emphasized that tests should be given according to the procedures listed in the test manual. Norms should also be provided so that teachers may help students compare their performances with the performance of students of the same age at local, state, and national levels. In addition to the criteria of validity, reliability, objectivity, and norms, administrative feasibility must also be considered. Class size, equipment, supplies and facilities, and other factors often dictate what tests may be used. Sources for the selection of tests for some of the lifetime sports may be found in Appendix C.

Subjective evaluations refer to the procedure of comparing the performances of students with predetermined criteria. Subjective evaluations should be used to complement, rather than replace, objective evaluations. Obviously, both types of evaluations will be needed to assess the educational results of lifetime sports-oriented physical education programs. The use of rating scales helps to improve the quality of subjective evaluations.

The application of measurement and evaluation to improve instruction was stressed. Measurement and evaluation may contribute to the selection of objectives, curricular content, learning experiences, and the procedures for instruction. The supervision of teachers becomes more meaningful and objective when based upon the results of measurement.

Grading is a controversial topic. The type of evaluation should be compatible with the style of teaching; that is, behaviorists should use grading procedures that will enable them to carefully evaluate the student's current status and growth toward the objectives of the program. Practical considerations, such as time and number of students, dictate, in part, the type of grading that may be used. Lifetime sports-oriented approaches to physical education require sensitive grading practices so that students will find physical activity a rewarding, pleasurable experience.

STUDY QUESTIONS

1. Define measurement and evaluation.
2. What is a behavioral objective?
3. Define education.
4. Define formative and summative evaluation. When should each type of evaluation be utilized?
5. What is the meaning of the word "accountability"?
6. How should behavioral objectives be classified?
7. What fundamental criteria should be met in writing behavioral objectives?
8. When selecting behavioral objectives, what guidelines should be used?
9. What steps does Mager propose for writing behavioral objectives?
10. What guidelines may be applied when formulating objectives for the affective domain?
11. Explain the continuum approach to the understanding of affective behaviors.

12. What criteria should be incorporated in the selection of evaluation instruments?
13. What five basic questions should be answered to assess the adequacy of normative data?
14. Explain the use of subjective evaluation.
15. What questions should be answered before making subjective evaluations?
16. Explain the use of rating scales to improve subjective evaluations.
17. What is the "halo" effect, and how may it be avoided?
18. How may measurement and evaluation be utilized to improve instruction?
19. Explain Tyler's conceptualization of the instructional process.
20. What is the function of supervision of instruction, and how may supervision be improved through the use of measurement and evaluation?
21. What type of grading procedures should be utilized in lifetime sports-oriented approaches to physical education?

REFERENCES

BARROW, H. M., and R. McGEE. *Measurement in Physical Education.* Philadelphia: Lea & Febiger, 1971.

BAUMGARTNER, T. A., and A. S. JACKSON. *Measurement for Evaluation in Physical Education.* Boston: Houghton Mifflin Company, 1975.

BLOOM, B. S. *Taxonomy of Educational Objectives—Handbook I: Cognitive Domain.* New York: David McKay Co., Inc., 1956.

BLOOM, B. S., J. T. HASTINGS, and G. T. MADAUS. *Handbook of Formative and Summative Evaluation of Student Learning.* New York: McGraw-Hill Book Company, 1971.

BOOKWALTER, K. W., and H. J. VANDERZWAAG. *Foundations and Principles of Physical Education.* Philadelphia: W. B. Saunders Company, 1969.

BUCHER, C. A. *Administration of School Health and College Health and Physical Education Programs.* St. Louis, Mo.: C. V. Mosby Company, 1972.

CRONBACH, L. E. *Essentials of Psychological Testing.* New York: Harper and Row, Publishers, 1960.

EBEL, R. L. *Essentials of Educational Measurement.* Englewood Cliffs, N.J.: Prentice-Hall, Inc., 1972.

————. *Measuring Educational Achievement.* Englewood Cliffs, N. J.: Prentice-Hall, Inc., 1965.

FOX, E. R., and B. L. SYSLER. *Lifetime Sports for the College Student—A Behavioral Objective Approach.* Dubuque, Iowa: Kendall-Hunt, 1971.

FRANKS, B. D., and H. DEUTSCH. *Evaluating Performance in Physical Education.* New York: Academic Press, Inc., 1973.

GLASSOW, R. B., and M. R. Broer. *Measuring Achievement in Physical Education.* Philadelphia: W. B. Saunders Company, 1938

GRONLUND, N. E. *Stating Behavioral Objectives for Classroom Instruction.* London: Macmillan, 1970.

HULAC, G. M. *The Construction of an Objective Indoor Test for Measuring Effective Tennis Serves.* Unpublished Master's thesis, The Woman's College of the University of North Carolina, 1958.

JEWETT, A., et al. "Educational Change Through a Taxonomy for Writing Physical Education Objectives," *Quest,* 16 (1971), 35.

KRATHWOHL, D. R. *Taxonomy of Educational Objectives—Handbook II: Affective Domain.* New York: David McKay Co., Inc., 1964.

LA PORTE, W. R. *Health and Physical Education Score Card, I, II.* Los Angeles, Calif.: Parker Publishing Company, 1951.

McCLOY, C. H. *Philosophical Bases for Physical Education.* New York: F. S. Crofts, 1940.

MAGER, R. F. *Preparing Instructional Objectives.* Palo Alto, Calif.: Fearon Publishers, 1962.

MATHEWS, D. K. *Measurement in Physical Education.* Philadelphia: W. B. Saunders Company, 1963.

MORRIS, H. H. "Assessment and Evaluation." Unpublished manuscript. 1975.

POPHAM, W. J., and E. L. BAKER. *Establishing Instructional Goals.* Englewood Cliffs, N.J.: Prentice-Hall, Inc., 1970.

ROGERS, C. R. *Freedom to Learn.* Columbus, Ohio: Charles E. Merrill Publishing Company, 1969.

RUSHALL, B. S., and D. SIEDENTOP. *The Development and Control of Behavior in Sport and Physical Education.* Philadelphia: Lea & Febiger, 1972.

SAFRIT, M. J. *Evaluation in Physical Education.* Englewood Cliffs, N.J.: Prentice-Hall, Inc., 1973.

SCHMIDT, R. A. *Motor Skills.* New York: Harper and Row, Publishers, 1975.

SCOTT, M. G., and E. FRENCH. *Measurement and Evaluation in Physical Education.* Dubuque, Iowa: Wm. C. Brown Company, Publishers, 1959.

SINGER, R. N., and W. DICK. *Teaching Physical Education.* Boston: Houghton Mifflin Company, 1974.

SKINNER, B. F. *The Technology of Teaching.* New York: Appleton-Century-Crofts, 1968.

STANLEY, J. C. *Measurement in Today's Schools.* Englewood Cliffs, N.J.: Prentice-Hall, Inc., 1964.

TYLER, R. W. "The Functions of Measurement in Improving Instruction," in *Educational Measurement,* E. L. Lindquist, ed. Washington, D.C.: American Council on Education, 1951.

VANDERHOOF, E. R. *Beginning Golf Achievement Tests.* Unpublished Master's thesis, State University of Iowa, 1956.

WERNER, P. "Preparing Behavioral Objectives," *The Ohio High School Athlete,* 32 (1973), 116–20.

CHAPTER 7

LIFETIME SPORTS
FOR THE
EXCEPTIONAL CHILD

A lifetime sports approach to physical education focuses attention on the needs of *all* students, particularly those boys and girls who need it the most—exceptional children. These children, in contrast to normal ones, usually suffer from some type of disability which prevents them from full participation in sports that may be played throughout life. Some children have physical handicaps, such as poor vision, hearing deficits, abnormal bone structures, or muscular weaknesses. Others are emotionally disturbed, mentally retarded, or possess multiple handicaps. Recently it has been found that some children appear normal but experience learning disabilities—that is, they are unable to learn to read, spell, and perform other cognitive tasks as well as their peers.

Formerly ignored or assigned to special classes, exceptional children are now participating in a wide variety of individual, dual, and team sports. The increment in participation is due, in part, to (1) the invention of assistive devices, such as braces, outrigger skis; (2) the modification of sports to meet the needs of the handicapped; and (3) the interest in working with exceptional children by physical education teachers and recreation leaders. As a result of these factors, creative approaches have been developed to make it possible for exceptional children to enjoy the thrills of sports participation. And, greater participation and involvement in sport has resulted in increased physical fitness, skill, and socialization. An often overlooked, but significant outcome, is the growth that normal children experience from participation with exceptional children.

It is beyond the scope of this text to present a detailed coverage of lifetime sports for exceptional children but the author would be remiss if he did not give an overview of this important topic. In keeping with this intent, the chapter's contents will include (1) a definition of the term "exceptional children"; (2) general suggestions for working with these boys and girls; and (3) the presentation of six lifetime sports, showing their modification for exceptional children. Special consideration is given to the use of assistive devices to help handicapped children participate in these activities.

THE EXCEPTIONAL CHILD DEFINED

Many names have been used in the past to describe children who possess physical, mental, emotional, and other deficits. Modern terminology suggests the use of the term "exceptional child." "A child is educationally exceptional if his deviation is of such kind and degree that it interferes with his development under ordinary classroom procedures and necessitates special education, either in conjunction with regular class or in a special class or school, for his maximum development" (Kirk, 1962, p. 5). Basically, the exceptional child deviates from the average or normal child in one or more of the following categories: (1) neuromuscular or physical characteristics, (2) sensory abilities, (3) mental characteristics, (4) social or emotional behavior, and (5) communication abilities. One of the major problems associated with the education of exceptional children in the past was the lack of trained personnel. Many physical education teachers and recreation therapists did not know how to work with them; they were poorly prepared to modify games and sports so that these children could play them. Some modification of school programs are required in order for them to continue development and to reach their full potential. This practice is especially true in physical education where there is some danger of injury to exceptional children from participation in regular classes. Changing rules and equipment often permits them to participate safely with normal ones in several lifetime sports.

GENERAL SUGGESTIONS
FOR THE PHYSICAL EDUCATION PROGRAM

Working with exceptional children requires special knowledge, skill, and understanding. Dolores Geddes (1974) provides a number of helpful suggestions that should be used when working with persons with special disabilities. First, a full understanding of each participant's medical background is essential before activities are designed for him or her. In addition, recognition of neuromuscular, sensory, mental, social-emotional, and communication limitations must be made before programs are developed to meet the interests and needs of handicapped boys and girls. Once teachers are aware of these problems they will be better able to design and implement programs for these children. In brief, the type of handicap dictates what you can do to help them.

Geddes (1974) also suggests that physical education teachers and recreation leaders should work closely as a member of the Rehabilitation-Education team. The team consists of physicians, social workers, psychologists, psychiatrists (occupational, physical, and corrective), recreational and speech therapists, and support personnel. The program for each patient is established by team members as they work cooperatively to develop a comprehensive approach to the solution of the child's problem. Too often, in the past, the communication among various workers was lacking. The team approach was developed to try and avoid, or at least lessen, this problem. Indications suggest that the team approach is working well and that physical education teachers are becoming better prepared to perform this important function.

Behavior modification techniques may be used to strengthen various types of desirable behaviors. To do this it is essential that each person's reinforcers be identified early and then applied to reinforce those behaviors that are to be developed. Since handicapped persons have the same need for social approval as other people, praise should be administered whenever possible to help them acquire the skills to better adjust to their environmental situation. However, if praise is given indiscriminately it will cease to reinforce the desired behavior. Psychologists have found that the quickest way to establish a given behavior is to reinforce it initially every time the person makes the correct response. Once the behavior is well established, less frequent reinforcement is needed to maintain it over a long period of time.

Geddes goes on to say that if you are not used to working with handicapped boys and girls you will need to remember that provisions should be made for periodic rest periods and change of activities. Sometimes their endurances are low and they tire easily. Likewise, their attention spans may be short and a change in activities will be needed in order

to stimulate them. During rest periods it is a good idea to involve handicapped children and adults in social intercourse. Many times persons
with handicaps are insecure and because of environmental deprivation
they are lacking in social skills. Once you have established rapport with
them they will usually work very hard to please you.

One of the most essential qualifications for success in teaching the
handicapped is patience. Repeating directions or saying the same thing
in different ways is important in getting boys and girls with visual,
auditory, or other impairments to understand what you are trying to
get them to do. Many are self-conscious of their impairments and do not
possess good psychological health. Being able to motivate them to want
to practice various skills is an important aspect of teaching success.

As you work with the handicapped you will acquire further in-
sights into the teaching-learning process. Do not be afraid to try new
techniques, to improvise and be creative in the design of equipment and
facilities to better meet their particular interests and needs. Although it
is interesting and sometimes productive to learn what others have to say
about working with the handicapped, personal experience is invaluable.
The team approach, as mentioned above, provides a setting for inservice
growth in the overall understanding of the exceptional child.

Several authorities have expressed the need for tactile stimulation
of retardates. Geddes (1974), for example, suggests toweling, brushing,
stroking, and contact with different textures as a means of providing
sensory input. These procedures are especially important for institutionalized persons who have very little contact with the outside world. Semi-
contact and contact sports may provide additional stimulation for those
who are able to play them.

PARTICIPATION IN LIFETIME SPORTS

Exceptional children, like normal ones, possess considerable interest
in sports that may be played throughout life. The quality of life may
be improved significantly through participation in sports that provide
physical, social, and emotional benefits. Hollis Fait (1966) is of the
opinion that individual sports such as archery, bowling, and golf, although not considered vigorous, place sufficient demands upon the body
to insure desirable development for handicapped players. Fait contends
that strength, coordination, flexibility, and other physical fitness components may be developed through participation in lifetime sports. Good
fellowship with nonhandicapped players is an important outcome of
these popular leisure-time sports.

The central purpose of this chapter is to show how the sports of bowling, archery, badminton, skiing, and swimming may be modified so that persons with handicaps may participate in them. The coverage is not all inclusive but is structured to show innovative adaptations in equipment design and teaching methodology. The coverage of each sport will be structured as follows: (1) historical developments, (2) desirable outcomes from participation, (3) the use of assistive devices, and (4) teaching techniques.

Bowling

Bowling is one of the most popular sports for the handicapped because it can be enjoyed by almost everyone, regardless of the extent of their physical, mental, or emotional disability. Although the use of regular bowling lanes is preferred, particularly for skillful bowlers, many of the fundamentals may be learned in the gymnasium, recreational hall, or other suitable facilities. Gym-bowl kits[1] consisting of polyethylene pins and balls have been developed for this purpose. If funds are not available for the purchase of these materials, plastic bottles may be used as pins and any type of playground ball may be substituted for the plastic ball.

HISTORICAL DEVELOPMENTS

Following World War II, bowling became a popular sport in Veterans Administration hospitals. At first the sport was popular with amputees and paraplegics but today it is enjoyed by many persons with physical, mental, emotional, and other types of disabilities. The popularity of the sport was increased considerably when assistive devices, such as the bowling frame unit and adapter-pusher device, were introduced in the late 1950s. They made it possible for persons with muscular weaknesses to enjoy the sport.

Wheelchair bowling was introduced in the National Wheelchair Games in New York in 1957 (Adams, et al., 1972). The American Blind Bowling Association, an affiliate of the American Bowling Congress, was formed in 1951 and has more than 1,200 members. Sanctioned tournaments for its members are held in the Middle Atlantic States, the South, and the Midwest.

WHEELCHAIR BOWLERS

Competition in wheelchair bowling is governed by the rules of the National Wheelchair Athletic Association. Bowlers are classified accord-

---

[1] Cosom Corporation, 6030 Wayzata Blvd., Minneapolis, Minnesota.

ing to their degree of physical impairment. The only major changes in the rules for regular bowlers is the elimination of the approach. If good upper-extremity arm and shoulder girdle strength is present, all the wheelchair bowler has to do is position his wheelchair near the foul line and use a pendulum swing of the arm to deliver the ball. It is helpful if the wheelchair is equipped with brakes so that it may be positioned and secured during the delivery process. If the wheelchair is not equipped with brakes, the chair should be supported from the rear during the bowling motion. This procedure will help to eliminate the backward thrust of the wheelchair as the ball leaves the hand of the bowler. When wheelchairs are not equipped with removable arm rests on the bowling arm side, a cushion is placed under the bowler to raise his body to allow the arm to swing more freely.

Some wheelchair bowlers may experience difficulty in retrieving the ball from the ball-return rack and should be assisted with this task. Usually, they can do this without assistance if they have good arm and shoulder girdle strength. While proceeding from the rack to the foul lane, the ball is securely positioned in the lap of the bowler so that the arms and hands are free to move the chair into position. The bowler will experience greater satisfaction if he is encouraged to do most of these tasks for himself. If, however, the bowler cannot perform these tasks safely, assistance should be provided.

ASSISTIVE DEVICES

Persons who have upper limb deficiencies such as structural and functional disorders are usually unable to bowl without some type of assistive device. Figure 7–1 shows a bowling frame unit that may be used

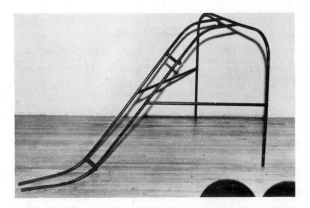

Figure 7–1 Bowling Frame Unit for Bowlers Who Are Unable to Lift Ball (Courtesy of Dr. Ronald C. Adams, Director Children's Rehabilitation Center, University of Virginia Hospital, Charlottesville, Virginia)

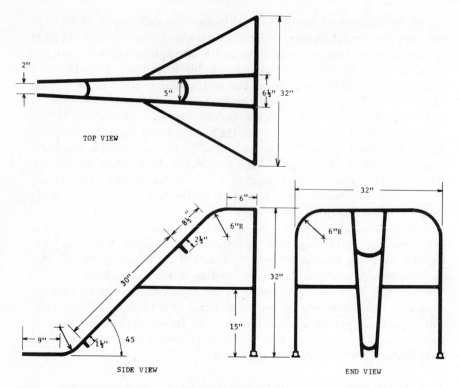

TOP VIEW

SIDE VIEW

END VIEW

Figure 7-2 Specifications for Bowling Frame Unit (Courtesy of Dr. Ronald C. Adams, Director Children's Rehabilitation Center, University of Virginia Hospital, Charlottesville, Virginia)

by those who have little or no use of their arms. This device requires an assistant to place the ball on the rack so that the handicapped bowler may give it a slight push to release it toward the pins. Specifications for making the device are shown in Figure 7–2.

Adapter-pusher devices (Figure 7–3) may also be utilized. These devices may be equipped with handlebar extensions for ambulatory bowlers unable to lift the ball. Wheelchair bowlers may also use the pusher device. These devices, however, require assistance in getting the ball from the rack and placing it in the mouth of the pusher.

BOWLING FOR THE BLIND

The development of a guide rail (Figure 7–4) has enabled many blind persons to enjoy bowling. Sanctioned tournaments are now held by the American Blind Bowlers Association, an affiliate of the American Bowling Congress.

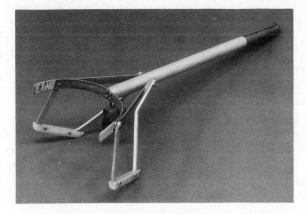

Figure 7–3 Adapter-Pusher Device (Courtesy of Dr. Ronald C. Adams, Director Children's Rehabilitation Center, University of Virginia Hospital, Charlottesville, Virginia)

The beginning blind bowler is first taught the pendulum swing followed by the one-, two-, three-, and four-step deliveries. The guide rail is used by the blind bowler to position himself at the start of delivery. When the ball is positioned at the side of the bowler the guide rail is in direct line with the center of the lane. In a sense, the blind bowlers "spot" bowls from the rail.

Figure 7–4 Blind Bowler Using the Guide Rail (Courtesy of Dr. Ronald C. Adams, Director Children's Rehabilitation Center, University of Virginia Hospital, Charlottesville, Virginia)

Most blind people become very dependent on sound for sensory feedback. The blind bowler is no exception because he is frequently able to tell how many pins he has knocked down by the sound. Devices are now being developed so that he will be able to feel the pins which remain standing from an indicator at the scorer's table. If this device is not available, someone tells the blind bowler the number of pins remaining and their specific locations. Since socialization is one of the important goals of programs of this nature, the presence of an assistant for each bowler helps to accomplish this goal. However, the bowler should also gain the feeling that he is in control of the outcome of the game; that is, do not bowl for him. The actual release of the ball must be performed by the blind person. The use of a "bowling buddy" system has been succcessful in teaching the blind to bowl.

POTENTIAL OUTCOMES

Participation in bowling by the handicapped may result in physical, social, emotional, and other benefits. Often overlooked is the sheer enjoyment that comes from participation in sports, games, and activities of this type. Although considered to be a mild form of physical activity, some physical fitness value may be gained from bowling. For handicapped persons, increments in strength, flexibility, and muscular endurance may result if a regular exercise regimen is established. Learning to take turns and to keep score are also important outcomes derived from the program.

The social and emotional values from bowling participation are well known. These outcomes are fostered in programs conducted in an atmosphere of friendly competition. When the situation becomes too competitive, oftentimes socialization and emotional growth may be lost. When the "bowling buddy" system is used, rapport is usually developed between the two partners. Use great care in the assignment of "buddies." If you observe that rapport is not being developed, make changes that you feel are needed.

Besides the physically handicapped, other exceptional children such as the mentally retarded or emotionally disturbed also may participate in this sport. However, permission should be obtained before patients with severe disabilities—for example, cardiac cases—should be allowed to participate.

Maureen Magee (1971, pp. 47–48) conducted a study to determine the ability of mentally retarded children to execute bowling skills and to demonstrate the effect of training and practice on the development of these skills. The subjects of the study were nine children, two boys and seven girls, whose ages ranged from 7–9 years. Their mental ages ranged from 3–7 years. In a word, they were educable mentally retarded children. Furthermore, one child was diagnosed as emotionally disturbed, two as perceptually handicapped, and one as trainable with an IQ below 50. Another child had cerebral palsy affecting all four limbs. Using plastic animal figures for pins and crushed newspapers wrapped with masking tape for balls, Magee taught modified bowling in a regular classroom for nine days. She concluded at the end of her study that all children enjoyed bowling and that their motor educability had improved. However, by the seventh day, some children began to lose interest. Magee said that there was no relationship between intelligence level and loss of interest.

Archery

Archery, a mild form of physical exercise, is also a popular sport of handicapped persons. However, it is a potentially dangerous activity and requires close supervision. During the last fifteen years it has become one of the most important rehabilitation sports for the paraplegic. Since becoming an official Olympic activity in 1972, the popularity of the sport has continued to rise. It has been estimated that approximately 150,000 contestants participate in target archery competition each year (Adams, et al., 1972).

HISTORICAL DEVELOPMENTS

Archery has been called "the sport of man since time began" because it has played such an important role in everyday life. It was not until the invention of gunpowder that archery became obsolete in combat and changed into a pure sport. Brasch (1970) compares the importance of archery to that of the wheel and fire. It was only after man learned to use the bow and arrow that he could confront the mighty beast of the jungle. In brief, the bow and arrow helped man to survive and to create his civilization.

WHEELCHAIR ARCHERY

Archery is one of the oldest sports for the physically handicapped. During the past several years it has become increasingly popular because of its rehabilitation potential. For example, shoulder girdle strength may be developed through the use of bows which require different pounds of pull to come to the full draw position. The overload principle suggests that systematic increases in strength will develop if this procedure is used. Wheelchair target archery makes up an important part of the

National Wheelchair Games. Much of archery's popularity is due to the fact that it may be conducted indoors or outdoors, and a number of variations of the sport have been developed such as archery golf and clout shooting.

ASSISTIVE DEVICES

Many types of assistive devices such as bow slings, below elbow amputee adapters, and wheelchair bow-stringers have been developed to make it possible for persons with various types of disabilities to participate. The crossbow (Figure 7–5), positioned on a tripod, is recommended for amputees who have loss of both grip and shooting hands. The crossbow is particularly suitable for individuals with general muscle weakness or upper shoulder girdle handicaps. These persons are usually unable to utilize the conventional bow because they cannot come to the full draw position. Quadriplegics may be equipped with crossbows that may be released with their mouths (Figure 7–6). A harness is utilized to hold the stock of the crossbow against the shooter's shoulder. Some assistance will, however, be required if quadriplegics are to participate in this activity. Good safety procedures are of course essential.

ARCHERY FOR THE BLIND

Telescopic sights have been developed for archers who are partially blind, and even the totally blind have participated successfully in target archery. Close supervision, however, is required to avoid accidents. A one-to-one instructor-student ratio is recommended. For the totally blind

Figure 7–5 Amputee Wearing an Opposition Plate Prothesis to Hold the Crossbow (Courtesy of Dr. Ronald C. Adams, Director Children's Rehabilitation Center, University of Virginia Hospital, Charlottesville, Virginia)

Figure 7-6 Quadriplegic Releasing Crossbow with Mouth (Courtesy of Dr. Ronald C. Adams, Director Children's Rehabilitation Center, University of Virginia Hospital, Charlottesville, Virginia)

archer, a tow line is suspended from the middle of the target to a nail attached to a toe board. This line enables the archer to position the bow correctly and to retrieve his own arrows. Self-scoring is encouraged. If each circle on the target is covered with a different textured material, the blind archer may score each arrow by feeling the texture of the target in which it is located. When he returns to the footboard, he records his score in braille.

POTENTIAL OUTCOMES

Using a bow requires the coordination of the muscles of the back, shoulders, arms, and eyes. For these reasons archery is a favorite activity among therapists and physical educators working with the physically disabled. It also possesses the potential to contribute to the emotional, social, and psychological development of the individual. Improved posture and increments in hand-eye coordination are important outcomes of participation in archery. Since bows vary in the amount of force required to bring them to the full-draw position, the strength of shoulder girdle muscles may be improved systematically through the use of overload training procedures.

Good mental health is also fostered through archery competition. The nature of this sport is such that shooting distances may be altered to fit the needs of each archer, thus providing continual challenge. The Columbia Round, for example, requires the archer to shoot twenty-five arrows from each of three distances: fifty, forty, and thirty yards.

Robert Peters (1971, pp. 39–40) reported that he experienced success in teaching archery to multiple-handicapped men (mean age 21 years) at the Fort Custer State Home, Augusta, Michigan. Class size was limited to seven men per class that met weekly. He reported no unusual administrative or supervisory problems. Some had difficulty, however, nocking an arrow because they were color blind. Nevertheless, Peters said that archery was a great benefit to these men. Increments in their morale was evident as they gained some skill in hitting the target.

Badminton

Badminton is a more vigorous game than either bowling or archery and requires greater mobility on the part of the handicapped person. As a result, it has the potential to contribute significantly to cardiovascular and cardiorespiratory endurance. Like archery, badminton may be played indoors or outdoors. Several adaptations of the game have been made so that persons with various types of disabilities may play it. Balloons, for example, are sometimes used when limited hand-eye coordination makes it impossible to play with regular birds. Table tennis paddles have also been substituted for racquets, and several players have played on each side of the net when the mobility of participants is limited. In addition, larger birds have been developed for backyard games. In brief, badminton may easily be adapted to meet the physical requirements of the participants.

HISTORICAL DEVELOPMENTS

The game was originated in India by the English military in the early 1870s. At first called "poona," the name "badminton" was adopted by a group of English officers home on leave from India in 1873. They played the game at Badminton, the country estate of the Duke of Beaufort, in Gloucestershire, England. The International Badminton Federation (IBF), the world governing body of the game, was founded in 1934.

Badminton has been played by the physically handicapped for many years. Although it is primarily played for fun, it has therapeutic value. For example, it requires the participant to move his upper arm, elbow, and wrist through ranges of movement. Thus, greater flexibility may be developed in these joints. It is also an excellent sport for fostering hand-eye coordination and neuromuscular integration of perceptual and motor mechanisms. Much of its popularity is due to the many adaptations that may be made to accommodate the handicapped. Balloon badminton, as mentioned previously, is one of the game's many variations.

ASSISTIVE DEVICES

Figure 7–7 shows a handicapped girl playing from a wheelchair. As shown, extension handle racquets have been developed to increase the

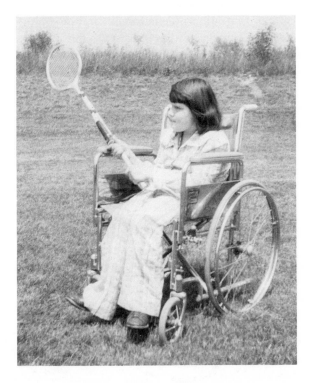

Figure 7–7 Brenda Wolcott, student at School for Children with Special Needs, Ithaca, New York (Tompkins, Seneca, Tioga Board of Cooperative Educational Services)

reach of these persons. Usually those playing on crutches or from wheel-chairs are positioned in the front court during modified doubles and triples play. Adams, et al. (1972), lists rules to govern these contests.

For amputees, a service tray (Figure 7–8) that attaches to their pros-theses has been developed. The bird is positioned on the tray and then lifted by the artificial arm so that it may be struck by the racquet in the hand of the unaffected limb.

POTENTIAL OUTCOMES

Because of the increased movement necessary to play the game, badminton has the potential to contribute significantly to cardiovascular and cardiorespiratory fitness. However, depending on the movement capabilities of the handicapped, the court size may be modified to reduce the amount of movement required. Play may be limited to half the single court or half the doubles court to accomplish this purpose.

The development of hand-eye coordination is also fostered through badminton competition. If arm movement is limited, the use of the wrist to provide force to the bird is suggested. The velocity of the bird in flight has been reported to reach 110 miles per hour during high-level competition (Adams, et al., 1972). This type of play, although infrequent by the handicapped, has the potential to develop fast reaction and move-ment time.

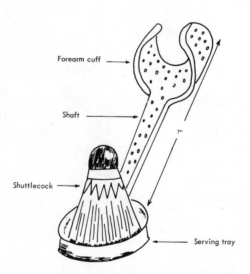

Forearm cuff

Shaft

7"

Shuttlecock

Serving tray

Figure 7–8 Service Tray for Amputees (From Adams, Daniel, and Rull-man, 1972)

Skiing

Amputee ski clubs were organized in the Scandinavian countries shortly after World War II. Within recent years, three-track skiing has become a popular sport for amputees in the United States. The National Amputee Skiers Association has been organized to foster the development of this sport. Adams, et al. (1972), report that one of the most active programs in the United States is located at the Willy Schaeffler Ski School, Arapahoe Basin, Colorado. Another program that is reported to be very successful is conducted at the Greek Peak ski area in Virgil, New York. Called TRIP, Therapeutic Recreation for Inconvenienced People, the program is run on Sunday mornings for blind skiers.

HISTORICAL DEVELOPMENTS

The word "ski" has a northern European linguistic root describing a splinter cut from a log. A method of transportation in regions with heavy snowfall, skiing as a sport originated in Norway and Sweden in the early 1800s. Immigrants from these countries introduced the sport to Americans in the mid-1800s. Representatives of twenty-six countries formed the Federation Internationale de Ski (FIS) in 1924.

As a sport for the handicapped, called three-track skiing, amputee ski clubs were first organized in Scandinavian countries shortly after World War II. The National Amputee Skiers Association is the major governing body in the United States.

ASSISTIVE DEVICES

It is recommended that leather protectors be worn by above-knee amputees to protect the stump. These devices may be made by a prosthetist or a leather worker. The invention of an outrigger ski (Figure 7–9) has made it possible for many amputees to enjoy this sport. This device increases the base of support and enables the skier to obtain better balance. A plunger, attached to the bottom of the outrigger and hand operated by the amputee, provides a braking action when needed.

The ski program for amputees requires careful supervision and expert instruction. It is costly in terms of equipment, but the values that may be obtained far exceed the costs. Skiing gets the handicapped outdoors and enables them to participate in a vigorous winter sport.

POTENTIAL OUTCOMES

Getting the handicapped to participate in a vigorous sport like skiing has great value. The fresh air, exercise, and the beautiful snow-

Figure 7–9 The Outrigger Ski Device (From Adams, Daniel, and Rullman, 1972)

covered slopes have the potential to help them forget their problems. Once some proficiency is achieved, many hours of enjoyable and beneficial exercise may be attained.

Like badminton, participation in skiing has the potential to develop good cardiovascular and cardiorespiratory fitness. Muscular strength, flexibility, and other fitness components may be developed through participation in skiing. In addition, socialization is fostered when they take part in a learn-to-ski program with others.

Swimming

One of the best lifetime sports for the handicapped is swimming. In addition to providing experiences with gross motor movements, swimming has therapeutic value. Even persons with multiple handicaps have learned to swim. Unlike other sports, however, swimming requires a one-to-one relationship because of the potential dangers involved. Learn-to-swim programs have become integral parts of adapted, developmental, and remedial programs for the handicapped. The added confidence that is acquired by the handicapped from participation in these programs is truly remarkable.

Historical Developments

The early Greeks and Romans placed great value on the therapeutic and hygienic use of water. Hydrotherapy was very popular in the late 1800s in the United States at spas such as Hot Springs, Arkansas; Saratoga, New York; and Warm Springs, Georgia. The use of hydrotherapy in hospitals, particularly orthopedic centers, is well known.

Much of the credit for the expansion of swimming activities for therapeutic purposes must be given to Carroll S. Bryant, former chief of Water Safety Service and Accident Prevention of the American National Red Cross, and Dr. Charles L. Lowman (Daniels and Davies, 1965). Dr. Lowman was largely responsible for discovering the use of group swimming for handicapped persons. Today, most all adaptive programs include swimming as one of the most popular and valuable sports.

Assistive Devices

A number of different floatation devices have been developed to enable the handicapped to enjoy aquatic activities. Once the person has overcome the fear of the water and has learned to stay afloat, the amount of support may be reduced. Ernie Davis (1971, p. 90) uses what he calls the "washcloth" approach. He has each youngster bring a washcloth to class and then proceeds to introduce them to the water through a series of washcloth exercises. According to Davis, methods which are familiar to the student and foster security are the most effective with the mentally retarded. Other instructors use towels to support the child in the water in a hammock-like position. This method is particularly suited to teaching children too small to touch bottom at the shallow end of the pool. Some teachers have found a plank (2" x 6" x 8') to be an effective aid in teaching swimming to handicapped persons. As the student gains confidence he is encouraged to use arm movements to propel the board along. Still other instructors use a length of rope to introduce the handicapped student to the water. In Evansville, Illinois, Louise Keffer used a Hubbard Tank[2] (5,000 gallon capacity) filled three-quarters full at a water temperature of 88 degrees to teach preschool deaf children (2–5 years of age) to swim. She floated ping-pong balls on the surface and had the boys and girls attempt to blow them across the water. Gradually, the children learned to say "blow" and put their mouths underwater and blow. Getting young children to put their heads in the water may be a difficult

---

[2] A shallow tank that is utilized by therapists for hydrotherapy treatments.

task but, according to Keffer, the ping-pong ball approach paid off. Hers did it in one lesson.

POTENTIAL OUTCOMES

Swimming offers more values to handicapped persons than any other sport. In addition to therapeutic values, swimming develops skill, endurance, flexibility, and other fitness parameters. The buoyancy of the body aids weakened muscles to perform movements that are difficult or impossible out of the water. Instead of medically prescribed exercises, the natural movements of swimming are utilized to build strength, flexibility, and cardiovascular and cardiorespiratory endurance. In addition to the obvious physical and physiological values, swimming contributes to psychological and social outcomes. Improved self-concept and social competence usually result from participation in aquatic activities. Adams, Daniel and Rullman (1972) suggest para-canoeing as an appropriate activity for paraplegics.

SUMMARY

Lifetime sports-oriented physical education programs are for everyone—including the exceptional child. Often misunderstood, ignored, or assigned to special classes, exceptional children are now being provided with opportunities to participate in a wide variety of lifetime sports. The potential outcomes of these programs contribute to the physical, social, emotional, and psychological well-being of this special group.

The increments in participation have been due to a dedicated group of teachers, therapists, and recreational leaders and to the development of assistive devices such as the outrigger ski, bowling frame, etc. The central purpose of this chapter was to show the application of these devices to the lifetime sports of bowling, archery, badminton, skiing, and swimming.

STUDY QUESTIONS

1. Define the term "exceptional child."
2. What are some general suggestions that may be made for working with the handicapped?
3. How may the lifetime sports be modified so that exceptional children and handicapped adults may participate in them?
4. Identify and describe the use of assistive devices that have been developed so that handicapped persons may participate in lifetime sports.

REFERENCES

ADAMS, R. C., A. N. DANIEL, and L. RULLMAN. *Games, Sports and Exercises for the Physically Handicapped.* Philadelphia: Lea & Febiger, 1972.

American Alliance for Health, Physical Education and Recreation. *Physical Activities for the Mentally Retarded—Ideas for Instruction.* Washington, D.C.: AAHPER, 1968.

————. *The Best of Challenge.* Washington, D.C.: AAHPER, 1971.

————. *The Best of Challenge.* Washington, D.C.: AAHPER, 1974.

ARNHEIM, D. D., D. AUXTER, and W. C. CROWE. *Principles and Methods of Adapted Physical Education.* St. Louis, Mo.: C. V. Mosby Company, 1969.

BRASCH, R. *How Did Sports Begin?* New York: David McKay Co., Inc., 1970.

CHRISTENSEN, D. "Creativity in teaching physical education to the physically handicapped child," *Journal of Health, Physical Education and Recreation,* 41 (1970), 73–74.

CLARKE, H. H., and D. H. CLARKE. *Developmental and Adapted Physical Education.* Englewood Cliffs, N.J.: Prentice-Hall, Inc., 1963.

CLEIN, M. I. "The early historical roots of therapeutic exercise," *Journal of Health, Physical Education and Recreation,* 41 (1970), 89–91.

CRUICKSHANK, W. M. *The Exceptional Child in Contemporary Education.* Syracuse, N.Y.: Syracuse University Press, 1952.

DANIELS, A. S., and EVELYN A. DAVIES. *Adapted Physical Education.* New York: Harper & Row, Publishers, 1965.

DAVIS, E. "Fresh Approaches for Combating Persistent Problems," in *The Best of Challenge.*" Washington, D.C.: AAHPER, 1971, p. 90.

ERSING, W. F. "The nature of physical education programming for the mentally retarded and physically handicapped," *Journal of Health, Physical Education and Recreation,* 45 (1974), 89–91.

FAIT, H. *Special Physical Education: Adopted, Corrective, Developmental.* Philadelphia: W. B. Saunders, 1974.

GEDDES, DOLORES. "Physical Activity: a necessity for severely and profoundly mentally retarded individuals," *Journal of Health, Physical Education and Recreation,* 45 (1974), 73–76.

————. *Physical Activities for Individuals with Handicapping Conditions.* St. Louis, Mo.: C. V. Mosby Company, 1974.

KEFFER, L. "Introduction to Swimming for the Deaf," in *The Best of Challenge.* Washington, D.C.: AAHPER, 1971, p. 92.

KIRK, S. A. *Educating Exceptional Children.* Boston: Houghton Mifflin Company, 1972.

LOGAN, G. A. *Adapted Physical Education.* Philadelphia: William C. Brown Company, 1972.

MAGEE, M. T. "An Experiment with Bowling Skills and the Mentally Retarded," *The Best of Challenge.* Washington: D.C.: AAHPER, 1971, pp. 47–48.

PETERS, R. "Bullseye!" *The Best of Challenge.* Washington, D.C.: AAHPER, 1971, pp. 39–40.

The University of the State of New York, State Education Department. *Conference Proceedings: Physical Education for Handicapped Children and Youth.* Albany, N.Y.: The University of the State of New York, State Education Department, Division of Secondary Curriculum Development, 1972.

————. *Physical Education for the Exceptional Child.* Albany, N.Y.: The University of the State of New York, State Education Department, Bureau of Curriculum Development, 1970.

CHAPTER 8

PUBLIC
RELATIONS

If you were to ask the average citizen about the physical education program in a particular school within the community in which he lived he would probably reply: They have an excellent baseball, football, wrestling, or basketball team. Seldom will the layman interpret your question in terms of the physical education instructional program for all students. This fact alone tells us that physical educators have not done a very good job in interpreting the objectives of their programs to the public. What "Mr. Citizen" interprets as physical education is in essence interscholastic athletics.

This interpretation of physical education is unfortunate and surprising, considering the fact that practically all citizens have taken physical education while they were in school. Actually, this attitude is the result of our failure as teachers and administrators to correctly interpret our profession to our students. Athletics, although an important part of physical education, is not the entire program.

On the other hand, it is understandable why this misinterpretation has come about. In most communities, the only part of the program to receive public attention through newspaper, radio, and television media is interscholastic sports. The purpose of this chapter is to present ideas which will help physical education teachers and recreation leaders to interpret all aspects of their programs to the public. Sound public relations will result in better financial and moral support for physical education and recreation. When the public becomes better informed about the objectives of class instructional, intramural, extramural, and interscholastic aspects of the program, they will support it in principle and financially. In an era of rapid gains in taxes and a shrinking economy, financial support is needed.

Despite the importance of public relations, however, they will not serve as a substitute for good programs. Nor is it a good practice to try and deceive the public into thinking that quality education is being provided if it is not. It is a basic tenet of sound public relations that the public has the right to know the truth. After all, they are paying the bill. When a credibility gap exists, the school will eventually suffer from lack of support. Usually, attitudes toward the school and its programs are expressed during bond issues, the annual budget, board of education meetings, and other functions. The results of these events express, in an indirect way, the public's opinions about the school, its personnel, and its programs, including physical education. In a word, the school cannot avoid public relations. As Matthew Resick, Beverly Seidel, and James Mason (1970, p. 225) pointed out, "By law, schools are public business."

REACHING THE PUBLIC

Public relations experts realize that they need to reach many different groups of people if their programs are to be effective. They speak of publics—not public. All too often, public relations in physical education are directed only at parents and members of booster clubs. Actually, there are at least five different publics which need to be considered. They are: (1) students, (2) teachers, (3) administrators, (4) parents, and (5) the general public, including alumni. Each of these groups plays a vital role in the success of your programs. Of particular importance is the fact that public relations procedures need to be designed specifically for each audience. Since they have different interests in education and view the school from diverse vantage points, they will need to be serviced differently.

The students are actually involved in the educational process and acquire first hand information about the quality of the courses in which they are enrolled. The quality of teaching, interpersonal relationships with teachers, and other factors shape their opinions. Since they communicate their beliefs to their parents and friends, students play an important role in the success of any public relations program. And, since they are future taxpayers and parents, they carry with them, after they leave school, the impressions which shape their own children's attitudes about education.

Other teachers form impressions about your programs too. Since they come in direct contact with athletes and students enrolled in P.E. classes, they formulate their attitudes by the way in which students speak of their experiences in these activities. Some teachers attend intramural and interscholastic contests; a few serve as coaches of junior and senior high school teams. Perhaps more than any other factor, the coaches' attitudes toward the educational process influence the opinions of fellow teachers. If, for example, coaches are academically inclined themselves and impress upon their athletes the importance of acquiring a good education while they are in school, other teachers are likely to support their programs. On the other hand, if coaches portray "the jock" image, they will likely turn some of their fellow teachers off. The personality of the coach and the way in which he views his program as a part of the total educational process are important factors in shaping public opinion. Aristotle's premise about the effects of prestige on persuasion lend credence to the above thoughts. He said:

> We believe good men more fully and more readily than others: this is true generally whatever the question is, and absolutely true where exact certainty is impossible and opinions are divided. . . . It is not true, as some writers assume in their treatises on rhetoric, that the personal goodness revealed by the speaker contributes nothing to his power of persuasion; on the contrary, his character may almost be called the most effective means of persuasion he possesses (Aristotle, tr. W. Phys Roberts, 1954, p. 25).

Incidentally, Elliot Aronson (1972, pp. 58–59), prominent social psychologist, reports that Aristotle's premise has been tested[1] a number of times and found to be tenable. In a word, these data suggest that coaches will have more "clout" when they are winning.

School administrators possess various philosophical positions regarding the place of physical education and athletics within their schools. Physical education teachers, coaches, and directors should know the administrator's beliefs so that they may contribute to the expectations of

---

[1] See Carl Hovland and Walter Weiss, "The Influence of Source Credibility on Communication Effectiveness," *Public Opinion Quarterly*, 15 (1951), pp. 635–50.

the total school program. For example, how important is winning? What about the emerging role of interscholastic sports for girls? How important is elementary physical education? Knowing the answers to these and other questions will enable you to deal more effectively with principals, superintendents, and boards of education. In brief, good public relations begin with knowing the expectations of chief school officers and other administrative personnel with whom you work.

You reach the parents through students. Basically, if they like the program the parents will support it; if they don't, parental support may be lacking. Although keeping everyone happy is an impossible task, a broad program in which there are many opportunities for students to participate at different levels of competition is one of the best public relations devices we have to help gain support for physical education in our schools. Schools that focus on the few rather than the many usually run into difficulty particularly when their teams are losing.

The general public is composed of those people who are not directly involved in school activities, who usually rely on mass media to gain information about school activities. They become more school-centered at critical periods when bond issues, budgets, and other money-producing activities affect them. In the past school officials have usually not attempted to keep these persons informed about school business. Today, however, there is a more concerted attempt to keep all community citizens aware of school activities. Good public relations is not a hit or miss business; it is, instead, an outgrowth of quality education designed to keep the public informed about what is happening in our schools.

THE SATISFIED CUSTOMER

The first cardinal principle of sound public relations is to produce satisfied customers. In business, if you have a good product people will want to buy it. In fact, some businessmen contend that if the product is good enough, it will sell itself. Very little attention will be needed in the form of advertisements, free samples, or other gimmicks.

The same principle may be applied to public relations in physical education. If the program is good enough, if the children like it, they will be your best salesmen. Unfortunately, however, some have not enjoyed physical education while they were in school, and as a result of their experiences they have become quite negativistic about the place and value of physical education in our schools. Laurence Morehouse and Leonard Gross (1975, p. 46) wrote that physical educators suffer from what they called ergomania—a craze for work. That is, ". . . an almost obnoxious enthusiasm for exercise." When individuals who have put up with the tyranny of fitness teachers become members of boards of education, the physical education program usually suffers.

Although it is difficult to please everyone, much of the problem has centered around the traditional nature of our programs and the lock-step way in which they have been conducted. Let's face it, traditional instruction with emphasis on mass calisthenics to rhythmic count, rigid dress and behavioral requirements, and teacher-centered instructional methodologies left little room for individual choice and atypical behaviors. In contrast, lifetime sports-centered programs stressing selective-elective opportunities for students and the teaching of the "why" as well as the "how" of physical activity should develop students who value physical activity and the benefits that may result from lifelong participation in sports. This change in emphasis is in keeping with changing societal values that stress individuality, creativity, and self-fulfillment.

USE OF MASS MEDIA

Producing a nation of participants, rather than a nation of spectators, is not an easy task. Mass media such as newspaper, radio, and television have the potential to help us accomplish this worthy goal. And, in support of this approach, the President's Council on Physical Fitness and Sport during the past several years has spent large sums of money to provide exposure to physical education and recreation. It is apparent that these commercials are helping to better inform the public of the values of physical activity and the need for quality programs in our schools. Charles Page (1973, p. 4), well-known sociologist at the University of Massachusetts, addressed this point when he said that television coverage of sporting events has not produced a nation of spectators. Page contends that there is mounting interest in sport in almost all major social groups and that the appetite for sport has never been so insatiable in the United States. Statistics show that "at least one out of five people bowl, about a third as many play golf or tennis, and millions of post-school adults, men and women, take up such mushrooming sports as skiing, water skiing, surfing, and skin diving" (Talamini and Page, 1973, p. 4). They continue that about sixty-five million people watched the 1972 Super Bowl, and this fact alone tells us something about the public's interest in sport.

In addition to the President's Council's attempt to influence public opinion, the American Alliance for Health, Physical Education and Recreation (AAHPER) has embarked upon a Physical Education Public

Information project (Pepi). While under the capable direction of Dr. Fay Biles, Pepi produced one of the best films ever made on lifetime sports-centered programs. "All the Self There Is" shows how lifetime sports may be integrated into physical education programs in secondary schools. The colored, fifteen-minute film, which may be rented or purchased through AAHPER, stresses self-fulfillment through enjoyable physical activity. At the present time, this film is one of the best public relations tools we have available to show students, parents, members of boards of education, and community citizens. The members of the New York State Lifetime Sports Association (NYSLSA) purchased two copies of the film and mail it free of charge to school districts in New York state on request.

Some school districts, colleges, and universities have adopted bumper sticker campaigns to help foster their programs. Recently, the members of NYSLSA purchased 2,000 "Lifetime Sports Extends Life" stickers and distributed them at the annual meeting of the New York State Association for Health, Physical Education and Recreation. Evidently, it was a popular idea. All 2,000 stickers disappeared during the first day of the three-day conference. It is apparent that catchy slogans have a way of stimulating awareness that may lead to greater support for our programs.

DEMONSTRATION CENTERS

The President's Council on Physical Fitness and Sport initiated a Demonstration Centers project several years ago to increase the attention given to physical fitness in our schools. The project was conducted in cooperation with State Education Departments throughout the various states. In order to qualify as Demonstration Center Schools each school had to meet at least four specific criteria. They were as follows:

- Periodic health appraisal for all pupils.
- Identification of the physically underdeveloped and measures to eliminate or alleviate their problems.
- Periodic physical achievement tests to evaluate and motivate pupil progress.
- A daily period of physical education emphasizing physical fitness for all pupils.

Individual states were expected to impose additional criteria to assure that Demonstration Center Schools were representative of the best within their states. Many states imposed additional criteria. The

New York State Education Department personnel, for example, said that schools had to meet the following additional criteria[2]:

- A written curriculum guide appropriately identifying goals, policies, procedures, and a cogent, sequential series of units at all grade levels.
- Purposeful instruction based on progressive, coordinated, and articulated experiences in body dynamics, games, self-testing activities, rhythms, dance, and aquatics.
- Daily vigorous, sustained physical activity adapted to the capabilities of the individual pupil as an integral part of instruction.
- Scheduling procedures which deploy teachers and groups for maximum effectiveness.
- A pupil-teacher load of not more than 200 different pupils.
- One indoor teaching station for each 200 pupils enrolled and essential outdoor teaching areas.
- The granting of credit for successful completion of physical education in the secondary school.

Schools that were selected agreed to schedule regular visitation periods, including appropriate demonstrations. As a result of being selected, each school received a handsome pennant and a certificate of appreciation for its service. Appropriate newspaper, radio, and television coverage was provided at the local level. Usually, a member of the Division of Physical Education and Recreation visited the school and awarded the pennant at an assembly program. Most of the Directors of Physical Education thought that the program helped physical education in their schools and throughout the state.

This project, still in process in many states, helped to increase the quality of physical education in our schools. Being a Demonstration Center School brought local, state, and national recognition. These kind of projects do a great deal to educate citizens about the goals of physical education.

LIFETIME SPORTS MODEL SCHOOLS

To infuse the lifetime sports concept of physical education into our schools members of the New York State Lifetime Sports Association (NYSLSA) have proposed a Lifetime Sports Model Schools project (LSMS). So as not to be in conflict with the efforts of the President's Council on Physical Fitness and Sport, NYSLSA members have suggested

---

2 "Quality in Physical Education" (Albany, N.Y.: The State University of New York, State Education Department, 1973).

that the two projects be combined. Demonstration Centers and Lifetime Sports Model Schools would draw attention to the need for fitness through lifetime sports participation. Although the President's Council has been receptive to the idea, cut-backs in staff may prevent New York State's Division of Physical Education and Recreation from implementing the project. Some of the suggested criteria for Lifetime Sports Model Schools, in addition to those already established for Demonstration Centers, are as follows:

- The faculty, including resource personnel, is qualified to teach a broad range of lifetime sports.
- Beginning, intermediate, and advanced levels of instruction are provided in a variety of lifetime sports.
- Adequate facilities, equipment and supplies are available for teaching a broad range of lifetime sports.
- Optimum use is made of community resources, such as golf courses, tennis courts, horseback riding stables, ski slopes, etc.
- Optimum use is made of resource personnel, such as ski, tennis, water-safety, and ice skating instructors.
- Selective-elective opportunities are provided for students.

Of course, other criteria could and should be added. However, staff, facilities, and equipment and supplies are the most essential features for quality lifetime sports-oriented programs.

OPEN FACILITIES TO PUBLIC

One of the best public relations devices to obtain support for our programs is to open our facilities to community use at appropriate times, e.g., at nights and on weekends. People who use our facilities for recreational purposes seem to be more willing to support our programs; a rapport that tends to spill over in support of physical education is established.

Not only should facilities be provided for public use but instructional programs should also be provided in the lifetime sports such as tennis, golf, swimming, etc. As skills and interest increase, participation also seems to increase.

Of course, proper supervision is needed. In some school districts city recreation departments conduct these programs at the end of the school day, evenings, and weekends. In some instances physical education teachers are paid additionally for their services. When school and recreation department people work well together these programs contribute significantly to good public relations. Some districts are making physical education and recreation activities integral parts of their continuing education programs. In some areas, there is a great demand for classes in golf, tennis, archery, and even belly dancing.

NEWSPAPER ARTICLES

Some school districts have found it desirable to periodically prepare newspaper releases about various aspects of their physical education programs. Considering the fact that so much newspaper, radio, and television coverage is given to interscholastic athletics, these releases, when done well, help to interpret class instructional, intramural, and extramural aspects of the program. Special events and innovative practices are also given special attention in mass media presentations. Programs for community citizens should also receive special coverage. With heart disease prevention programs becoming increasingly important, they may serve as excellent examples of how school districts meet the needs of community citizens.

Releases should be prepared by the Director of HPER and his staff and approved by the central administration before being released to the press. Following proper channels will help eliminate the controversy that sometimes results from the release of stories controversial in nature. Whenever possible appropriate photographs should accompany releases because of their ability to enhance the story that is being presented.

Great care should be taken to make sure that the releases are realistic; that they reflect the true nature of the program. The extent and quality of the program is too often distorted. Usually, poor public relations result from this type of publicity.

Daniel Ziatz (1975) recommends that a newsletter be written and sent home to parents four to six times a year. The purpose of the newsletter is to keep parents informed of the activities, objectives of the program, and evaluation procedures that are being used in physical education. Figure 8–1 shows a copy of a newsletter developed for this purpose. Additionally, the author suggests that (1) different colored paper be used for each issue, (2) drawings of sports figures be included, and (3) the content be limited to one page.

ADVISORY COUNCIL

Within recent years many school districts have found it desirable to establish advisory councils composed of students, faculty, administration, and community citizens. These councils serve as sounding boards for the establishment of new programs and the revision of older ones.

PHYSICAL

EDUCATION

NEWSLETTER

Dear Parents:

May I take this opportunity to tell you about our
new physical education program at Podunk High School.
During this past summer the members of our P. E.
Department, with the help of several students, completely updated our curriculum. We are very excited
about the new course of study that will be implemented this Fall. Let me tell you about it!

The program is lifetime sports-oriented. That is, we have decided to teach
a wide variety of sports that may be played throughout life. For example,
tennis, golf, bowling, badminton, archery, skiing and other sports with high
carryover value are now included in the curriculum. In addition, at grades
10 and 11, students may select those sports which they enjoy the most. Instruction will be given at beginning, intermediate and advanced levels so
that students may become highly skilled in the sports they have selected.
It is our opinion that unless boys and girls acquire a fairly high skill
level they will not participate during the adult years.

At the 10th and 11th grade levels, the curriculum is completely elective in
nature. It is also coeducational in non-contact sports. We see no reason
why boys and girls can not learn sports skills together. We are hopeful
that this change will produce better socialization and lead to increased
understanding among young people.

We are still very much concerned about physical fitness but our approach to
it has changed. In brief, the new program requirements call for a "gentle"
approach to exercise. That is, we hope that students will become physically
fit through participation in enjoyable activities. We still plan to give
fitness tests twice a year but we are not trying to condition your son or
daughter the way we prepare our athletes for interscholastic sports competition.

In the very near future we plan to hold "open house" so that you may come
to school and see our program in operation. At that time you may ask
questions, participate yourself if you like, and meet the members of our
P. E. faculty. We look forward to meeting you at this function.

Sincerely yours,

William F. Straub
Director of Physical Education

Figure 8–1   The Physical Education Newsletter

From a public relations point of view, advisory councils provide
interested members of the school and community with a voice in the
establishment of policies concerning physical education. Although the
board of education is the legal policy-making body, the recommendations

of the Advisory Council often influence its decisions. Incidentally, it is desirable to have a member of the board of education serve on the council so that a close tie-in with the board may be established. However, all policies must be cleared through the members of the central administration. Knowing how policies are established and utilizing appropriate channels is absolutely essential if good public relations are to be fostered. When such groups become too forceful and overpowering they can destroy rather than build sound public relations.

DEMONSTRATIONS

Giving the public a chance to actually observe the program in operation is another way of promoting good public relations. As mentioned previously, the public often gets a distorted view of physical education because of the emphasis and publicity given to interscholastic athletics. When demonstrations are scheduled they should be realistic so that they present a proper view of the curriculum, and the time allocated to preparation should be minimal. It is a good idea to ask each class to demonstrate some aspect of the program. When this policy is followed practices may be held during class periods. One or two dress rehearsals with all members of the cast present will help to alleviate problems that may develop during the actual performance.

Invitations to parents, members of the board of education, the press, and community citizens should be sent well in advance of the demonstration. Often the cooperation of other department members may be secured to help with special aspects of the demonstration. For example, the music department may provide appropriate music and the department of home economics may assist with the construction of costumes. Securing the cooperation of these and other departments is essential if good demonstrations are to be provided. Demonstrations are a lot of work but their potential for the development of support from school and community citizens is great.

OUTSIDE GROUPS

Another way to promote physical education in your community is to schedule demonstrations by outside groups. Springfield College's Demonstration Gymnastics team, for example, has held many excellent performances. Traveling groups from abroad may also be scheduled when they are in the area. Continual interest in physical education may be developed by inviting alumni back for games, award dinners, and other functions. Annual award dinners are frequently utilized for this purpose as well as getting parents, community officials, and others interested persons to recognize athletes who have played on various teams throughout the school year.

Guest speakers should be chosen for these functions with great care. They possess the potential to enhance or destroy the image which you are trying to build for your school. Choose someone who is articulate, a good story teller, and respected by people in the community. His address could have quite an impact on your program.

These events are usually very popular with the public, students, and faculty and have the potential to contribute significantly to building support for quality physical education programs. It is true that the promotion of demonstrations do take time but their potential worth to the physical education program far outweighs the time required.

SUMMARY

When physical education teachers and administrators broaden the scope of their programs to include the use of community resources they have the potential to significantly influence public opinion. All too often the school becomes a closed community in and of itself, and as a result of this practice community citizens are not provided with opportunities to observe the various programs in operation. This unfortunate practice results in an isolationism that destroys financial and moral support. Making people feel a part of the school through participation in its many diverse activities has the potential to build the kind of support that is needed in an era of high taxes and other economic pressures.

In this chapter ideas were presented for the development of sound public relations programs. The first cardinal principle of public relations is to provide a quality experience for all community citizens, especially school-age boys and girls. When young people enjoy and profit from their experiences in physical education they will sell the program to their parents, friends, and other members of the community.

Basically, good public relations is brought about through good interpersonal relations. When physical education department personnel are respected in the community this helps to foster positive attitudes toward the school and, in particular, the physical education program. However, public relations should not be left to chance. Each school should plan a public relations program that will build support for all aspects of its total school curriculum. Physical education, as an integral part of the total school curriculum, has the potential to contribute toward this goal.

Since no other part of the school curriculum is challenged as often as physical education to support its place in the total curriculum, sound public relations are vital to the success of these programs. Without strong public support these programs are often viewed as frills and eliminated or drastically curtailed when budget cuts are made. Public relations will continue to play a vital role in the operation of physical education programs in the years ahead. And although differences in background, education, and expectation result in different social and political values, most citizens will support physical education programs that educate for lifelong participation in sport.

STUDY QUESTIONS

1. What is the need for sound public relations in physical education?
2. How may the use of mass media such as radio, newspaper, and television help develop public awareness?
3. What contribution (s) has the President's Council on Physical Fitness and Sport made to the development of public relations in physical education?
4. What is the Pepi project?
5. What is the purpose of the Demonstration Center and Lifetime Sports Model Schools project?
6. Identify three ways in which physical educators may increase public awareness of their programs.
7. What is the interrelationship between public relations and interpersonal relations?
8. What contributions may Advisory Councils make to public relations programs?
9. How may demonstrations be utilized to improve public relations?

REFERENCES

ARISTOTLE, "Rhetoric," in *Rhetoric and Poetics,* trans. W. Rhys Roberts. New York: Modern Library, 1954, p. 25.

DAUGHTREY, G., and J. B. WOODS. *Physical Education Programs: Organization and Administration.* Philadelphia: W. B. Saunders Company, 1971.

MOREHOUSE, L. E., and L. GROSS. *Total Fitness in 30 Minutes a Week.* New York: Simon and Schuster, 1975.

PAGE, C. H. "The World of Sport and Its Study," in *Sport and Society—An Anthology,* J. T. Talamini and C. H. Page, eds. Boston: Little, Brown and Company, 1973.

RESICK, M. C., B. L. SEIDEL, and J. G. MASON. *Modern Administrative Practices in Physical Education and Athletics.* Reading, Mass.: Addison-Wesley Publishing Co., 1970, pp. 223–36.

ZIATZ, D. H. "Practical Realistic Public Relations," *Journal of Health, Physical Education and Recreation,* 46:1 (January 1975), p. 69.

CHAPTER 9

FACILITIES

The lifetime sports concept of physical education suggests that maximum use be made of facilities and equipment, both in school and in the community. When scheduling procedures permit, use is made of community bowling lanes, ice arenas, gymnasia, tennis courts, ski areas, golf courses, riding stables, and other facilities. Greater use is also made of outdoor activity areas adjacent to the school on a year-round basis. Many schools have outdoor space for such activities as snow shoeing, cross country skiing, orienteering, winter camping, backpacking, and ice skating. Outdoor areas provide additional teaching stations and enable directors of HPER to conduct more comprehensive programs.

Lifetime sports-oriented programs require the availability of a wide range of facilities. Unless appropriate facilities are provided, the scope of the program is limited. All too often facilities have been constructed before the curriculum has been developed. When this unfortunate practice occurs, the curriculum is limited by the design of the facilities: for example, instruction in aquatics is impossible because a pool was not provided. It is also true that the construction of the gymnasium specifically to accommodate basketball has limited the use of this facility for other purposes. Wagner, Evans and Nowak (1961, p. 17) spoke of this point when they said: "The basis of the problem seems to be the tendency to build the entire building around a single purpose space, the basketball court." To avoid this situation, a number of progressive communities have constructed field houses rather than the traditional gymnasium. The field house, when designed well, is much better suited to lifetime sports-centered instruction. The flexibility of the design provides more wide-open space where large-group instruction may take place in a variety of lifetime sports. Therefore, it is a cardinal principle of facility planning to first design the curriculum and then build facilities to help accomplish the objectives of the program.

The purpose of this chapter is to provide information that will be helpful in the design and construction of facilities for the lifetime sports. The coverage is not inclusive but is representative of some of the innovative activity areas needed to implement a comprehensive program. The objective is the most economical and efficient use of total community resources.

THE PLANNING PROCESS

The basic purpose of lifetime sports-centered programs is to provide all boys and girls with skills, knowledge, and attitudes so that they will be able to participate in physical activity throughout life. With this thought in mind, facilities should be designed and constructed to enable school officials to accomplish this objective. The increased attention that has been given to facility planning and construction during the past several years has been due to increased leisure time and a growing realization that recreation, and especially physical activity, is a fundamental need essential to the well-being of all people. This concept is in keeping with the thought that the purpose of education is not only to help one acquire the competencies needed to make a living but should contribute to the quality of life itself.

The widening impact of athletics, public recreation, and physical education on our culture calls for a careful assessment of those factors that should be considered in planning facilities for the lifetime sports. Cooperation and joint planning help to eliminate the duplication and overlapping of facilities found in many communities. The pooling of resources usually results in the construction of facilities that better meet the needs of all community citizens.

The following guidelines should be utilized when planning facilities for lifetime sports-centered instructional programs.

- A master plan, based on community needs, should be established.
- Use should be made of individuals who are qualified to give expert advice and assistance in planning areas and facilities.
- The type, location, and size of essential areas and facilities should be related to recreational needs of the entire community.
- Areas and facilities should be planned according to the social and economic characteristics of the community.
- Plans for areas and facilities must conform to local and state regulations.
- All interested organizations, individuals, and groups should have an opportunity to share in the planning of areas and facilities intended for public use.
- There should be close cooperation among all public and private agencies concerned with the location, acquisition, development and operation of areas and facilities.
- Widespread publicity, sound interpretation, and public discussion should be held to gain support for the project.
- Planning should include provisions for the needs of exceptional children.[1]

A check list for facility planners is in Appendix D.

THE PARK-SCHOOL CONCEPT

The Park-School concept of facility planning provides areas that serve both education and public recreation. It is most appropriate for inclusion here since it encompasses the lifetime sports spirit of physical education and recreation for all community citizens. Since the park-school concept combines on a single site the neighborhood recreational area, the elementary school, the community recreational area, and the secondary school, it has the potential to contribute to the worthy use of leisure by all community citizens. The result of joint planning by community citizens, the community park-school provides outdoor-indoor facilities to house an integrated program of education, recreation, and community activities. When school and municipal authorities decide to pool their resources, not only is there considerable improvement in the extent and quality of areas and facilities but there is also economy in land acquisition and use, construction, operation and maintenance. The economy of dual use idea has gained wide acceptance for the park-school concept, especially today in an era of rising building costs.

As a part of the park-school concept, some school districts may wish

---

[1] *Planning Facilities for Athletics, Physical Education and Recreation* (Chicago: The Athletic Institute, 1974), pp. 2–3.

to develop resident camps, nature trails, primitive areas for outpost camping and exploration, and other areas and facilities. Many schools are also making use of state owned and operated recreational areas for camping, backpacking, orienteering,[2] and other activities.

SELECTION OF THE ARCHITECT

One of the most important decisions in the planning process is made when an architect is selected. The planning team, consisting of school and community citizens, should jointly select the architect after they have interviewed several candidates. Functional, efficient, and economical buildings result from a well-coordinated team effort. The architect, as a member of the team, plays a central role in accomplishing this important objective. Interviews, inspection of buildings they have designed, and conferences with clients they have served provide valuable information about the qualifications of architects. Knowledge, past experiences, personality, and ability to establish rapport are some of the criteria that should guide the selection process.

Once the architect has been selected, the planning team must work with him to (1) determine specific and comprehensive program requirements, (2) determine size, (3) designate functions, and (4) delineate operational patterns. To accomplish these objectives, regular meetings must be held, agendas prepared and followed, and minutes taken of all sessions. Much of the architect's time will be spent in developing and preparing detailed drawings. Usually, the architect will develop the final plans for the building(s) after progressing through (1) programming, (2) schematic design, (3) design development, (4) construction documents, (5) bidding documents, and (6) construction phases.

NEW CONCEPTS

The lifetime sports concept of physical education requires a new approach to traditional building design and construction. Since lifetime sports-centered instruction places emphasis on the total development of the individual and enables all students to become active participants in the program, activity areas and facilities must be constructed so that these outcomes are realized. Inadequate facilities, equipment, and supplies restrict the attainment of these goals. If boys and girls are to carry the habit of fitness into adulthood, they need to acquire skills,

---

[2] A combination of cross-country running and land navigation with the aid of a topographical map and a compass.

interests, knowledge, and appreciation of the values of regular physical activity while they are in school. Utilization of the natural environment for human activity helps to foster this objective. The park-school, located on a large tract of land in a natural setting, is an ideal site for this type of program.

During the past three decades, school building construction has undergone an almost complete transformation. Oiled wood floors have been replaced by easily maintained surfaces constructed of materials, such as tartan, vinyl, carpeting, terrazzo, and other products. Bright colors have replaced "institutional ivory" and create a more stimulating environment in which to learn. Students now study in an environment of controlled lighting, acoustically treated rooms enclosed by large areas of glass and thermostatically regulated by air-conditioning systems. Moveable walls enable administrators to create instant classrooms to better meet the needs of new instruction methods. Flexibility is an earmark of these innovations in schoolhouse design.

Throughout this transition in design and construction, however, one part of the school plant, the gymnasium, remained largely unchanged. Until recently, we had the usual rectangular shaped structure complete with wood floors, high windows, exposed trusses, and suspended heating and ventilating units, with basketball goals protruding from fixed or moveable structures.

Outdoors the usual interscholastic areas are provided, such as the baseball diamond, football field, track, soccer field, etc. Only recently have some schools constructed sports facilities that have high carry-over value like tennis courts, archery ranges, putting greens, and golf driving ranges. Obviously, from an analysis of facilities, it appears that physical education programs, by and large, have focused attention on the star athlete rather than on those boys and girls who comprise the large segment of our school population. And, although star athletes, both male and female, deserve their share of attention, those persons who need physical education the most should not be forgotten.

The investment in total space requirements for physical education is large compared to the rest of the total school program. A conservative estimate is that approximately 70 percent of the total school property is devoted to physical education (Wagner, Evans and Nowak, 1961). In 1960 alone, it is estimated that four hundred and eighty million dollars were spent on new physical education facilities (Wagner, et al., 1961). In other words, about 15 to 20 percent of the school building dollar is spent on physical education facilities. Clearly, the investment in physical education is large and the outcomes should be commensurate with this expenditure. Lifetime sports-oriented programs make this large investment worthwhile.

Innovative Facilities

THE LIMITED SHELTER

In practically every region of the United States, a new kind of facility, the limited shelter, has appeared with increasing regularity. The design of this facility is in keeping with the lifetime sports emphasis of taking some part of the curriculum out of doors on a year-round basis. Figure 9–1 shows limited shelters designed to provide protection against wind, low temperatures, hot weather, and precipitation.

According to Wagner, Evans, and Nowak (1961), three factors should influence the design of these structures. They are (1) climate, (2)

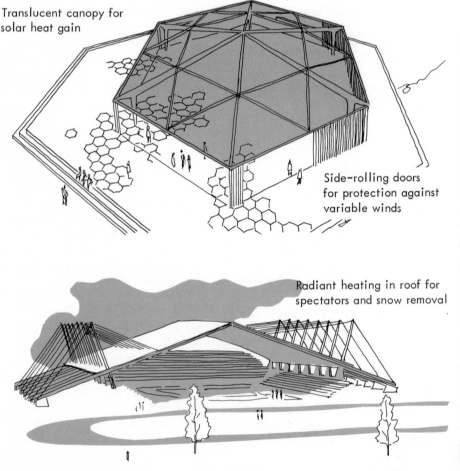

Translucent canopy for
solar heat gain

Side-rolling doors
for protection against
variable winds

Radiant heating in roof for
spectators and snow removal

Figure 9–1   The Limited-Shelter (From Wagner, Evans, and Nowak, 1961)

degree of utilization required, and (3) the size and scope of the program. The ingenuity of the designer and his knowledge of the climate conditions in the area under consideration will greatly influence the type of structure that is designed and constructed.

If high utilization is desired, the architect must develop methods to control air movement and radiation. Trees, shrubs, terrain contours, and other natural elements help to control air movements. The architect may also provide walls, roofs, louvers, screens, and mechanical devices, such as fans, to provide climate control. Depending on situational factors, it may be necessary to shield a shelter from the wind or to provide increased air flow.

Solar radiation is controlled through the use of opaque, translucent, or transparent roof structures. If solar radiation is not adequate, infrared heating units may be installed. All-weather floor surfaces, equipment storage, and drinking fountains may also be provided.

The basic criterion for evaluation of these facilities is: how well does it accommodate the activities for which it was designed? A cheap building that does not function well can be very expensive.

NEW DESIGN IDEAS

Changing concepts of physical education, such as lifetime sports-oriented programs, call for new building design features. This trend along with coeducational instruction, interscholastic sports for girls, and other developments require innovative approaches to the design, construction, and utilization of activity areas and facilities. Basically, these curricular trends require more practice facilities and teaching stations with multiple-use capabilities. As expected, the design of facilities has not kept up with these new developments. Therefore, it is the purpose of this section to explore some of the solutions to these problems.

To create a series of new and different design concepts for physical education activities, three well-known architects, Lomar Kelsey, Fred Kolflat, and Robert Schaefer, were secured by *The Nation's Schools* to provide innovative approaches to facility design and construction. Much of their work was shaped by the statement of Harold Gores, President of the Educational Facilities Laboratory: "K–12 physical education facilities should provide all the program opportunities on an acre of grass, with proper equipment, in a climate like a perpetual June day in the mountains."[3]

Referred to as their "acre of June," the architects came up with the following ideas:[4]

---

[3] "New Generation Gyms," *The Nation's Schools*. 34:6 (December 1969), p. 42.
[4] Kelsey, L., F. Kolflat, and R. Schaefer, "New Generation Gym," in *The Nation's Schools*, 84, 1969, pp. 41, 56.

Figure 9–2 Colorful Dropped Nets Form Barrier to Absorb the Impact of Golf Balls, Baseballs, and Arrows.

- Construct dropped nets and canvas partitions—to form barriers to absorb the impact of golf balls, baseballs, and arrows (Figure 9–2).
- Install instant replay video tape television systems to provide immediate feedback to participants.
- Utilize grass-like synthetic materials and plastic ice (Figure 9–3).
- Create a new environment that provides fresh air, sound control, visual harmony, thermal comfort, and controlled lighting (Figure 9–4).
- Construct pivot walls that may be utilized as bangboards for tennis practice, projection and writing surfaces, tackboards, and room dividers.
- Increase comfort for participants and spectators through glass separated pool and spectator areas (Figure 9–5).
- Install huge overhead doors to provide inside/outside continuity of space (Figure 9–6).
- Construct rigid "people platforms" that may be lowered from the ceiling to accommodate activities such as fencing, dancing, etc.
- Utilize motorized storage platforms that are raised to the ceiling when not in use.
- Design forced air ventilated lockers.
- Open corridors and lobby areas to present panoramic views into physical education activity spaces (Figure 9–7).

The above innovations are only an example of what creative architects are capable of doing when they focus attention on the design and construction of physical education facilities. These changes are welcome

the floor

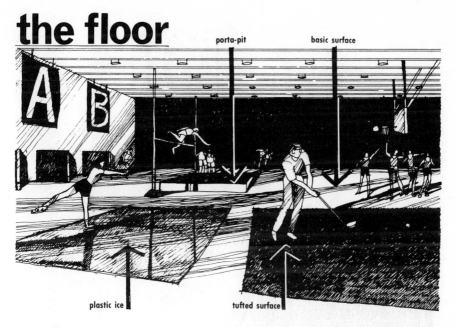

porta-pit   basic surface

plastic ice   tufted surface

Figure 9–3   New Floor Design Complete with Plastic Ice, Tufted Surface, Porta Pit, and Basic Surface

additions to the box-like structures and drab surroundings that have permeated physical education facilities for many years. They present greater flexibility and are capable of adapting to the new and changing philosophies of physical education.

SYNTHETIC SURFACES

One of the major changes in the construction of indoor and outdoor activity areas within the past several years is the utilization of synthetic surfaces. Known by various trade names such as tartan, astroturf, Uniturf, etc., these surfaces may be categorized into two basic types. They are (1) artificial grasses and (2) flat finished, multi-purpose surfaces. Advertised originally to cut down on injuries in sports such as football, these surfaces appear not to have achieved this objective. However, they have helped to solve other problems as: (1) allow recreation or athletic competition immediately after a rain storm, (2) allow use of a gymnasium area at any time without having to be concerned about the floor surface, and (3) allow the setting of chairs without leaving the surface scarred or indented.

Most of the synthetic surfaces fulfill the above requirements; how-

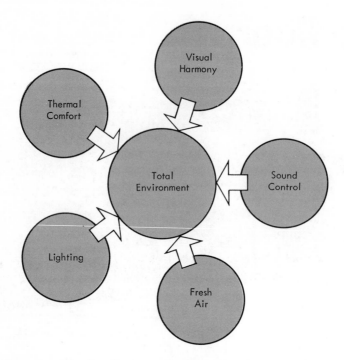

Figure 9–4   The New Environment (From "New Generation Gym," *The Nation's Schools,* 84:6, December 1969, p. 44)

ever, some problems still remain. Although the problem of fire hazard appears to have been overstated, the dropped flaming cigarette butt leaves a small elliptical black mark that will not wash off. And, although it does not affect the use of the surface, it is unsightly.

According to P. Richard Theibert (1971), consultant with Educational Facilities Laboratories (EFL), no one material is best for every installation. Each installation needs to be studied carefully before the type of floor covering material is specified. Edward Steitz (1970) reported that the exponents of synthetic surfaces contend that they (1) eliminate the problem of refinishing and sanding, (2) avoid glare, (3) eliminate dead spots, and (4) do not show the wear and tear of heavy play. Others have reported that synthetic surfaces lessen the incidence of shin splints and leg fatigue. And, although synthetic surfaces cost more than conventional ones, the difference is compensated by the lessening of maintenance requirements. With the cost of labor soaring, this factor cannot be overlooked.

Synthetic surfaces, when installed well, appear to be more appropriate for the lifetime sports. H. W. Woods (1972) is of the opinion that synthetic flooring is the surface of the future. He bases his claim on

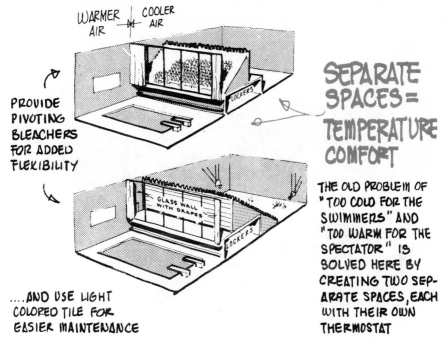

WARMER | COOLER
AIR —▶◀— AIR

PROVIDE
PIVOTING
BLEACHERS
FOR ADDED
FLEXIBILITY

LOCKERS

GLASS WALL
WITH DRAPES

LOCKERS

....AND USE LIGHT
COLORED TILE FOR
EASIER MAINTENANCE

SEPARATE
SPACES =
TEMPERATURE
COMFORT

THE OLD PROBLEM OF
"TOO COLD FOR THE
SWIMMERS" AND
"TOO WARM FOR THE
SPECTATOR" IS
SOLVED HERE BY
CREATING TWO SEP-
ARATE SPACES, EACH
WITH THEIR OWN
THERMOSTAT

Figure 9–5 Pivot Bleachers and Glass Separated Pool and Spectator Areas (From "New Generation Gym," *The Nation's Schools*, 84:6, December 1969, p. 44)

its (1) high strength and resiliency, (2) indestructibility, and (3) ability to reduce bruises, skin burns, and muscular sprains. In essence, according to Woods, these surfaces transform gymnasiums into all-purpose field houses.

AIR STRUCTURES

Air structures were first utilized in the late 1940s by the U.S. Government to encapsulate large areas of space in radomes. Since that time air structures have been utilized in a wide variety of building designs. EXPO '70, the U.S. Pavilion at Osaka, Japan, represented the use of vinyl-coated fiberglass fabric to enclose a large area of space (100,000 square feet). This was done with success and efficiency. The air-supported structure required the circulation of 40,000 cubic feet of air per minute. The popularity of air and cable-supported structures in recent years has been due to their ability to enclose large amounts of space with the least amount of money. They also provide the least amount of internal supports and encumbrances so that there is maximum layout

Figure 9-6 .Overhead Doors Provide Inside/Outside Continuity of Space (From "New Generation Gym," *The Nation's Schools,* 84:6 December 1969, p. 51).

flexibility. These structures are fire-safe, weather-resistant, translucent or opaque, strong, and easy to fabricate. With advances in technology, fabric structures will be built higher and wider than ever before. The cost is estimated to be less than half of the cost for traditional brick and mortar buildings, and that includes heating equipment, structural envelope, above-grade attachment hardware, inflation equipment, lighting fixtures, and installation fees.

Air- and/or cable-supported structures may be utilized to cover skating rinks, swimming pools, tennis courts, riding stables, and other outdoor facilities so that they may be used on a year-round basis. It is now possible to enclose an entire football stadium with a fabric roof, so that the field may be utilized for many other purposes. Unmatched for cost, efficiency, durability, maintenance, flexibility, and speed of construction, air-supported and/or cable-supported structures are now being built for educational, commercial, and civic purposes.

The major limiting factor of the first membrane coverings was their five-to-seven-year life expectancy. Recently, however, application of a

Better Use of Space

Figure 9–7 Open Up Lobby and Corridor Areas for a View into the Physical Education Spaces (From "New Generation Gym," *The Nation's Schools,* 84:6 December 1969, p. 52).

fiberglass fabric coated with teflon flurocarcon resin has protected the surface from the sun to produce a life expectancy of twenty years. Additionally, these fabrics may also be reconditioned at half their original cost. And, according to Harold Gores of the Educational Facilities Laboratories, a new material has been developed that is reported to have a life expectancy of nearly forty years.[5]

Many colleges and universities have found air domes to be successful and satisfactory structures (Gardner, 1971). La Verne College (Los Angeles, California), in a bold break with the past, combined a Drama Center and Student Union facility to provide an acre and a quarter of usable space (Figures 9–8 and 9–9). The fabric roof is supported by a network of cables extending from structural members to compression rings around a concrete block foundation.

Harvard University installed a new 45,000 square feet vinyl-coated nylon track facility that cost less than ten cents per cubic foot. Kingsborough Community College (Brooklyn, New York) erected two (his and hers) air-supported structures (100′ by 125′) that serve as boys' and girls' physical education teaching stations. The cost, reported to be 10 percent of the cost for permanent buildings the same size, was $68,000. It has been reported that this structure can withstand 80 m.p.h. winds and is coated with a translucent vinyl to permit outside light.

---

[5] Conference with the author on March 31, 1975.

Figure 9–8 La Verne College's Student Activities Center (Courtesy of Educational Facilities Laboratories)

In order to gain full advantage of its open air Memorial Sports Stadium, the University of Minnesota is currently evaluating plans to enclose the stadium with an air-supported fabric roof of fiberglass coated with teflon. Severe weather conditions have made it one of the most underutilized open air fields in the country.

Figure 9–9 Interior of La Verne College's Student Activities Center (Courtesy of Educational Facilities Laboratories)

A small, private college in Brooklyn, hemmed in by skyscrapers, installed an air structure on top of the physics building to solve the problem of lack of space for physical education.

Santa Clara University has a completed structure which houses a swimming pool, spectator seating for 6,000 persons, locker and shower facilities, student activity center, dining area, and study complex. Two low-profile, air-supported structures, enclosing more than 60,000 square feet, were designed and constructed to solve the space problem. The domes are supported by 1 $\frac{7}{8}$-inch diameter restraining cables.

Professional sports facilities are also promoting air-supported structures. Now under construction is the new Detroit Lions Stadium in Pontiac, Michigan. The 80,000 seat structure's fabric roof will cover 10 acres.

At the secondary school level, air-supported structures have been erected at the Forman School, Litchfield, Connecticut; the Hinchley School, Hinchley, Maine; and at the Bettendorf (Iowa) Middle School. The Iowa facility was constructed at a cost of only four dollars per square foot compared to about twenty-four dollars per square foot for a regular gymnasium.

From all indications, the new, bubble-like structures appear to be working out very well. Their principal advantages, as mentioned previously, are low cost, unlimited area coverage, on-site assembly, portability, low maintenance, resistance to fire, and ability to handle the elements (Pierson and Snyder, 1972). Their use in lifetime sports-oriented physical education programs will contribute significantly to the development of additional teaching stations for a wide variety of individual, dual, and team sports.

The Architects Collaborative (Robertson, 1968) drew up a 10-point checklist that should be followed when installing air-supported structures. The important factors are as follows:

- Provide positive anchorage.
- Provide positive drainage.
- Protect the envelope from sharp objects during erection.
- Provide protection against sharp protrusions inside the bubble.
- Control air leakage from envelope (a taut skin is required to withstand high winds, storms).
- Remove snow unless internal pressure is sufficient to compensate for maximum snow load.
- Protect fan inlets from snow or other obstruction.
- Periodically check inflation equipment (worn or loose fan belts can cause a loss of air pressure).

• Provide auxiliary generators to maintain blower operation in case of power failure.
• Attach lights to poles rather than to bubble skin.

THE MOBILE GYMNASIUM

With the utilization of off-school sites becoming a central aspect of lifetime sports-oriented programs, the need for mobile gymnasiums is increasing. This thought is not as farfetched as it might at first seem, and its potential to bring physical education to the people, wherever they are located, is in keeping with the lifetime sports concept of physical education.

Clyde E. Cole, former Chief, Bureau of Physical Education, New York State Education Department, designed a mobile shower and locker room facility and a prototype model was constructed (Figure 9–10). This facility could be positioned adjacent to air-supported structures to provide power for auxiliary devices such as lighting, forced air, heating, etc., as well as shower and dressing areas.

The mobile gymnasium along with already available innovations—artificial turf, plastic ice, modular buildings, roof-top fields, foam and membrane structures and other devices—will enable physical educators and recreation leaders to better meet the interests and needs of all students and community citizens. The school-community concept provides coordinated programs and dual use of facilities.

ROOFTOP FIELDS

The practice of locating physical education facilities at the edge of the campus or in remote areas away from centers of population has not produced high utilization of these areas. To eliminate this problem and to encourage more people to participate, rooftop fields are becoming increasingly popular. Portland State University, for example, located tennis courts on top of its physical education complex. A urethane surface doubles as a playing surface for tennis and as a waterproof roofing material. Fencing encloses the entire rooftop area.

Greater utilization of rooftop structures is provided when they are covered by air-supported and/or cable-supported membranes. Since an increasing number of students are no longer content to enjoy sports vicariously through groups of football or basketball players representing their school or college, the demand for more space to participate is increasing. The rooftop concept provides additional space for sports which may be played throughout life.

a. 10 x 44 ft. All-metal towed trailer

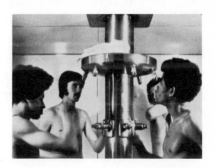

b. Bradley 6-unit columnar shower

c. Fully equipped "Locker Room-on- Wheels"

d. Attractive functional interior

Figure 9–10 The Sportsmobile (Courtesy of Mr. Clyde Cole, Boycol Corporation, Delmar, N.Y.).

Utilization of rooftops for sports participation is not limited to the lifetime sports. Rooftop intercollegiate fields for football and baseball are being planned at Knoxville College in Tennessee and for football and track at Miles College in Alabama. The objective is to locate these facilities in the center of the campus so that they are easily available to students and community citizens. And, although the cost of an elevated field is high, it is considerably less than a separate recreational building and sports stadium (Theibert, 1973).

SURFING POOLS

Although surfing has not been given much attention in the United States as a lifetime sport, it may increase in popularity with the invention of wave generating machinery. In Hachioji, Japan, a surfing pool, complete with landscaped interior, has been in use for several years. When not in use for surfing, the pool becomes a swimming facility. The large pool is shelved at one end for the waves to funnel out or to allow small children to enter the water gradually, as they would at a beach. The interior landscaping helps to dispel the sterile environment usually present in these facilities. Figure 9–11 shows a picture of a surfing pool that was constructed in Tempe, Arizona. Water surging from the base of the reservoir wall creates waves at 50-second intervals.

Figure 9–11   Surfing Pool (Courtesy of Big Surf, Inc., Tempe, Arizona)

PORTABLE POOLS

Within recent years portable swimming pools have been utilized by schools, recreational agencies and other organizations with increasing regularity. They are particularly suitable for teaching "drownproofing," a floating technique for staying alive in water for long periods of time. Some communities have installed portable pools on flat bed truck platforms and moved them about as the need arises. The city of Winnipeg purchased two pools, 15 feet long and 6 feet wide and 31 inches deep, capable of being joined together to form a larger swimming area. The smaller size pools are capable of being fitted into classrooms so that valuable gym space is not lost. Each pool is equipped with its own filtration and chlorination units. Twenty-gauge vinyl liners are held in position by sixteen-gauge galvanized panels. The cost of the pools was reported to be $8,960.

In setting up these structures a number of factors should be considered. First, the floor must be strong enough to support the pool when it is filled with water. The Winnipeg pools, for example, weighed in excess of 179,000 pounds. Second, adequate plumbing (sewer and water), electrical, and dressing and shower facilities need to be provided. Third, adequate ventilation and humidity control are necessary in indoor facilities utilized for this purpose. Water heating units may also need to be purchased. And, fourth, control of splash water and condensation should be provided.

The Big Space Concept

The gym is dead. But, the multi-purpose sports center lives. With more people playing more sports than ever before, the gymnasium, as we know it, cannot meet today's and tomorrow's needs. Special-purpose facilities, such as the traditional rectangular gymnasium, are too inflexible to accommodate the demands for comprehensive lifetime sports programs. In most cases, gymnasia are too small and house too few activities. Traditional gyms, for example, are seldom large enough for sports such as tennis, jogging, and indoor practice for football and baseball. Hopefully, we will not continue to build $20,000,000 stadiums that are utilized only four or five times a year. P. Richard Theibert (1971, p. 14) spoke to this point when he said: "We do it backwards. We'll build a quarter million dollar track for 18 boys." Theibert's comment is typical of the reactions of a growing number of parents, students, and other citizens who desire to change the emphasis in physical education. In brief, the goal for physical education should not be to produce pros at exorbitant costs, but to stress lifetime physical fitness for all citizens.

Basically, the problem as Theibert sees it is that boards of education choose designs for interscholastic athletics instead of intramural physical education facilities. The showmanship for two or three major sports dictates, in many cases, the design of the entire sports complex. Browne (1971), an architect, is in agreement with Theibert's proposal. He is in favor of the big space concept, the construction of multi-purpose facilities capable of housing a wide variety of individual, dual and team sports. Renting stadiums for intercollegiate and interscholatic sports may be a far better alternative than building special areas incapable of housing comprehensive programs for all students and community citizens. However, Browne (1971) contends that any multi-purpose situation is accompanied by limitations, tradeoffs, and compromises. But, he believes that a facility which will provide space for a large number of activities, at 90 percent efficiency, is far better than a structure that provides the ultimate for only a few uses.

Planning for change is also an important aspect of facility design. After 15 to 20 years the structure will probably be obsolete. Big open areas are more easily converted to new concepts of the place of sport, physical education, and recreation in our culture. Additionally, plans should make it possible for expansion of facilities if the need arises.

The secret in design, according to Theibert and Browne, is the encapsulating of enough space, use of the right synthetic surfaces, and the correct roof design. When asked to design physical education facilities for a secondary school, Theibert said that he would give these areas more freedom—more open space. Both authorities also advocate the use of sophisticated conversion systems that remove one floor surface to reveal another. These systems are being constructed at the University of Missouri and in the New Orleans Superdome. What we need is a universal surface suitable for grass sports as well as smooth-court games. An artificial ice suitable for hockey would also be a welcome addition.

The use of multicolored floor surfaces and marking lines for various courts may create a handsome effect or a confusing situation (Browne, 1971). Electrification of painted lines would prevent the unsightly mass lined problem. It is not unrealistic to believe that in the near future we should be able to turn the various court layouts on and off with a switch.

These innovations along with the development of teflon-coated fiberglass to extend the life expectancy of air-supported structures to about twenty years should improve the utilization of physical education facilities for lifetime sports instruction.

Platform Tennis Systems

Platform tennis, sometimes called Paddle, is an exciting new American sport that is growing very rapidly. The sport was introduced in 1928 by a small group of tennis-minded businessmen who decided to build a deck for all-year-round outdoor play. What evolved was an elevated surface that would drain easily of rain and snow.

Platform tennis incorporates the same basic rules of tennis, with several variations. The court is 60′ by 30′—one-fourth the size of a tennis court. Governed by the American Platform Tennis Association (APTA), there are more than 250 clubs in existence at the present time. Nationally televised tournaments are held each year by APTA.

Courts are constructed of wood or steel, equipped with tension facing, nightlights, and low maintenance nonslip surfaces (Figure 9–12). It is possible to lease courts from North American Recreation: Platform Tennis Systems Division, Bridgeport, Connecticut. Tennis offers school districts a chance to utilize limited areas on a year-round basis for recreation.

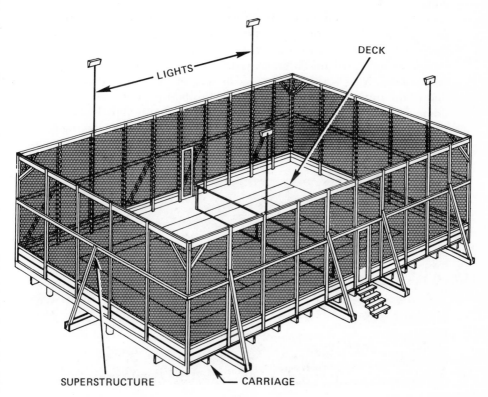

Figure 9–12 Platform Tennis (Courtesy of North American Recreation, Platform Tennis Systems Division, Bridgeport, Connecticut)

Geodesic Dome

Particularly at the college level, geodesic dome construction is becoming increasingly popular. One of the principal reasons for this trend is that this method of construction reduces the weight of the structure by placing materials in axial compression. The result is a large enclosed activity area uncluttered by support devices.

Notre Dame's $8.6 million athletic convocation center is a twin-domed complex, 750 feet by 630 feet, and contains 460,000 square feet of air conditioned space. When completed in 1975 the Louisiana Super-dome will enclose 125 million cubic feet of space. The activity area is 680 by 900 feet. Sections of the stadium will move for various sport events. At Elmira College, Elmira, New York, three interconnected geodesic domes (Figure 9–13) are utilized to house an ice arena, basketball court, and space for the lifetime sports. In addition, a swimming pool was constructed with a roll-back roof to provide space for aquatic activities.

At the high school level, Washington High School, eight miles south of Tacoma, Washington, has a triax dome that houses a 90 by 94 feet basketball area, surfaced with tartan over a concrete slab floor. A geodesic dome, prefabricated in Torrance, California, was shipped 3,000 miles to Ogdensburg, New York. It houses ice hockey, basketball, and other school and community activities and is reported to be the largest all-aluminum dome constructed in the United States. It is made up of 1,300 diamond-shaped, gold anodized panels. Assembled in only forty-five working days, the structure rises 70 feet from the ground level to apex and has an out-

Figure 9–13 Elmira College's Triple Geodesic Domes (Courtesy of Mr. Paul Brand, Director of Athletics, Elmira College)

side diameter of 234 feet. The 51,000 square feet of floor space was constructed at a cost of $1,300,000. Because of the long cold winter months, a special resilient flooring was utilized so that it is possible to move outdoor sports such as baseball, track, and golf under the dome, when not frozen for hockey, ice skating, or figure skating.

REDESIGN

To this point we have talked about the construction of new facilities to house lifetime sports-oriented programs. Nothing has been said about the redesign or renovation of existing teaching stations. In other words, if you have facilities already erected to house the traditional teams sports, what can you do to make them also acceptable for instruction in the lifetime sports? Many directors of physical education find themselves in this unfortunate situation.

After having completed the Lifetime Sports Community Resources Inventory (LSCRI), you will be better able to answer this question. As mentioned previously, the pool which you are lacking in your school may be found in town, minutes away from school. Bowling lanes, horseback riding stables, tennis courts, ice arenas, and other facilities may also be found and used to expand your program.

To provide more teaching stations, investigate the possibility of making use of activity areas adjacent to the school on a year-round basis. For example, elevated platform tennis courts may be purchased and installed on all-weather areas. Some schools have hills nearby that could be developed for beginning and intermediate level ski instruction. Other schools have wooded areas for camping. Cross-country skiing is also possible in parts of the country where snow is available. In brief, the possibilities are unlimited. Innovation and improvisation will help to solve many of your most pressing facilities problems.

Even the old "band-box" type of gymnasium may be altered to teach the fundamentals of the sports of tennis, golf, bowling, badminton, and archery. Installation of netting, which may be hoisted to the ceiling when not in use, provides protection for delicate wall structures in auditorium-gymnasium situations. Figure 9–14 shows the use of swing-out walls to convert gymnasiums to teaching stations for handball, paddleball, and squash. A basement room may serve as a teaching station for fencing, dance, or other activities. If you have outdoor areas such as tennis courts, all-weather areas or a pool, think about encapsulating them with bubble-like structures so that you may use them all year long. Renting these facilities to outside groups when they are not being utilized for school

Figure 9–14 Swing-out walls may be used to convert gymnasiums to handball, paddleball, and squash practice facilities (Courtesy of J. E. Gregory Company, Spokane, Washington).

activities will help to defray the initial cost of maintenance of these facilities.

Since each school situation is unique it is impossible to present a blueprint for the redesign of these structures. The best advice is to consult an architect who is knowledgeable about the renovation of physical education teaching stations. However, you should inform him of the needs for each sport that you want to add to your program. Working together will usually produce the solution that is best suited for your situation.

MAINTENANCE

While serving as a supervisor of physical education and recreation, Division of Physical Education and Recreation, New York State Education Department, I could usually tell the quality of the physical education program by looking at how well facilities were maintained. Schools which had well-manicured fields, pool, and gymnasia usually, but not always, had quality physical education and athletic programs. Well-maintained facilities indicate that someone cares about the program and takes pride in the way in which it is presented to the public. The appearance of the school indicates to taxpayers and other citizens how well their monies are being utilized. It makes little sense to pay large sums of money for fields, pools, gymnasiums and other expensive teaching stations and then let them deteriorate because of poor maintenance.

The person in administrative charge of maintenance is usually the director of physical education. He should periodically inspect all facilities with the head custodian to see if repairs are needed. It is a good idea to make out a check list for each teaching station so that important items are not overlooked. The coaches of the various interscholastic teams should be consulted too, since they are utilizing the facilities and have first-hand information about how well they are maintained. Procedures should be established so that requests for maintenance will be handled without delay. If the repair problem may lead to the injury of athletes or students in physical education classes, immediate repairs should be made. Broken glass, stones, and other debris may lead to serious injury. Potholes sometimes contribute to serious ankle injuries. Usually, the board of education designates one of its members to serve on the Buildings and Grounds Committee. As director, it is a good idea to bring to the attention of the members of this committee, through your chief school officer, long-range maintenance and site development problems. Large budget requests for field development must be made well in advance of annual budget preparations for the district. Not only should you keep your immediate superiors informed of what is needed but you should develop a strong rationale or reasons for the proposed request. Cost estimates are helpful to economy-minded board members.

Since facilities are used from early in the morning to late at night, the night shift usually handles the daily cleaning and minor repairs of each teaching station. It is helpful if you spell out, in written form, exactly what type of daily maintenance is required. This is particularly important in activity areas that house aquatic and wrestling activities. Mats need to be disinfected daily, and pool, locker and shower areas need careful cleaning. Although knowing what to do is important, someone must see to it that maintenance tasks are actually completed. The head custodian is usually in charge of workers who are paid to perform these tasks and he should make sure that all areas are maintained well.

Some school districts, realizing the large expenditure of funds for physical education facilities, have workers who maintain only these areas. This is a step in the right direction since they become knowledgeable about how fields are to be mowed, fertilized, lined, etc. Each sport requires special skills and knowledge about installation and maintenance procedures. From time to time it is also a good idea to bring in an outside expert to advise you about specific problems. If you are having difficulty with turf, water circulation in the pool, or other technical problems, consult someone who can give you first-hand advice.

Of course, the initial design of the facility will have a great deal to do with the amount and quality of care needed. For example, hard-surfaced tennis courts are much easier to maintain than clay or grass surfaces. Synthetic turf fields are usually easier to ready for play than natural grass ones. The all-weather track is a striking example of the use of technology to lessen maintenance problems.

Unfortunately, some schools maintain areas for interscholastic sports well, but let their facilities for physical education classes deteriorate badly. Students, physical education conscious parents, and community citizens sense this oversight, and it tells them a great deal about the philosophies of the director and his staff. The next time you visit a school take a look at its outdoor and indoor teaching stations. You will be able to obtain some idea of the scope of the program by noting the number, design, and maintenance of each area.

Lifetime sports-oriented programs require many different kinds of activity areas. Each sport, as previously mentioned, requires special types of facilities that have their own maintenance requirements. Outdoor archery, for example, requires some type of mound of earth to stop arrows that have missed the target. Although some of the fundamentals of bowling may be taught in a gymnasium, when students advance to intermediate and advanced levels, bowling lanes are needed. The use of community facilities makes advanced levels of instruction possible. And, it also avoids the great cost of up-keep for these kinds of facilities.

In a word, get your students to take pride in the proper use of equipment, supplies, and activity areas. After all, learning how to use, maintain, and repair facilities and equipment is an important part of their education. Teachers who set good examples are usually more successful in getting their students to do this than those who are careless in these matters.

Proper supervision of facilities during and after school hours reduces maintenance and repair costs. Insist that there is a responsible person on duty at all times when facilities are being used by out-of-school groups. Many problems occur when proper supervision is lacking.

ARCHITECTURAL "GOOFS"

If you are involved in the construction of a new building or the renovation of an existing one, you should be concerned with avoiding architectural "goofs." "Goofs" refer to errors in design that create problems for the users of the structure once it is completed. For example, the most talked-about outlandish instance was by the architect who designed an elegant, twelve-story apartment building only to discover that he had forgotten to sketch in any elevators. Supposedly, the hapless architect was punished by being forced to live in an apartment on the top floor.

Architects in the United States have become goof-prone. One of the most notable boo-boos in sports architecture is the new Philadelphia Spectrum. Four months after it was completed, the 12-million dollar structure had 100 feet of roof blow off in a high wind storm.

The jumbo goof of them all, however, may be the Rayburn Building in Washington, a $100 million structure done in a style called "Mussolini Modern." It was designed to provide office space for U.S. Congressmen. As far as physical education is concerned, the major goof was the one in which workmen found the roof of the $500,000 swimming pool too low for diving after they had installed a diving board.

At the professional baseball level, San Francisco's Candlestick Park is another architectural legend. Not only do players and fans have to live with the elements such as high winds and fog but the absence of elevators or escalators forces elderly spectators to climb the equivalent of ten floors of ramps inside the park. Furthermore, there isn't a water cooler in the place.

Lack of attention to detail may result in expensive damage. At a college in the University of the State of New York system, someone apparently forgot to turn a water tap off, and a 150,000 gallon swimming pool overflowed in a new $4.1 million physical education building under construction. The damage to the SUNY facility was reported to be at least $15,000.

The failure to recess folding doors in gymnasia is one of the most widely known "goofs" in high school physical education facilities design and construction. This practice frequently inhibits spectators from viewing the action at one end of the court. Failure to adequately ventilate locker and shower rooms is another pressing problem. One school lined the gymnasium walls with beautiful wood paneling. It looked nice, but proved to be a very poor rebound surface for drills requiring wall volleying. Not only did the plastic wood come out of the nail holes but baseballs could not be thrown in the gym for fear of damaging the walls. In a word, it was not practical for multiple use.

The failure to install flush door sills prevents apparatus, such as parallel bars and side-horses, from being moved in and out of physical education teaching stations. When this unfortunate situation occurs, the rubber cups on the bottom of the apparatus are pulled off as the equipment is dragged across the elevated door sills. As a result, wooden floors are damaged, and the apparatus cannot be positioned securely to avoid injury to participants.

Failure to include windows in offices, laboratories, and other stations can cause problems when forced air and air conditioning systems malfunction. It is true that walls may be built cheaper without windows, but the average person does not like to work for long periods of time without seeing out of doors. The loss in productivity and emotional health is not, in my opinion, worth the savings in construction costs.

Another oversight is the failure to construct outdoor activity areas until a year or two after the building is completed. Not only does this practice seriously curtail the program, but damage to floors occurs from tracking into the building large amounts of dirt. Custodians will appreciate it if walkways, roads, and fields are constructed at the beginning of the building project.

Many other incidents could be cited; however, it is safe to conclude that closer inspection of architectural plans needs to be made by knowledgeable people. Once the structure has been erected it is costly and sometimes impossible to correct the mistakes that have been made. In a word, you live with the problem for the life of the building. Functional buildings, free of "goofs," are the result of careful planning by all members of the architectural team, including physical education teachers and administrators. So, take the time to review the working drawings very carefully.

SUMMARY

Changing concepts of physical education and recreation are calling for innovative approaches in the design and construction of sports facilities. The traditional "band-box"—like gymnasium appears to be dead. In its place large multi-use spaces, encapsulated by geodesic, air-supported and/or cable-supported structure, are appearing with increasing regularity. The challenge, in an era of rising costs, is to plan multipurpose facilities which can accommodate a wide variety of lifetime sports. What is needed are facilities that can serve indoor tennis, basketball, volleyball, badminton, track, archery, golf driving, and other sports.

Large activity areas, known as the big space concept, capable of being subdivided to reassign space from one activity to another, appear to be the ideal type of structure for lifetime sports-centered instruction. Trends in facilities should reflect trends in programs and require the development of new technologies, new materials, and new methods of instruction. The ability to obtain adequate and functional facilities will depend largely on cooperative planning by architects, physical educators, recreational leaders, school administrators, and community citizens.

Innovative concepts in facility design have occurred with increasing regularity in recent years. Theibert contends that our technology is years ahead of concepts and innovative thinking. Theibert's premise is supported by the thoughtless imitations of facilities that have appeared at schools, colleges and universities. Since the type of physical education and recreation program should depend on the particular interests and needs of each community, "stock" plans are not appropriate for these programs. All too often, program personnel are not involved, or involved only superficially, in the planning of new facilities. When this unfortunate practice occurs, new facilities often lack flexibility and expansibility to accommodate changing curricular practices. Harold Gores, President of Educational Facilities Laboratories, expressed this thought well when he said: ". . . a program that is dependent on the weather is primitive."[6] The need for careful, planned, and systematic study in the selection, acquisition, development, and utilization of school property is increasing.

The environmental effects of physical space on teaching and learning have also placed new demands on facility planners. With more people than ever before participating in a wide variety of lifetime sports, facilities must be designed to accommodate new teaching methods and greater use of audio-visual teaching aids and television. Today, there is a need for lifetime sports specialists who can teach not only the traditional sports of golf, tennis, bowling, archery, swimming, etc. but the lesser known and increasingly popular activities of orienteering, platform tennis, backpacking, scuba diving, surfing, water and snow skiing, winter camping, and other sports.

More imaginative and economically prudent solutions will be needed in order to rethink the classical facilities such as the box-shaped gymnasium for basketball and the stadium for only six afternoons in the fall. Facilities need to be designed with sensitivity to meet the desires of students to participate in games they can play after graduation.

---

6 Conference with the author on March 31, 1975.

STUDY QUESTIONS

1. What is the first cardinal principle of facility planning?
2. Describe the planning process that should take place when building physical education facilities.
3. What are two central purposes of physical education and how should they influence the design and construction of facilities?
4. What guidelines should be utilized in planning facilities for lifetime sports-oriented physical education programs?
5. Describe the Park-School concept.
6. What factors should be considered when selecting an architect?
7. Why have physical education facilities remained largely unchanged in an era of change in design and construction of other parts of the school plant?
8. Describe the investment in physical education facilities in terms of the cost of the total school plant.
9. Describe the design and construction of the Limited Shelter. What contribution can it make to lifetime sports-oriented physical education programs?
10. Identify three factors that should influence the design of Limited Shelters.
11. Identify and describe the innovations in facilities suggested by architects Kelsey, Kolflat, and Schaefer.
12. What factors should be considered when creating a new environment for physical education activities?
13. Identify and describe two types of synthetic surfaces. What advantages do these surfaces present? What problems still need to be solved in the utilization of synthetic surfaces?
14. What are the advantages and disadvantages of air-supported structures? Where may these structures be utilized?
15. Identify the ten factors, proposed by Architects Collaborative, that should be considered when installing air-supported structures.
16. Describe the mobile gymnasium and its potential use.
17. Describe the design and construction of rooftop fields. What advantages do they have for use in lifetime sports-oriented programs?
18. Will the construction of surfing pools lead to greater participation in surfing?
19. What factors should be considered in the use of portable pools?
20. Describe the "big space" concept of physical education facilities.
21. What are Theibert's and Browne's design ideas for physical education facilities?
22. Describe the facilities needed for platform tennis.

REFERENCES

"Air-inflatable track facility for winter use at Harvard." *American School and University,* 42 (1970), 32.

Athletic Institute, and the American Alliance for Health, Physical Education, and Recreation. *Planning Facilities for Athletics, Physical Education and Recreation.* Chicago: The Athletic Institute, 1974.

————. *College and University Facilities Guide—for Health, Physical Education, Recreation and Athletics.* Chicago: The Athletic Institute, 1968.

BROWNE, ROBERT L. "Innovations in Sports Facilities," *American School and University,* 42 (1971), 25–30.

CRAWFORD, W. H. *A Guide for Planning Indoor Facilities for College Physical Education.* New York: Teachers College, Columbia University, 1963.

GARDNER, J. C. "Air-supported Field House," *American School and University,* 43 (1971), 4.

"His and Hers," *American School and University,* 43 (1971), 42.

JOHNSON. W. A. "The Nielson Tennis Stadium," *Journal of Health, Physical Education and Recreation,* 41 (1971), 36.

KELSEY, L., F. KOLFLAT, and R. SCHAEFER. "New Generation Gym," in *The Nation's Schools,* 84 (1969), 41, 56.

MARTINI, J. "Poly's Rooftop Gym," *Scholastic Coach,* 40 (1971), 7.

"Notre Dame's Twin-domed Wonderland," *Scholastic Coach,* 39 (1971), 20.

"P. Richard Theibert on Facilities for Lifetime Sports." *American School and University,* 42 (1971), 14–18.

"Pennsylvania's Practice Track Bubble," *Scholastic Coach,* 37 (1968), 11.

Physical Recreation Facilities. New York: Educational Facilities Laboratories, 1973.

PIERSON, R. M., and C. E. SNYDER. "Enclosospace," *Park and Recreation,* 7 (1972), 36.

PUCKETT, JOHN. "Two promising innovations in physical education facilities." *Journal of Health, Physical Education and Recreation,* 43 (1972), 40–41.

ROBERTSON, N. *Air Structures for School Sports:* New York: Educational Facilities Laboratories, Inc., 1968.

SEITZ, E. "The synthetic surface revolutions," *Scholastic Coach,* 39: 22 (1970), 100–101.

SHULDINER, HERBERT, "Louisiana's New Superdome is World's Largest Sports Cover-up," *Popular Science,* 202 (1973), 84–85.

THEIBERT, P. "A Primer on Synthetic Surfaces," *American School and University,* 43 (1971), 44–45

"These Air Structures Excel at Sports," *American School and University,* 40 (1968), 30.

"Try Air Structures for Year-round Activities with a Minimal Investment for

Your District," *Physical Education Supplement,* 14 (1970), 2.

WAGNER, W. G., B. H. EVANS, and M. A. NOWAK. *Shelter for Physical Education.* College Station, Texas: Texas Engineering Experiment Station, Texas A. and M. College, 1961.

WOODS, H. W. "Vinyl Flooring: the Surfacing of the Future," *Athletic Journal,* 53 (1972), 16.

CHAPTER 10

INNOVATIVE
PROGRAMS

The lifetime sports concept of physical education encourages the use of innovative approaches to teaching and curriculum design. During the past several years innovation has become an integral part of many physical education programs. The use of team teaching, flexible scheduling, paraprofessionals, contract grading, and off-campus facilities attests to the willingness of teachers and administrators to recognize the need for change. Changing the curriculum to include instruction in sports that may be played throughout life is perhaps the most significant development that has occurred in physical education during the past ten years.

Some readers may find it difficult to speak of innovation and creativity in an era of budget slashing, loss of staff, and other economic pressures. It is true that change usually requires the purchase of new equipment and supplies, added teaching stations, more staff, etc. However, this is not always the case and in some instances savings in budget, staff time, facility utilization, and other aspects of the program may result from innovative practices. With alternate forms of education becoming such a central topic in education today it is apparent that physical educators and recreation leaders will be asked to devise new and better ways of meeting educational goals.

CHANGE FOR CHANGE'S SAKE

Most parents envision education as the means of achieving great expectations for their children. In order to accomplish this goal, physical education as a part of general education, must provide curricular experiences in learning environments that are conducive to the development of health, physical fitness, neuro-muscular skill, attitudes, and knowledge of the effects of activity on the organism. When changes in curriculum are made, they should be based upon the findings of carefully conducted research investigations. Change just for the sake of change often does not result in significant increments in the important outcomes of physical education. Once we know what our goals are, it is much easier to determine ways of achieving them. For example, at the present time we are experiencing a return to basic education or what is referred to as the traditional school with its emphasis on the 3 R's. Evidently, some parents, teachers, administrators, and members of boards of education are not satisfied with the results of open education. On the other hand, others espouse the values of optional learning environments and the important role which they play in the development of creativity and self-directed learners. There seems to be at least one thing certain about the educational process; all persons do not agree on the direction it should take.

THE PILOT STUDY

Before making drastic changes in curriculum, teaching methodology, or other aspects of the program, it is a good procedure to conduct pilot studies to determine the desirability of making these changes. If the pilot study goes well more extensive changes may be made. There are many values to be achieved from the results of well-conducted pilot investigations: First, massive changes disrupt some people. Alvin Toffler (1970, p. 2) coined the term "future shock" to describe the shattering stress and disorientation that we induce in individuals by subjecting them to too much change in too short a time. Therefore, based upon Toffler's premise, pilot studies let you wet the wrists before you dive into the water. Second, there are savings in staff time, equipment, supplies and other essentials. There is no sense in going out and purchasing equipment and supplies for a new sport unless you are going to put it in your program on a long-term basis. Third, pilot studies let you experiment without disrupting the entire educational process. Administrators are concerned with all aspects of education—not just physical education. Changes in physical education curriculums frequently affect other aspects of instruction. For example, it is common knowledge that, on the average, girls out-perform boys in educational achievement at the secondary school level. With the advent of interscholastic sports for girls, however, some guidance counselors have informed me that the grades for female athletes are now approaching those of male athletes. Finally, pilot studies produce important feedback from students about the educational process they have experienced. Before the activity is taught on a mass scale, changes may be made.

Pilot studies in various aspects of lifetime sports instruction have occurred with increasing regularity. For example, if downhill ski instruction is to be considered it may be desirable at first to have only one class for this purpose. After having participated in skiing for a semester, students will be able to provide teachers and administrators with definitive information about the quality of the program. From an administrative view, pilot studies allow school personnel to determine cost, bus schedules, injury rates, etc. Working out acceptable procedures for innovative activities is an important aspect of administration.

Pilot studies also help to evaluate the effectiveness of new teaching methods. For example, before changing the entire curriculum to a competency basis it may be desirable to utilize one class for this purpose. After a semester of experience with this procedure, students and teachers will be in a more advantageous position to comment about the outcomes of this method of instruction.

APPLIED RESEARCH

In addition to pilot studies, some physical education personnel may wish to conduct actual research investigations to determine the value of different curricular practices. Applied research, commonly referred to as action research, may be utilized by teachers to solve practical problems. For example, Sara Staub (1975) determined the contribution of traditional and lifetime sports-centered programs to the development of attitudes toward physical activity of senior high school boys and girls enrolled in three different secondary schools in the Finger Lakes Region of New York State. Her findings show that, in general, both types of programs produce positive attitudes toward physical activity. A number of subproblems were also considered. First, she found that female interscholastic athletes had more positive attitudes than female nonathletes.

However, this finding was not true when male athletes were compared to nonathletes. At the intramural sports level of competition, both male and female participants had significantly better attitudes toward physical activity than nonparticipants.

Staub's study is a perfect example of applied research. She showed that both traditional or team sports-oriented programs and lifetime sports-centered instruction produce positive attitudes toward physical activity. Willgoose (1974, p. 120) summarized well when he said: "To acknowledge the need for change is one thing; to effect it is another."

Another example of an applied research investigation is a study completed by Straub, Stair, and Hungerford (1975). The purpose of this study was to determine if changes had taken place since 1967 in lifetime sports instruction in New York state secondary schools. Baseline data were available from a study completed by Straub (1967) in which he determined the extent of instruction in five lifetime sports: tennis, golf, bowling, badminton, and archery. Surprisingly, the results of the 1975 study showed that a decrement in instruction had taken place since 1967. Percentagewise, fewer schools were providing instruction in golf, tennis, bowling, archery, and badminton than in 1967. One plausible reason for this change may have been due to the development of more diversified curriculums that included a greater number of lifetime sports such as skiing, backpacking, orienteering, etc. Others contend that budgetary cutbacks have forced schools to adopt the traditional team sports-oriented curriculum. The results of these investigations have led to many speculations about the future directions of lifetime sports-centered programs. Evidently, the Lifetime Sports Education Project did bring about curricular change but the long-term impact of the project is difficult to determine.

Maryanne Sanacore's 1972 study of the extent of lifetime sports activities in the physical education programs of twenty-eight Suffolk County School districts on Long Island, New York, is another example of an applied research investigation. This statement does not imply that her study did not have a theoretical basis. It does suggest that she was basically concerned with answering a number of practical questions. For example, at what grade level should various lifetime sports be introduced to elementary children? Table 10–1, from Sanacore's study, shows how a group of experts whom she consulted answered this question. Mrs. Sanacore concluded that the majority (66%) of the school districts met or exceeded the recommended criteria for lifetime sports instruction at the elementary and junior high levels. They did not, however, meet the recommended criteria at the senior high level (Sanacore, 1972, p. 58).

Table 10–1

Recommended Grade Level for Lifetime Sports Activities

L.S.A.	GRADES (b= boys, g= girls)															
	5		6		7		8		9		10		11		12	
	b	g	b	g	b	g	b	g	b	g	b	g	b	g	b	g
*Aerial Darts																
Archery	X	X	X	X	X	X	X	X	X	X	X	X	X	X	X	X
Badminton					X	X	X	X	X	X	X	X	X	X	X	X
Bicycling	X	X	X	X	X	X	X	X	X	X	X	X	X	X	X	X
Boating					X	X	X	X	X	X	X	X	X	X	X	X
Boccie																
Bowling - Lawn																
Bowling - Regular	X	X	X	X	X	X	X	X	X	X	X	X	X	X	X	X
Camping	X	X	X	X	X	X	X	X	X	X	X	X	X	X	X	X
Canoeing					X	X	X	X	X	X	X	X	X	X	X	X
Curling													X	X	X	X
Dance - Folk	X	X	X	X	X	X	X	X	X	X	X	X	X	X	X	X
Dance - Modern	X	X	X	X						X		X		X		X
Dance - Square	X	X	X	X	X	X	X	X	X	X	X	X	X	X	X	X
Fencing					X	X	X	X	X	X	X	X	X	X	X	X
Fishing	X	X	X	X	X	X	X	X	X	X	X	X	X	X	X	X
Flycasting	X	X	X	X	X	X	X	X	X	X	X	X	X	X	X	X
Golf	X	X	X	X	X	X	X	X	X	X	X	X	X	X	X	X
Gymnastics	X	X	X	X	X	X	X	X	X	X	X	X	X	X	X	X
Handball					X	X	X	X	X	X	X	X	X	X	X	X
Hiking - Alpine																
Hiking - General					X	X	X	X	X	X	X	X	X	X	X	X
Horseback Riding	X	X	X	X	X	X	X	X	X	X	X	X	X	X	X	X
Horsemanship																
Horseshoes					X	X	X	X	X	X	X	X	X	X	X	X
Judo																
Karate																
Orienteering																
Physical Fitness Activities	X	X	X	X	X	X	X	X	X	X	X	X	X	X	X	X
Sailing																
Scuba Diving											X	X	X	X	X	X
Shooting					X	X	X	X	X	X	X	X	X	X	X	X
Shuffleboard	X	X	X	X	X	X	X	X	X	X	X	X	X	X	X	X
Skating - Ice	X	X	X	X	X	X	X	X	X	X	X	X	X	X	X	X
Skating - Roller	X	X	X	X	X	X	X	X	X	X	X	X	X	X	X	X
Skiing - Snow					X	X	X	X	X	X	X	X	X	X	X	X
Skiing - Water											X	X	X	X	X	X
Slow Pitch Softball	X	X	X	X	X	X	X	X	X	X	X	X	X	X	X	X
Snow Shoeing													X	X	X	X
Squash											X	X	X	X	X	X
Swimming - Diving	X	X	X	X	X	X	X	X	X	X	X	X	X	X	X	X
Swimming - Regular	X	X	X	X	X	X	X	X	X	X	X	X	X	X	X	X
Tennis - Deck	X	X	X	X	X	X	X	X	X	X	X	X	X	X	X	X
Tennis - Paddle					X	X	X	X	X	X	X	X	X	X	X	X
Tennis - Regular	X	X	X	X	X	X	X	X	X	X	X	X	X	X	X	X
Tennis - Table					X	X	X	X	X	X	X	X	X	X	X	X
Track and Field	X	X	X	X	X	X	X	X	X	X	X	X	X	X	X	X
Volleyball	X	X	X	X	X	X	X	X	X	X	X	X	X	X	X	X
Weight Training									X		X		X		X	

* Activities modified according to grade level

SOURCE: Maryanne Sanacore, 1972, pp. 24–25.

PRESSURE GROUPS

Most every community is composed of pressure groups who attempt to influence the extent and quality of education. And, over the years, physical education has had to deal with persons who advocated aerobics, jazz dance, football, skiing, and other activities. Probably in no other area of education do we find so many self-designated "experts" than in physical education. Despite many attempts to deal with political, economic, religious, and social pressure groups, they still are a major problem in some communities. When advisory councils have been formed, however, these persons may be invited to meetings to present their proposals. Development of a broad and varied program based upon the interests and needs of boys and girls is the best way to answer the critics of your program. The fact remains, however, that it is difficult to please everyone. Emphasizing one aspect of the program at the expense of another is not in keeping with the goals of education. This philosophy, of course, should not lead to a closed-mind approach to curriculum construction. Educationally sound and defensible programs should always receive careful consideration. Reform is usually based upon need and practicality.

Sports booster clubs have been a problem in some communities when they have tried to take over some of the duties of the coach and his staff. These unfortunate situations have arisen when clear-cut operating codes have not been established—that is, the modus operandi must be carefully specified. If it is not, problems may arise and the helping function of the club may be lost. So, let the administrators administrate, the coaches coach, and the players play. The function of booster clubs should be to help these persons do their jobs better.

EXPERIMENTAL HIGH SCHOOLS

There are a number of experimental high schools that have utilized the lifetime sports concept of physical education as the basis for their innovative programs. At John Dewey High School in Brooklyn an eight-hour day is divided into 22 modules. Students' schedules are planned by computer. The regular school year is composed of five 7-week cycles. An additional 7-week cycle is held in the summer. The curriculum, according to Shulman (1973), in all subjects is divided into graded phases of content. During each cycle students master specific amounts of subject matter. At the end of each cycle students and parents receive written evaluations of how well students achieved specific behavioral objectives for each phase of work. The term "mastery" indicates that the student has solid understanding of material and may progress to the next cycle of the course. "Conditional mastery" allows the students to go on to the next cycle but there are some gaps in his knowledge of subject matter. Letter grades are not used in this evaluation system. The advantage of this approach is that if a student is having difficulty with a subject it is recognized immediately.

Much emphasis is placed on independent study. Each department has a resource center that is staffed all day by teachers and paraprofessionals who assist students with remedial work or homework. Dewey Independent Study Kits (DISKs) have been developed so that students may complete course requirements outside formal classrooms in independent study. After having completed the DISK, students are given written, oral, and/or laboratory examinations to establish course credit for graduation purposes. There is also a physical education resource center in the gymnasium when regular classes are not scheduled. Students may come to the center to practice the skills learned in classes.

Students must complete 18 cycles of physical education to graduate. In a given cycle as many as 22 different activities may be provided, depending on student requests. However, in the ninth and tenth grades, students are required to explore a variety of activities including team, individual, and dual sports. The program is completely elective for eleventh and twelfth grade boys and girls. Since Dewey has no varsity sports teams, emphasis is placed on an extensive intramural program for all students. Competition is organized within classes, and championships are held in a variety of traditional and lifetime sports.

Field work in physical education is also provided. The course meets for about four hours once a week. Students utilize community recreational facilities for ice skating, fishing, camping, etc.

At Irvin High School,[1] El Paso, Texas, instruction takes place in more than twenty different lifetime sports. The purpose of the program is to introduce a variety of physical activities that students may participate in as adults. Elective opportunities are provided for juniors and seniors who have completed the two-year physical education requirement. Coeducational classes are held in dance, softball, volleyball, archery, table tennis, roller skating, swimming, shuffle board, paddle tennis, and badminton. Instruction includes fundamentals, rules, strategy, and historical considerations of sports and games. Knowledge tests are given at the end of each unit. According to Ken McGuire, instructor at Irwin, a syllabus is being prepared for each activity.

The experimental programs at John Dewey High School and Irvin

---

[1] Reported by Lowell Klappholz in the *Physical Education Newsletter,* October 2, 1972, p. 2.

High School are indicative of the changing nature of physical education in our society. The number of innovative programs is unlimited. Unfortunately, however, the innovators are frequently too busy innovating to put their thoughts down on paper. Only once in a while do reports of programs get published in journals, newspapers, or other media. For example, Hanson Carroll, of the *New York Times*,[2] reported that kayaking is now a popular sport in many high schools, colleges, and universities. Evidently, interest in the traditional hunting craft of the Eskimos is intense in some parts of the country. Since kayaking in white water may be classified as a vertigo sport,[3] it may explain some of the increased interest among high-risk–seeking youth and adults. School officials are finding ways to make physical education more valuable and more palatable for all their students. Reports indicate that students love it and so do the teachers.

Despite the many innovations, C. A. Moore (1973) issues a word of caution. He indicates that the use of specialists to teach off-site courses may be putting many certificated teachers out of work. Moore is also opposed to offering courses that have potentially high risks of injury such as cave exploring or sky diving.

THE PROBLEM OF CURRICULUM REFORM

Although there are many enthusiastic and persuasive innovators, there is no coherent theory for making sound curricular decisions. Deciding "what" and "how" to teach has come about largely through trial and error. This problem is particularly true in physical education where new ideas and new procedures develop in an apparently random manner from one emphasis to another.

Although the need for a theoretical framework has been emphasized for at least twenty years, Beauchamp (1961) concluded after examining the status of curriculum theory, that there was no logical set of constructs for curriculum workers. Louis Alley (1972, pp. 1–2), former President for AAHPER, pointed out the need for a national research project to identify and describe a theoretical structure of physical education as an area of scholarly study and research. As soon as we define more clearly "what physical education is, what it can become, how it can best be interpreted to the public, and how it can best serve mankind," Alley said that we will be in a far better position to develop curricular practices to accomplish these goals. There is no good reason why progress in

---

2 "Kayaking Is Now So Popular That Some Schools Teach It," *New York Times,* January 12, 1975.
3 A sport that gives one the feeling of falling or tumbling in space.

physical education should be held back by lack of efficient planning and development.

The national demand for change in physical education has reached an all-time high. People are becoming more knowledgeable about the effects of physical activity on their bodies, the need for stimulating environments in which to recreate, and the important sociological, psychological, and emotional benefits that may come about through participation in sports. Bringing about change on a national level would require teams of school teachers, college lecturers and researchers, and advisory committees to draft new programs to be tried out in selected schools. Perhaps these teams would make better decisions about the selection and organization of the content of courses and about the relative merits of different teaching methods.

In developing a theoretical basis for curriculums in physical education a number of factors need to be considered. First, we need to arrive at some kind of agreement about educational objectives. Second, how may we take account of individual differences in children? Third, what are the contributions of philosophy, psychology, medicine, sociology, and other disciplines to our field? Perhaps a new area called curriculum studies should be developed to help answer these and other pertinent questions concerning the teaching-learning process.

Despite the confusion about "what" and "how much" should be taught, one factor has emerged in which most scholars agree. Kerr (1968, p. 19) summarized this point well when he said that the curriculum "ought to be a dynamic and continuously evolving system." Perhaps at this point in time the lifetime sports approach to physical education curriculum construction reflects the very essence of this dynamic process.

SUMMARY

Innovation and creativity are important aspects of lifetime sports-centered physical education programs. Curriculum should be viewed in this context as a dynamic and continuously evolving system.

Many changes have occurred in physical education during the past ten years. Flexible scheduling, the use of paraprofessionals, independent study, field work, and other innovations are just a few of the many and diverse changes that have been made. John Dewey High School in Brooklyn has implemented a unique physical education program that makes use of the newer concepts of lifetime sports-centered instruction.

Despite the need for change, physical educators have not provided a theoretical base on which to build the curriculum. As a result, change in physical education is often random and lacking in scientific validity. When change is made for change's sake, significant increments do not usually occur in skill, knowledge, and attitudes toward physical activity. To avoid this problem, physical educators should conduct pilot studies to determine the value of the procedures they desire to implement. Applied research investigations can help to determine the long-term effects of curricular practices. A national curriculum study is needed to determine the depth and scope of our field.

STUDY QUESTIONS

1. Identify and describe some of the innovative practices that have been utilized in physical education during the past ten years.
2. What are the values of pilot studies prior to making curricular changes?
3. Describe the program at John Dewey High School in Brooklyn.
4. Why should a theoretical base be developed for physical education?
5. Give an example of an applied research investigation.
6. How should physical educators handle pressure groups?

REFERENCES

ALLEY, L. "The Project," *Tones of Theory*. Washington, D.C.: American Alliance for Health, Physical Education and Recreation, 1972.

BEAUCHAMP, G. A. *Curriculum Theory*. Wilmette, Ill.: Kegg Press, 1961.

KERR, J. F., ed. *Changing the Curriculum*. London: University of London Press, 1968.

MOORE, C. A. "Changes: Relevance or Irresponsibility," *Journal of Health, Physical Education and Recreation*, 44 (1973), 27–28.

SANACORE, MARYANNE. "The Extent of Lifetime Sports Activities in the Physical Education Programs of Suffolk County School Districts." Unpublished Master's thesis, New York University, 1972.

SHULMAN, S. "An Experimental High School," *Journal of Health, Physical Education and Recreation*, 44 (1973), 23–24.

STAUB, SARA. *Attitudes toward Physical Activity of Senior High School Students Enrolled in Traditional and Lifetime Sports-centered Physical Education Programs*. Unpublished Master's thesis, Ithaca College, 1975.

STOWE, G. L., and J. C. BURTON. "A Fitness Park for Adults," *Journal of Health, Physical Education and Recreation*, 46:1 (1975), p. 31.

STRAUB, W. F. "The Status of Lifetime Sports Instruction in New York State Secondary Schools," *New York State Journal of Health, Physical Education and Recreation*, 20 (Fall, 1967).

STRAUB, W. F., D. L. STAIR, and B. W. HUNGERFORD. "The Status of Lifetime Sports Instruction in New York State Secondary Schools." Paper presented at National Convention, American Alliance for Health, Physical Education and Recreation, Atlantic City, New Jersey, March, 1975.

TOFFLER, ALVIN. *Future Shock*. New York: Random House, Inc., 1970.

WILLGOOSE, C. E. *The Curriculum in Physical Education*. Englewood Cliffs, N.J.: Prentice-Hall, Inc., 1974.

APPENDICES

APPENDICES

A

Questionnaire

WHAT DO YOU LIKE TO DO?

To the boys and girls answering these questions:

In order to make good school programs for boys and girls, it is important to know about the things you want to learn. The answers to these questions will help us know some of the things that are important to you. Will you follow the directions carefully.

1. Read each question. If your teacher reads the questions aloud, read with her silently.
2. After reading each question, put a check in the column which tells how important the activity is to you.
3. The first two questions are samples. They have been done for you to show how to mark yours.
4. Write your age and grade on the line below. Then check the word GIRL or BOY depending upon which you are. You do not need to sign your name.

Age _____ Grade _____ Boy _____ Girl _____

PART 1

Here is a long list of things which can be done in the gym or out of doors. Some of them you probably like to do, others you don't. There may be some on the list you have never heard of. As you read each activity on the list, mark it in this way:

Very Important. There will be some activities that mean a lot to you. Perhaps you do them very well and have a lot of fun doing them. Perhaps you do not do them well or don't even know how to do them, but want very much to learn because they are things your friends do well. Whatever the reason, you are telling the person who is reading your answers that here are the activities most important to you.

Important. There are probably some things you like to do that still are not quite as important as the ones described above. Perhaps there are some you want to learn, but not quite as badly as the ones described above. They are the activities you mark important.

Not at all Important. There are probably some activities that you are asked to do and that you do very well, but still to you, they don't matter

189

very much. Perhaps there are others that don't matter to you. They are the activities you mark not at all important.

How important is it to you to know how to:

	Very Important	Important	Not at all Important
1. Play touch football?			
2. Play basketball?			
3. Play jacks?			
4. Jump rope?			
5. Play softball?			
6. Play kick baseball?			
7. Travel on the traveling rings?			
8. Skip?			
9. Run fast?			
10. Do a high jump?			
11. Throw a baseball far?			
12. Throw a baseball accurately?			
13. Walk on stilts?			
14. Walk on the balance beam?			
15. Play tether ball?			
16. Shoot a bow and arrow?			
17. Social dance?			
18. Act to music, as in rhythms?			
19. Play soccer?			
20. Play captain basketball?			
21. Do tricks on the flying rings?			
22. Play hopscotch?			
23. Play badminton?			
24. Play tennis?			
25. Have a good posture?			
26. Catch a ball well?			
27. Climb a rope?			
28. Chin yourself several times?			
29. Punt a soccer ball?			

	Very Important	Important	Not at all Important
30. Punt a football?			
31. Play volleyball?			
32. Do square dancing?			
33. Lift heavy weights?			
34. Do folk dances?			
35. Do a head stand?			
36. Do a hand stand?			
37. Do a cart wheel?			
38. Do stunts?			
39. Swim?			
40. Ice skate?			
41. Hike a long distance?			
42. Ride horseback?			
43. Ride a bicycle?			
44. Roller skate?			
45. Box?			
46. Wrestle?			
47. Play horseshoes?			
48. Play on the jungle gym?			
49. Do tricks on the stall bars?			
50. Do a broad jump?			
51. Shoot baskets?			
52. Play line soccer?			
53. Play capture the flag?			
54. Play running games like tag?			
55. Play running games like red light?			
56. Play running games like hill dill?			
57. Play quiet games like Simon says?			
58. Play safely?			
59. Control your temper?			
60. Plan good plays in a game?			

	Very Important	Important	Not at all Important
61. Play different positions?			
62. Explain plays clearly?			
63. Practice skills you need in games?			
64. Have marching drills?			
65. Know how to referee?			
66. Play softball?			
67. Play quoits?			

PART II

Is it important to you:

	Yes	Sometimes	No
1. To be a captain?			
2. To be a good captain when you are one?			
3. To be a good team member?			
4. To get along well with your friends?			
5. To be on the winning team?			
6. To have your teacher choose captains?			
7. To have your class vote on captains?			
8. To have everyone in your class take turns being captain?			
9. To have only "the best" be captain?			
10. To have everyone in your class on a team?			
11. To have only "the best" on a team?			
12. To have boys and girls on the same team?			
13. To have boys and girls on separate teams?			
14. To be able to organize your own games?			
15. To have some say about planning games to be played or activities for the day?			
16. To be able to apologize when you make a mistake that hurts someone else or your team?			
17. To make up after a fight?			

	Yes	*Sometimes*	*No*
18. To have your classroom teacher play games with you?			
19. To have equipment at school you can borrow for games at noon or after school?			
20. To have equipment at school to use during school hours?			
21. To know rules for games?			
22. To know the history of games?			
23. To know how to take care of equipment?			
24. To have time during school for playing games?			
25. To have time after school for playing games?			
26. To have space after school for playing games?			
27. To have a teacher help with after school games?			
28. To have time during school with a teacher whose special job is to teach games and other skills?			
29. To see other teams play the games you like?			
30. To see movies about the games you like? (Movies in school to teach you about the games.)			

From: The University of the State of New York, State Education Department, Bureau of Research, Albany, New York.

B

CHECK LIST FOR EVALUATING
THE FINAL LIST OF OBJECTIVES

In the first three chapters, we told how to identify and define instructional objectives in behavioral terms. Our focus was on the stating of the objectives and the specific learning outcomes. Questions such as "Which objectives are most desirable for a particular instructional unit?" we leave to the curriculum specialist and subject expert. In evaluating your final list of objectives, however, you might want to appraise how adequate the list is, as well as how clearly the statements indicate your instructional intent. Therefore, general criteria for evaluating the final list of objectives and specific learning outcomes have been incorporated into this check list.

This check list is intended as a diagnostic tool for detecting and correcting errors in the final list of objectives. Any negative answer indicates an area where improvement is needed. The check list is also useful, of course, as a guide for developing the original list of instructional objectives.

CHECK LIST

Adequacy of the List of General Objectives	Yes	No
1. Does each general instructional objective indicate an appropriate outcome for the instructional unit? (See recommendations of curriculum and subject experts.)	____	____
2. Does the list of general instructional objectives include all logical outcomes of the unit (knowledge, understanding, skills, attitudes, etc.)?	____	____
3. Are the general instructional objectives attainable (do they take into account the ability of the students, facilities, time available, etc.)?	____	____
4. Are the general instructional objectives in harmony with the philosophy of the school?	____	____
5. Are the general instructional objectives in harmony with sound principles of learning (e.g., are the outcomes those that are most permanent and transferable)?	____	____

Statement of General Objectives	Yes	No

6. Does each general instructional objective begin with a verb (e.g., knows, understands, appreciates, etc.)? _____ _____

7. Is each general instructional objective stated in terms of student performance (rather than teacher performance)? _____ _____

8. Is each general instructional objective stated as a learning product (rather than in terms of the learning process)? _____ _____

9. Is each general instructional objective stated in terms of the students' terminal behavior (rather than the subject matter to be covered)? _____ _____

10. Does each general instructional objective include only one general learning outcome? _____ _____

11. Is each general instructional objective stated at the proper level of generality (i.e., is it clear, concise, and readily definable)? _____ _____

12. Is each general instructional objective stated so that it is relatively independent (i.e. free from overlap with other objectives)? _____ _____

Behavioral Definition of General Objectives

13. Is each general instructional objective defined by a list of specific learning outcomes that describes the terminal behavior students are expected to demonstrate? _____ _____

14. Does each specific learning outcome begin with a verb that specifies definite, observable behavior (e.g., identifies, describes, lists, etc.)? _____ _____

15. Is the behavior in each specific learning outcome relevant to the general instructional objective it describes? _____ _____

16. Is there a sufficient number of specific learning outcomes to adequately describe the behavior of students who have achieved each of the general instructional objectives? _____ _____

From: N. E. Gronlund. *Stating Behavioral Objectives for Classroom Instruction.* New York: Macmillan, 1970, pp. 51–52.

C

SOURCES FOR SELECTED SPORTS SKILL TESTS

This section is designed to provide the reader with references for a wide variety of sports skills tests that may be of interest to physical educators. Due to changes that have occurred in many sports over the years, some of the older tests may no longer be wholly appropriate for class usage. Nonetheless, numbers of these tests are included in this appendix because of their usefulness to the teacher in developing formative evaluation measures.

Archery

American Association for Health, Physical Education and Recreation. *Archery Skills Test Manual*. Washington, D.C.: AAHPER, 1967.

BOHN, R. W. "An Achievement Test in Archery." Unpublished Master's thesis, University of Wisconsin, Madison, 1962.

HYDE, EDITH I. "An Achievement Scale in Archery," *Research Quarterly*, VIII (1937), 109–16.

ZABICK, R. M., and A. S. JACKSON. "Reliability of Archery Achievement," *Research Quarterly*, XL (1969), 254–55.

Badminton

Department of Physical Education for Women, Badminton Report. An unpublished report prepared by the badminton committee, University of Wisconsin, 1963.

FRENCH, E., and E. STALTER. "Study of Skill Tests in Badminton for College Women," *Research Quarterly*, XX (1949), 257–72.

GREINER, M. R. "Construction of a Short Test for Beginning Badminton Players." Master's thesis, University of Wisconsin, Madison, 1964 (Microcard PE 670, University of Oregon, Eugene).

HALE, P. A. "Construction of a Long Serve Test for Beginning Badminton Players (Singles)." Master's thesis, University of Wisconsin, Madison, 1970 (Microcard PE 1133, University of Oregon, Eugene).

HICKS, J. V. "The Construction and Evaluation of a Battery of Five Badminton Skills Tests." Unpublished Doctoral dissertation, Texas Women's University, Denton, 1967.

LOCKHART, A., and F. A. MCPHERSON. "The Development of a Test of Badminton Playing Ability," *Research Quarterly*, XX (1949), 402–5.

McDONALD, E. D. "The Development of a Skill Test for the Badminton High Clear." Master's thesis, Southern Illinois University, Carbondale, 1968 (Microcard PE 1083, University of Oregon, Eugene).

MILLER, F. A. "A Badminton Wall Volley Test," *Research Quarterly*, XXII (1951), 208–13.

SCOTT, M. G. "Achievement Examinations in Badminton," *Research Quarterly*, XII (1941), 242–53.

SCOTT, M. G., and M. FOX. "Long Serve Test," in *Measurement and Evaluation in Physical Education*, M. G. Scott and E. French, eds. Dubuque, Iowa: Wm. C. Brown Company Publishers, 1959.

THORPE, J., and C. WEST. "A Test of Game Sense in Badminton," *Perceptual and Motor Skills*, XXVIII (1969), 159–69.

Bowling

MARTIN, J. L. "Bowling Norms for College Men and Women," *Research Quarterly*, XXXI (1960), 113–16.

MARTIN, J. L., and J. KEOGH. "Bowling Norms for College Students in Elective Physical Education Classes," *Research Quarterly*, XXXV (1964), 325–27.

OLSON, J. K., and M. R. LIBA. "A Device for Evaluating Spot Bowling Ability," *Research Quarterly*, XXXVIII (1967), 193–210.

PHILLIPS, M., and D. SUMMERS. "Bowling Norms and Learning Curves for College Women," *Research Quarterly*, XXI (1950), 377–85.

SCHUNK, C. *Test Questions for Bowling*. Philadelphia: W. B. Saunders Company, 1969.

Fencing

BOWER, M. G. "A Test of General Fencing Ability." Unpublished Master's thesis, University of Southern California, Los Angeles, 1961.

COOPER, C. K. "The Development of a Fencing Skill Test for Measuring Achievement of Beginning Collegiate Women Fencers in Using the Advance, Beat, and Lunge." Unpublished Master's thesis, Western Illinois University, Macomb, 1968.

FEIN, J. T. "Construction of Skill Tests for Beginning Collegiate Women Fencers." Unpublished Master's thesis, University of Iowa, Iowa City, 1964.

SAFRIT, M. J. "Construction of a Skill Test for Beginning Fencers." Unpublished Master's thesis, University of Wisconsin, Madison, 1962.

SCHUTZ, H. J. "Construction of an Achievement Scale in Fencing for Women." Unpublished Master's thesis, University of Washington, Seattle, 1940.

WYRICK, W. "A Comparison of the Effectiveness of Two Methods of Teaching Beginning Fencing to College Women." Unpublished Master's thesis, The Woman's College of the University of North Carolina, Greensboro, 1958.

Golf

BROWN, H. S. "A Test Battery for Evaluating Golf Skills," *Texas Association for Health, Physical Education and Recreation Journal* (May 1969), pp. 4–5, 28–29.

CLEVETT, M. A. "An Experiment in Teaching Methods of Golf," *Research Quarterly*, II (1931), 104–12.

COCHRANE, J. F. "The Construction of Indoor Skills Test as a Measure of Golfing Ability." Unpublished Master's thesis, University of Minnesota, Minneapolis, 1960.

MCKEE, M. E. "A Test for the Full Swinging Shot in Golf," *Research Quarterly*, XXI (1950), 40–46.

NELSON, J. K. "An Achievement Test in Golf," in *Practical Measurements for Evaluation in Physical Education.* B. L. Johnson and J. K. Nelson, eds. Minneapolis: Burgess Publishing Company, 1969.

VANDERHOOF, E. R. "Beginning Golf Achievement Tests." Master's thesis, State University of Iowa, Iowa City, 1956 (Microcard PE 306, University of Oregon, Eugene).

WATTS, H: "Construction and Evaluation of a Target on Testing the Approach Shot in Golf." Unpublished Master's thesis, University of Wisconsin, Madison, 1942.

WEST, C., and J. THORPE. "Construction and Validation of an Eight-iron Approach Test," *Research Quarterly*, XXXIX, No. 4 (1968), 1115–20.

Gymnastics

BOWERS, C. O. "Gymnastics Skill Test for Beginning to Low Intermediate Girls and Women." Master's thesis, Ohio State University, Columbus, 1965 (Microcard PE 734, University of Oregon, Eugene).

FAULKNER, J., and N. KOKEN. "Objectivity of Judging at the National Collegiate Athletic Association Gymnastic Meet: A Ten-year Follow-up Study," *Research Quarterly*, XXXIII (1962), 485–86.

Handball

CORNISH, C. "A Study of Measurement of Ability in Handball," *Research Quarterly*, XX (1949), 215–22.

GRIFFITH, M. A. "An Objective Method of Evaluating Ability in Handball Singles." Unpublished Master's thesis, Ohio State University, Columbus, 1960.

MONOTOYE, H. J., and J. BROTZMANN. "An Investigation of the Validity of Using the Results of a Doubles Tournament as a Measure of Handball Ability," *Research Quarterly*, XXII (1951), 214–18.

PENNINGTON, G. G. "A Measure of Handball Ability," *Research Quarterly*, XXXVIII (1967), 247–53.

Ice Skating

CARRIERE, D. L. "An Objective Figure Skating Test for Use in Beginning Classes." Unpublished Master's thesis, University of Illinois, Urbana, 1969.

LEAMING, T. W. "A Measure of Endurance of Young Speed Skaters." Unpublished Master's thesis, University of Illinois, Urbana, 1959.

RECKNAGEL, D. "A Test for Beginners in Figure Skating," *Journal of Health and Physical Education*, XVI (1945), pp. 91–92.

Skiing

ROGERS, H. M. "Construction of Objectively Scored Skill Tests for Beginning Skiers." Unpublished Master's thesis, University of Colorado, Boulder, 1960.

WOLFE, J. E., and H. H. MERRIFIELD, "Predictability of Beginning Skiing Success from Basic Skill Tests in College Age Females." Paper presented at the National American Association for Health, Physical Education and Recreation Convention in Detroit, Michigan, April 1971.

Stunts and Tumbling

COTTERAL, B., and D. COTTERAL. "Scale for Judging Quality of Performance in Stunts and Tumbling," *The Teaching of Stunts and Tumbling*. New York: The Ronald Press Company, 1936.

EDWARDS, V. M. *Test Questions for Tumbling*. Philadelphia: W. B. Saunders Company, 1969.

Swimming

BENNETT, L. M. "A Test of Diving for Use in Beginning Classes," *Research Quarterly*, XIII (1942), 109–15.

CHAPMAN, P. A. "A Comparison of Three Methods of Measuring Swimming Stroke Proficiency." Master's thesis, University of Wisconsin, Madison, 1965 (Microcard PE 738, University of Oregon, Eugene).

FOX, M. G. "Swimming Power Test," *Research Quarterly*, XXVIII (1957), 233–37.

HEWITT, J. E. "Swimming Achievement Scales for College Men," *Research Quarterly*, XIX (1948), 282–89.

MUNT, M. R. "Development of an Objective Test to Measure the Efficiency of the Front Crawl for College Women." Unpublished Master's thesis, University of Michigan, Ann Arbor, 1964.

ROSENTSWIEG, J. "A Revision of the Power Swimming Test," *Research Quarterly*, XXXIX (1968), 818–19.

WILSON, C. T. "Coordination Tests in Swimming," *Research Quarterly*, V (1934), 81–88.

WILSON, M. R. "Wilson Achievement Test for Intermediate Swimming," in

H. M. Barrow and R. McGee, *A Practical Approach to Measurement in Physical Education.* Philadelphia: Lea & Febiger, 1972, pp. 313–19.

Table Tennis

Mott, J. A., and A. Lockhart. "Table Tennis Backboard Test," *Journal of Health and Physical Education,* XVII (1946), 550–52.

Tennis

Benton, R. "Teaching Tennis by Testing," in *Selected Tennis and Badminton Articles,* D. Davis, ed. Washington, D.C.: Division of Girl's and Women's Sports, American Association for Health, Physical Education and Recreation, 1963.

Broer, M. R., and D. M. Miller. "Achievement Tests for Beginning and Intermediate Tennis," *Research Quarterly,* XXI (1950), 303–13.

Cobane, E. "Test for the Service," in *Tennis and Badminton Guide—June 1962– June 1964.* Washington, D.C.: Division of Girls' and Women's Sports, American Association for Health, Physical Education and Recreation, 1962.

DiGennaro, J. "Construction of Forehand Drive, Backhand Drive, and Service Tennis Tests," *Research Quarterly,* XL (1969), 496–501.

Dyer, J. T. "Revision of the Backboard Test of Tennis Ability," *Research Quarterly,* IX (1938), 25–31.

Edwards, J. "A Study of Three Measures of the Tennis Serve," Master's thesis, University of Wisconsin, Madison, 1965 (Microcard PE 746, University of Oregon, Eugene).

Felshin, J., and E. Spencer. "Evaluation Procedures for Tennis," in *Selected Tennis and Badminton Articles,* D. Davis, ed. Washington, D.C.: Division of Girls' and Women's Sports, American Association for Health, Physical Education and Recreation, 1963.

Hewitt, J. E. "Revision of the Dyer Backboard Tennis Test," *Research Quarterly,* XXXVI (1965), 153–57.

————. "Classification Tests in Tennis," *Research Quarterly,* XXXIX (1968), 552–55.

Hubell, N. C. "A Battery of Tennis Skill Tests for College Women." Unpublished Master's thesis, Texas Women's University, Denton, 1960.

Hulac, G. M. "Hulac Rating Scale for the Tennis Serve," in H. M. Barrow and R. McGee, *A Practical Approach to Measurement in Physical Education.* Philadelphia: Lea & Febiger, 1972, pp. 325–26.

Hulbert, B. A. "A Study of Tests for the Forehand Drive in Tennis." Master's thesis, University of Wisconsin, Madison, 1966 (Microcard PE 818, University of Oregon, Eugene).

Johnson, J. "Tennis Serve of Advanced Women Players," *Research Quarterly,* XXVIII (1957), 123–31.

JOHNSON, J. "Tennis Knowledge Test," in *Selected Tennis and Badminton Articles*, D. Davis, ed. Washington, D.C.: Division of Girls' and Women's Sports, American Association for Health, Physical Education and Recreation, 1963.

KEMP, J., and M. F. VINCENT. "Kemp-Vincent Rally Test of Tennis Skill," *Research Quarterly*, XXXIX (1968), 1000–1004.

MALINAK, N. R. "The Construction of an Objective Measure of Accuracy in the Performance of the Tennis Serve." Unpublished Master's thesis, University of Illinois, Urbana, 1961.

RONNING, H. E. "Wall Tests for Evaluating Tennis Ability." Master's thesis, Washington State University, Pullman, 1959 (Microcard PE 441, University of Oregon, Eugene).

SCOTT, M. G. "Achievement Examinations for Elementary and Intermediate Tennis Classes," *Research Quarterly*, XII (1941), 40–49.

SCOTT, M. G., and E. FRENCH. "Scott-French Revision of the Dyer Wallboard Test," *Measurement and Evaluation in Physical Education*. Dubuque, Iowa: Wm. C. Brown Company, Publishers, 1959, pp. 222–25.

Volleyball

American Association for Health, Physical Education and Recreation. *Volleyball Skills Test Manual*. Washington, D.C.: AAHPER, 1967.

BASSETT, G., R. B. GLASSOW, and M. LOCKE. "Studies in Testing Volleyball Skills," *Research Quarterly*, VIII (1937), 60–72.

BLACKMAN, C. J. "The Development of a Volleyball Test for the Spike." Unpublished Master's thesis, Southern Illinois University, Carbondale, 1968.

BRADY, C. F. "Preliminary Investigation of Volleyball Playing Ability," *Research Quarterly*, XVI (1945), 14–17.

BROER, M. A. "Reliability of Certain Skill Tests for Junior High School Girls," *Research Quarterly*, XXIX (1958), 139–45.

BRUMBACH, W. B. "Brumbach Service Test," in B. L. Johnson and J. K. Nelson, *Practical Measurements for Evaluation in Physical Education*. Minneapolis: Burgess Publishing Company, 1969, pp. 365–66.

CLIFTON, M. "Single Hit Volley Test for Women's Volleyball," *Research Quarterly*, XXXIII (1962), 208–11.

CROGAN, C. "A Simple Volleyball Classification Test for High School Girls," *The Physical Educator*, IV (1943), 34–37.

CUNNINGHAM, P., and J. GARRISON. "High Wall Volley Test for Women," *Research Quarterly*, XXXIX (1968), 486–90.

FRENCH, E. L., and B. I. COOPER. "Achievement Tests in Volleyball for High School Girls," *Research Quarterly*, VIII (1937), 150–57.

HELMEN, R. M. "Development of Power Volleyball Skill Tests for College Women." Paper presented at the Research Section of the 1971 American

Association for Health, Physical Education and Recreation National Convention, Detroit, Michigan.

JACKSON, P. L. "A Rating Scale for Discriminating Relative Playing Performance of Skilled Female Volleyball Players." Master's thesis, University of Alberta, Edmonton, 1966 (Microcard PE 931, University of Oregon, Eugene).

KESSLER, A. "The Validity and Reliability of the Sandefur Volleyball Spiking Test." Unpublished Master's thesis, California State College, Long Beach, 1968.

KRONQUIST, R. A., and W. B. BRUMBACH. "A Modification of the Brady Volleyball Skill Test for High School Boys," *Research Quarterly*, XXXIX (1968), pp. 116–20.

LATCHAW, M. "Measuring Selected Motor Skills in Fourth, Fifth, and Sixth Grades," *Research Quarterly*, XXV (1954), 439–49.

LIBA, M. R., and M. R. STAUFF. "A Test for the Volleyball Pass," *Research Quarterly*, XXXIV (1963), 56–63.

LONDEREE, B. R., and E. C. EICHOLITZ. "Reliabilities of Selected Volleyball Skill Tests." Paper presented at the Research Section of the 1970 American Association for Health, Physical Education and Recreation National Convention, Seattle, Washington.

LOPEZ, D. "Serve Test," in *Volleyball Guide—July 1957–July 1959*. Washington, D.C.: Division of Girls' and Women's Sports, American Association for Health, Physical Education and Recreation, 1957.

MOHR, D. R., and M. J. HAVERSTICK. "Repeated Volleys Tests for Women's Volleyball," *Research Quarterly*, XXVI (1955), 179–84.

RUSSELL, N., and E. LANGE. "Achievement Tests in Volleyball for Junior High School Girls," *Research Quarterly*, XI (1940), 33–41.

RYAN, M. F. "A Study of Tests for the Volleyball Serve." Master's thesis. University of Wisconsin, Madison, 1969 (Microcard PE 1040, University of Oregon, Eugene).

SLAYMAKER, T., and V. H. BROWN. *Test Questions for Power Volleyball*. Philadelphia: W. B. Saunders Company, 1969.

SNAVELY, M. "Volleyball Skill Tests for Girls," in *Selected Volleyball Articles*, A. Lockhart, ed. Washington, D.C.: Division of Girls' and Women's Sports, American Association for Health, Physical Education and Recreation, 1960.

THORPE, J., and C. WEST. "A Volleyball Skills Chart with Attainment Levels for Selected Skills," *Volleyball Guide—July 1967-July 1969*. Washington, D.C.: Division of Girl's and Women's Sports, American Association for Health, Physical Education and Recreation, 1967.

WATKINS, A. "Skill Testing for Large Groups," in *Selected Volleyball Articles*, A. Lockhart, ed. Washington, D.C.: Division of Girls' and Women's Sports, American Association for Health, Physical Education and Recreation, 1960.

WEST, C. "A Comparative Study between Height and Wall Volley Test Scores as Related to Volleyball Playing Ability of Girls and Women." Unpublished Master's thesis, The Woman's College of the University of North Carolina, Greensboro, 1957.

Adapted from: M. J. Safrit. *Evaluation in Physical Education.* Englewood Cliffs, N.J.: Prentice-Hall, Inc., 1973, pp. 273–284.

D

CHECK LIST FOR FACILITY PLANNERS

As an aid to those responsible for planning facilities for athletics, physical education, and recreation, a check list has been prepared. The application of this check list may prevent unfortunate and costly errors.

Place the appropriate letter in the space indicated in the right-hand margin after each statement.

A—The plans meet the requirements completely.

B—The plans meet the requirements only partially.

C—The plans fail to meet the requirements.

Soundly conceived plans for areas and facilities are not achieved by chance or accident, but by initiative and action of knowledgeable people acting individually, in groups, and as agencies.

GENERAL

1. A clear-cut statement has been prepared on the nature and scope of the program, and the special requirements for space, equipment, fixtures, and facilities have been dictated by the activities to be conducted. _____

2. The facility has been planned to meet the total requirements of the program as well as the special needs of those who are to be served. _____

3. The plans and specifications have been checked by all governmental agencies (city, county, and state) whose approval is required by law. _____

4. Plans for areas and facilities conform to state and local regulations and to accepted standards and practices. _____

5. The areas and facilities planned make possible the programs that serve the interests and needs of all the people. _____

6. Every available source of property or funds has been explored, evaluated, and utilized whenever appropriate. _____

7. All interested persons and organizations concerned with the facility have had an opportunity to share in its planning (professional educators, users, consultants, administrators,

engineers, architects, program specialists, building managers, and builder—a team approach). _____

8. The facility and its appurtenances will fulfill the maximum demands of the program. The program has not been curtailed to fit the facility. _____

9. The facility has been functionally planned to meet the present and anticipated needs of specific programs, situations, and publics. _____

10. Future additions are included in present plans to permit economy of construction. _____

11. Lecture classrooms are isolated from distracting noises. _____

12. Storage areas for indoor and outdoor equipment are of adequate size. They are located adjacent to the gymnasiums. _____

13. Shelves in storage rooms are slanted toward the wall. _____

14. All passageways are free of obstructions; fixtures are recessed. _____

15. Facilities for health services and the first-aid and emergency-isolation rooms are suitably interrelated. _____

16. Buildings, specific areas, and facilities are clearly identified. _____

17. Locker rooms are arranged for ease of supervision. _____

18. Offices, teaching stations, and service facilities are properly interrelated. _____

19. Special needs of the physically handicapped are met, including a ramp into the building at a major entrance. _____

20. All "dead space" is used. _____

21. The building is compatible in design and comparable in quality and accommodation to other campus structures. _____

22. Storage rooms are accessible to the play area. _____

23. Workrooms, conference rooms, and staff and administrative offices are interrelated. _____

24. Shower and dressing facilities are provided for professional staff members and are conveniently located. _____

25. Thought and attention have been given to making facilities and equipment as durable and vandalproof as possible. _____

26. Low-cost maintenance features have been adequately considered. _____

27. This facility is a part of a well-integrated master plan. _____

28. All areas, courts, facilities, equipment, climate control, security, etc., conform rigidly to detailed standards and specifications. _____

29. Shelves are recessed and mirrors are supplied in appropriate places in rest rooms and dressing rooms. _____

30. Dressing space between locker rows is adjusted to the size and age of students. _____

31. Drinking fountains are conveniently placed in locker-room areas or immediately adjacent thereto. _____

32. Special attention is given to provision for locking service windows and counters, supply bins, carts, shelves, and racks. _____

33. Provision is made for the repair, maintenance, replacement, and off-season storage of equipment and uniforms. _____

34. A well-defined program for laundering and cleaning towels, uniforms, and equipment is included in the plan. _____

35. Noncorrosive metal is used in dressing, drying, and shower areas except for enameled lockers. _____

36. Antipanic hardware is used where required by fire regulations. _____

37. Properly placed hose bibbs and drains are sufficient in size and quantity to permit flushing the entire area with a water hose. _____

38. A water-resistant, coved base is used under the locker base and floor mat, and where floor and wall join. _____

39. Chalkboards and/or tackboards with map tracks are located in appropriate places in dressing rooms, hallways, and classrooms. _____

40. Book shelves are provided in toilet areas. _____

41. Space and equipment are planned in accordance with the types and number of enrollees. _____

42. Basement rooms, being undesirable for dressing, drying, and showering, are not planned for those purposes. _____

43. Spectator seating (permanent) in areas that are basically instructional is kept at a minimum. Roll-away bleachers are used primarily. Balcony seating is considered as a possibility. _____

44. Well-lighted and effectively displayed trophy cases enhance the interest and beauty of the lobby. _____

45. The space under the stairs is used for storage. _____

46. Department heads' offices are located near the central administrative office, which includes a well-planned conference room. _____

47. Workrooms are located near the central office and serve as a repository for departmental materials and records. _____

48. Conference area includes a cloak room, lavatory, and toilet. _____

49. In addition to regular secretarial offices established in the central and department-chairmen's offices, a special room to house a secretarial pool for staff members is provided. _____

50. Staff dressing facilities are provided. These facilities may also serve game officials.

51. The community and/or neighborhood has a "round table" for planning. _____

52. All those (persons and agencies) who should be a party to

planning and development are invited and actively engaged in the planning process.   _____

53. Space and area relationships are important. They have been carefully considered.   _____

54. Both long-range and immediate plans have been made.   _____

55. The body comfort of the child, a major factor in securing maximum learning, has been considered in the plans.   _____

56. Plans for quiet areas have been made.   _____

57. In the planning, consideration has been given to the need for adequate recreational areas and facilities, both near and distant from the homes of people.   _____

58. Plans recognize the primary function of recreation as being enrichment, and the achievement of self-potential.   _____

59. Every effort has been exercised to eliminate hazards.   _____

60. The installation of low-hanging door closers, light fixtures, signs, and other objects in the traffic areas has been avoided.   _____

61. Warning signals—both visible and audible—are included in the plans.   _____

62. Ramps have a slope equal to or greater than a one-foot rise in twelve feet.   _____

63. Minimum landings for ramps are 5 by 5 feet, they extend at least one foot beyond the swinging arc of a door, have at least a 6-foot clearance at the bottom, and have level platforms at 30-foot intervals on every turn.   _____

64. Adequate locker and dressing spaces are provided.   _____

65. The design of dressing, drying, and shower areas reduces foot traffic to a minimum and establishes clean, dry aisles for bare feet.   _____

66. Teaching stations are properly related to service facilities.   _____

67. Toilet facilities are adequate in number. They are located to serve all groups for which provisions are made.   _____

68. Mail services, outgoing and incoming, are included in the plans.   _____

69. Hallways, ramps, doorways, and elevators are designed to permit equipment to be moved easily and quickly.   _____

70. A keying design suited to administrative and instructional needs is planned.   _____

71. Toilets used by large groups have circulating (in and out) entrances and exits.   _____

CLIMATE CONTROL

1. Provision is made throughout the building for climate control —heating, ventilating, and refrigerated cooling.   _____

2. Special ventilation is provided for locker, dressing, shower, drying, and toilet rooms. _____

3. Heating plans permit both area and individual-room control. _____

4. Research areas where small animals are kept and where chemicals are used have been provided with special ventilating equipment. _____

5. The heating and ventilating of the wrestling gymnasium have been given special attention. _____

ELECTRICAL CONTROL

1. Shielded, vapor-proof lights are used in moisture-prevalent areas. _____

2. Lights in strategic areas are key-controlled. _____

3. Lighting intensity conforms to approved standards. _____

4. An adequate number of electrical outlets are strategically placed. _____

5. Gymnasium and auditorium lights are controlled by dimmer units. _____

6. Locker-room lights are mounted above the space between lockers. _____

7. Natural light is controlled properly for purposes of visual aids and avoidance of glare. _____

8. Electrical outlet plates are installed three feet above the floor unless special use dictates other locations. _____

9. Controls for light switches and projection equipment are suitably located and interrelated. _____

10. All lights are shielded. Special protection is provided in gymnasiums, court areas, and shower rooms. _____

11. Lights are placed to shine between rows of lockers. _____

WALLS

1. Movable and folding partitions are power-operated and controlled by keyed switches. _____

2. Wall plates are located where needed and are firmly attached. _____

3. Hooks and rings for net are placed (and recessed in walls) according to court locations and net heights. _____

4. Materials that clean easily and are impervious to moisture are used where moisture is prevalent. _____

5. Shower heads are placed at different heights—four feet (elementary) to seven feet (university)—for each school level. _____

6. Protective matting is placed permanently on the walls in the wrestling room, at the ends of basketball courts, and in other areas where such protection is needed. _____

7. An adequate number of drinking fountains are provided. They are properly placed (recessed in wall). _____

8. One wall (at least) of the dance studio has full-length mirrors. _____

9. All corners in locker rooms are rounded. _____

CEILINGS

1. Overhead-supported apparatus is secured to beams engineered to withstand stress. _____

2. The ceiling height is adequate for the activities to be housed. _____

3. Acoustical materials impervious to moisture are used in moisture-prevalent areas. _____

4. Skylights, being impractical, are seldom used because of problems in waterproofing roofs and the controlling of sun rays (gyms). _____

5. All ceilings except those in storage areas are acoustically treated with sound-absorbent materials. _____

FLOORS

1. Floor plates are placed where needed and are flush-mounted. _____

2. Floor design and materials conform to recommended standards and specifications. _____

3. Lines and markings are painted on floors before sealing is completed (when synthetic tape is not used). _____

4. A coved base (around lackers and where wall and floor meet) of the same water-resistant material used on floors is found in all dressing and shower rooms. _____

5. Abrasive, nonskid, slip-resistant flooring that is impervious to moisture is provided on all areas where water is used—laundry, swimming, pools, shower, dressing, and drying rooms. _____

6. Floor drains are properly located, and the slope of the floor is adequate for rapid drainage. _____

GYMNASIUMS AND SPECIAL ROOMS

1. Gymnasiums are planned so as to provide for safety zones (between courts, end lines, and walls) and for best utilization of space. _____

2. One gymnasium wall is free of obstructions and is finished with a smooth, hard surface for ball-rebounding activities. _____

3. The elementary school gymnasium has one wall free of obstructions, a minimum ceiling height of 18 feet, a minimum of 4,000 square feet of teaching area, and a recessed area for housing a piano. _____

4. Secondary school gymnasiums have a minimum ceiling height of 22 feet; a scoreboard; electrical outlets placed to fit with bleacher installation; wall attachments for apparatus and nets; and a power-operated, sound-insulated, and movable partition with a small pass-through door at one end. _____

5. A small spectator alcove adjoins the wrestling room and contains a drinking fountain (recessed in the wall). _____

6. Cabinets, storage closets, supply windows, and service areas have locks. _____

7. Provisions have been made for the cleaning, storing, and issuing of physical education and athletic uniforms. _____

8. Equipment is provided for the use of the physically handicapped. _____

9. Special provision has been made for audio and visual aids, including intercommunication systems, radio, and television. _____

10. Team dressing rooms have provisions for the following:
    a. hosing down room _____
    b. floors pitched to drain easily _____
    c. hot- and cold-water hose bibbs _____
    d. windows located above locker heights _____
    e. chalk, tack, and bulletin boards, and movie projection _____
    f. lockers for each team member _____
    g. drying facility for uniforms _____

11. The indoor rifle range includes the following:
    a. targets located 54 inches apart and 50 feet from the firing line _____
    b. 3 to 8 feet of space behind targets _____
    c. 12 feet of space behind firing line _____
    d. ceilings 8 feet high _____
    e. width adjusted to number of firing lines needed (one line for each three students) _____
    f. a pulley device for target placement and return _____
    g. storage and repair space. _____

12. Dance facilities include the following:
    a. 100 square feet per student _____
    b. a minimum length of 60 linear feet for modern dance _____
    c. full-height viewing mirrors on one wall (at least) of 30 feet; also a 20-foot mirror on an additional wall if possible _____

d. acoustical drapery to cover mirrors when not used and for protection if other activities are permitted _____

e. dispersed microphone jacks and speaker installation for music and instruction _____

f. built-in cabinets for record players, microphones, and amplifiers, with space for equipment carts _____

g. electrical outlets and microphone connections around perimeter of room _____

h. an exercise bar (34 to 42 inches above floor) on one wall _____

i. drapes, surface colors, floors (maple preferred), and other room appointments to enhance the room's attractiveness _____

j. location near dressing rooms and outside entrances _____

13. Training rooms include the following:

a. rooms large enough to administer adequately proper health services _____

b. sanitary storage cabinets for medical supplies _____

c. installation of drains for whirlpool, tubs, etc. _____

d. installation of electrical outlets with proper capacities and voltage _____

e. high stools for use of equipment such as whirlpool, ice tubs, etc. _____

f. water closet, hand lavatory, and shower _____

g. extra hand lavatory in the trainers' room _____

h. adjoining dressing rooms _____

i. installation and use of hydrotherapy and diathermy equipment in separate areas _____

j. space for the trainer, the physician, and for the various services they provide _____

k. corrective exercise laboratories located conveniently and adapted to the needs of the handicapped _____

14. Coaches' rooms provide the following:

a. a sufficient number of dressing lockers for coaching staff and officials _____

b. a security closet or cabinet for athletic equipment such as timing devices _____

c. a sufficient number of showers and toilet facilities _____

d. drains and faucets for hosing down the rooms where this method of cleaning is desirable and possible _____

e. a small chalkboard and tackboard _____

f. a small movie screen and projection table for use of coaches to review films _____

From: American Alliance for Health, Physical Education and Recreation. *Planning Facilities for Athletics, Physical Education and Recreation.* Chicago: The Athletic Institute, 1974, pp. 7–9.

INDEX

DATE DUE

GAYLORD			PRINTED IN U.S.A.